Journey Among the Economists

Journey
Among
the Economists

by ARRIGO LEVI

Translated by Muriel Grindrod

Library Press Incorporated
LaSalle, Illinois
1973

First published in the United States of America
in 1974 by
Library Press, LaSalle, Illinois 61301

Printed in Great Britain
by Watmoughs Limited
Bradford and London

Contents

Contents

Foreword

This book reproduces, with many later additions and expansions, in some cases substantial ones, the text of articles published in *La Stampa* of Turin between June 1969 and the winter of 1970 under the general title of "Whither modern economics?". This journey of mine among the economists was suggested, encouraged and made possible by the then editor of *La Stampa*, Alberto Ronchey. It is the journey of an economic amateur, undertaken from the standpoint of a journalist, and its chief aim has been to facilitate the not always easy communication between economists and the general public. A second fundamental aim has been to illustrate the similarity between the problems facing economists in the Western and the Communist worlds and the convergence not infrequently to be found in their respective solutions. Economic revisionism in Eastern Europe was the subject of a course of lectures given by me at the Bologna Center of Johns Hopkins University during the academic year 1967–68.

In order to take into account more recent developments, I subsequently, in the summer of 1972, addressed a supplementary questionnaire to several of the people I had interviewed. The results of this are embodied in Chapter 34, "The Debate Goes On".

My wife and daughter, in patiently putting up with my long absences from Rome, made it possible for me to write this book.

A.L.

Preface

by John Pryor

WERE ECONOMICS universally accepted as an exact science it is improbable that Arrigo Levi would have been prompted to write *Journey among the Economists*. Most people are prepared to concede that economics is a formal activity requiring the exercise of logic and numerate precision—which is not at all the same thing as its being a precise science.

As far as I know no one has written a book of journeyings among the crystallographers or the specialists on steel structures or the pure mathematicians. It is rather hard to imagine an author being moved to do so. It is not unreasonable to suppose that crystal structure or stress in steel or the systematic manipulation of the concepts of quantity, number, and increment have as much to do with life as we all live it as has economic analysis. But what these overt displays of precision lack and economics possesses is an inescapable association with human emotion and ideology. Economists, whether they like it or not—and the members of a perfectly respectable tradition of academic economics do not like it at all—are bound up in the human condition.

I have not the slightest doubt that both professional and lay readers will gain from Mr Levi's remarkable odyssey a much more clearly illuminated view of the probable future of this condition, of the material environment, than they would otherwise have had. But this is not the central point of *Journey among the Economists*. It is *per se* not yet another piece of economic prognosis, of which so many have been written in the past quarter-century. As the title indicates, it is essentially a highly informed tourist's album of portraits of intellects and personalities at work in a widely misunderstood field of endeavour.

9

Disagreement about a general external definition of economics—the question of whether the community at large expects economics to be pursued as an exact science or not—is unfortunately only one of many problems confronting the interested layman. Within the profession itself there is a fundamental dispute about what economics is and what, if anything, it is for. Those economists who, as I suggest above, dislike the idea of direct involvement with ideology or human *persona* want their activity to be a "neutral" science of choice. Their concession to "reality" would be that the phenomenon of economic choice must be set against the background of resources, supply, wants and needs which in a real-life way are finite and measurable, if only by an algebraic "x". A different "school" is intellectually just as respectable, though in the present nature of things socially more acceptable. This school or tradition insists that economics is the science (or analytical art) of human behaviour in relation to the material things of life. As such it illuminates and monitors the variables which, in many combinations and circumstances, determine changes in human wealth and material wellbeing. This fundamental debate has been going on since Keynes re-invented economics after the World Depression and probably for very much longer than that. What we have to ask ourselves now is why, in the mid-1970s, we should take a new, particularly intense look at the economists themselves, as distinct from the economy or even economics as such. In other words, we can legitimately ask why this book has been written.

IN PART, AT LEAST, both Mr Levi and his public are moved to look again at the leading practitioners of this enthralling science, art or whatever it is, by the observable condition of the world in the third quarter of the century. In material terms, most of us manage well enough, but we are aware that something has gone wrong with disturbing suddenness in the latter years of the 1960s and the early 1970s. On one hand, it is true, fewer people in most countries than ever before are actually on the breadline—the underdeveloped world and America's New Poor notwithstanding. For the most part what has happened is that the threshold of unacceptable poverty has been raised, thanks largely to the introduction of welfare politics in many countries.

On the other hand, however, we are aware of a condition of perennial stress, almost of neurosis, in the international economy and many of the national economies. We identify the chief decision-makers on material affairs not as the economists, but as the politicians with their civil service advisers (only some of whom are economists by discipline, and then of highly variable levels of attainment and intellect); the business leaders; and the leaders of organised labor. There is widespread disillusionment with party politics; with some of the objectives of the "capitalist" profit motive; and with the seemingly limited, selfish aims of the unions.

It may well be, indeed, that we are coming towards the end of one of those periods of exponential change which have been observable in history: at the height of the Roman Empire before the death of Marcus Aurelius; at the peak of the Italian Renaissance; and again at the climax of the age of political and industrial revolution in the late 18th and early 19th centuries. In such periods the time taken between the introduction or conception of a technological or social or political novelty and its permanent acceptance (or rejection) becomes shorter and shorter. Innovation breeds innovation at ever increasing speed.

AT TIMES LIKE THESE the community, the public, begins to look behind the obvious sources of policy and decision in material affairs to see if there are other factors or personalities to be blamed for the contemporary condition—or to try to discover alternative sources of explanation, reassurance, and practical help. By the 1970s, the politicians seem not to have mastered techniques for clearing away the final obstacles to the "wealth of nations". At the time of writing this preface, the world was still confronted with the problem of how to counter various kinds of inflation without killing economic growth. Its leaders were still groping for a permanent replacement for the Bretton Woods fixed parity system of international exchanges largely abandoned in 1971. There was still no final answer to such questions as how to forestall trade wars, or to measure and control the effects of the growing spread of multinational companies. A vast tariff-free market was being created in the enlarged European Community—but with little notion among the politicians about what effects, baleful or beneficial, might break upon the people arbitrarily embraced within that market.

THIS BOOK DEALS mainly with the leading originators in the field of economics. But one thing which can be said with certainty about economists in the mid-1970s is that there are a great many of them around. If we ask "Can the economists now stand up and help?" we must remember that we are speaking not just of the hundred or two major intellects, but also of the many thousands who have been trained in various branches of the discipline since the second World War, who have filled newly-created teaching posts in the universities, have joined large and not so large companies and banks and have swollen the retinues of advisers in governments and state agencies.

Will all these trained people now stand up and speak their minds about what is needed to achieve stability and prosperity? Alas, the immediate answer must be No. Economists, like philosophers and theologians, spend much of their working lives and efforts addressing each other rather than the community at large. This is inevitable given the vast increase in size of the profession in the past 30 years. The only way of assuring that one's career continues and develops is constantly to submit oneself to judgements of technical competence by those able to make such judgements—other economists.

Similiar considerations apply to the matter of agreement about basic economic situations. If an economist finds he has only a very uncertain audience among the policy-makers—the politicians—he can make an impression on his "public", meaning mostly his professional peers, by product differentiation, by producing a deliberately "different" analysis of a situation from that of his contemporaries.

But we should not despair that economists and economics seem so far to have "failed" in the sense of producing a single final answer to a particular economic problem or crisis which has immediately recommended itself in the corridors of power as the right answer. For their part, the economists can afford to be more communicative, less disputatious just for the sake of being different, and more involved in decision-making *as economists*. The way ahead from one analytical discipline, economics, is not to infiltrate into other disciplines as so many professional economists have recently done by subtly changing themselves into sociologists or ecologists. Nor is it helpful to re-shape economic argument so as to make it fit a particular party political ideology—which is not the same thing as criticising an economist for deriving a personal political view from his economic findings. We are asking too much if we demand that the economists agree in detail on the remedies for all our material maladies. But if, as Mr Levi has done, we encourage professional economists to pursue more "open" analysis, less self-consciously market-oriented towards other economists, the activity called economics would, at worst, be seen to reassert itself as a valuable contribution to human self-knowledge.

We cannot demand of the economists that they cure economic ills single-handed. As Professor Hayek has insisted in his well-known criticism of excessive numeracy in economics, we cannot expect economists to make spot-on predictions of every economic eventuality, however distant or close at hand. But we can and should encourage economists to continue to assemble all possible circumstantial evidence on the material condition of the human race, and to be more assertive (though perhaps less deliberately idiosyncratic) than in the past in communicating that evidence to the power centres and the policy makers. In this way, at the very worst, the margin of error in dealing with material problems could be progressively reduced.

April 1973   *John Pryor*

Introduction

The turn of the wheel in cultural fashion is not particularly favourable at present to economics viewed as the science of development and wellbeing; but perhaps for that very reason it merits consideration.

Economics had its period of greatest cultural and popular prestige at the beginning of the 1960s. The Kennedy slogan of the "new economics" in Western countries, and the movement for economic reforms in the post-Stalin societies of the East, promised a large and constant growth of production and consumption, the elimination of poverty and other social ills, and even an expansion of political liberties.

In 1930, at the time of the world crisis, John Maynard Keynes had prophesied, in an essay called *Economic Possibilities for our Grandchildren*, that it would take at least a hundred years to solve the economic problem arising from the perennial scarcity of resources. This prospect of universal prosperity, at least among the more advanced nations, was brought much nearer by the *new economics* in the West and by *market socialism* in the East. Advances in production were to make possible long before 2030 that "leap by humanity from the reign of necessity to the reign of freedom" of which Marx and Engels spoke.

The 'sixties have not, in fact, seen the failure of these promises on the purely economic and productive plane. In particular, the "new economics" in the West has fulfilled its promise: rates of development have been rapid, and crises localised and transitory.* Nevertheless this economic progress has not produced the social and political results that many people expected. On the contrary, certain tensions have become more acute and anxieties have been transferred from the social to the political sphere, as, for example, in post-Kennedy America, in France in 1968, or in Italy in 1969. In post-Stalinist societies, the economic road to reforms has proved difficult and fraught with unexpected obstacles. It may be that failures, both in the West and in the East, are to be attributed not to the new economics but to old political concepts. In any case some of the

* See next page.

symptoms of unrest and imbalance arise from the speed and violence of economic progress itself. Modern man, as the social scientist Geoffrey Vickers says, has conquered knowledge and power, but he has made use of them to make a world that is increasingly unpredictable and uncontrollable.

The prestige of economic science has suffered from this evolution. As the 'sixties drew to a close, economic forecasts for the last third of the century continued to be vigorously optimistic;† but faith has waned in the myth of economics as a science capable of solving every political and moral ill on the basis of a revolutionary expansion of productive structures.

Is this disappointment justified? Is this anti-economistic reaction on the part of public opinion reasonable, or is it

* Judgements of the extent to which economic crises between the mid-1960s and 1973 have been "localised and transitory" are necessarily subjective and, as emerges from this book as a whole, there is less agreement among professional economists than among the political managers of economic policy and among business leaders about what constitutes a "crisis" at a given moment. The author's journeyings among the economists were largely undertaken and his basic text prepared before the serious, even radical nature of some of these "crisis" events in the late '60s and early '70s was fully recognised. One refers particularly to the world-wide onset of various forms of inflation—steeper than at any time since the early '30s; to the preliminary round of monetary upsets in 1967–69; and to the more fundamental disturbance in 1971–72 of the 1944 Bretton Woods system, involving the end of the gold convertibility of the dollar and the floating of other currencies, including the £ sterling.

On the other hand it could still be said at the moment of the enlargement of the European Community in January 1973 that these disturbances, if they were fundamental crises likely to have lasting repercussions, retained throughout the character of "controlled" crises. Despite the partial overthrow of the old monetary order in 1971–72, an elaborate network of international monetary institutions and agreed procedures, as well as governments' ability to intervene in times of monetary and other economic imbalance, had become politically well established. By the early 1970s, therefore, it still seemed improbable that the continuing disturbances and distortions in the international economy would ever be permitted to reach the outright crisis proportions of the depression of the late 1920s and early '30s. Readers are referred in this context particularly to the author's supplementary investigations in Chapter 34 and to his discussions with Lord Balogh in Chapter 25. —J. P.

† At least in the industrialised countries. Forecasts for the less-developed world, particularly in respect of capital transfers, "imported" inflation and the food balance—the so-called calorie gap—were somewhat more pessimistic.

exaggerated and cyclical? How does the economists' scientific and civil involvement express itself in concrete terms? How have they reacted to their successes and setbacks, and what technical and social objectives are they aiming to achieve?

With these questions in mind, I went to visit some of the main centres of economic research in the United States, the Soviet Union, and Eastern and Western Europe. It seemed sensible to start with America since there is a general conviction among economists that that country is today in many respects (though not all) in the vanguard of research. Thirty years ago an inquiry of this kind would inevitably have begun in Cambridge, England, in the country of Adam Smith and Ricardo and at Keynes's university. Today it has seemed more advisable to start with Cambridge, Massachusetts, where the world's highest concentration of economic talent is to be found in the two great universities of Harvard and the Massachusetts Institute of Technology.

The prestige of American economics today derives less from the United States' primacy in production and technology than from two other factors: the very large number of European scholars who have gone there since the war, and the great leap forward in research through an astonishing proliferation of research centres. "The MIT", the economist Paul Samuelson told me at Cambridge four years ago, "is the greatest technical university not only in America but in the world. But it does not belong to America alone, any more than Shakespeare belongs only to England. We have today what can be called an explosion of knowledge, a boom in brains." This phenomenon is not confined to America. It has similar manifestations in Russia and Europe.

What concrete results has this boom in grey matter, "the only raw material that counts today", produced in America and in the world? This has been one of my key questions in my inquiry; and my plan in carrying it out has been to seek, not for a global ideological answer to resolve all doubts, not for other myths or slogans, but for precise results of work and concrete researches for deeper knowledge. Of what use is the most generous reforming impulse, the most genuine zeal for social improvement, the most sincere political protest, if it cannot express itself in bringing about concrete change? Of what use is politics if it has no root in reality? Knowledge is of its very nature revolutionary.

Knowledge is also, and always, limited and conscious of its limitations, and therefore critical of itself; it can neither permit a complacent pause on familiar ground nor offer revelations. The scientific mentality, Bertrand Russell said, is nourished on "constructive and fertile scepticism", not on "dogmatic beliefs . . . of militant certainty about objectively dubious matters". The dominant attitude in economic research today, it seems to me, is not millennial optimism but an experimental, analytical cast of mind: in the course of this inquiry I have found not prophets or wizards, but scholars and scientists. This is not the era of broad syntheses; but the field of research is very wide indeed.

The ideas of economists, so Keynes said, are objectively important and more powerful than is generally supposed: the world is governed by those ideas, and even practical men "are usually the slaves of some defunct economist".

I

AMERICA

AMERICA

1. Samuelson: We are not Magicians

At the Massachusetts Institute of Technology, in his room on the third floor of the Sloan Building, Paul Samuelson talked to me about Schumpeter. Behind him a big open window looked out on the Charles River which separates Cambridge from Boston. There were sailing-ships on the river, and beyond it the shining skyscrapers of Kennedy's city. A stormy wind was blowing from the Atlantic. Samuelson said: "I'd like to talk to you about Schumpeter, who was one of my teachers. Some time ago I was re-reading his great book, *Capitalism, Socialism and Democracy*, and in that book Schumpeter says that a mixed economy is as sterile as a mule. He used to talk to us at Harvard, in the early 1940s, about 'capitalism in an oxygen tent'. Reading the book again and looking back, I thought to myself how wrong he was. He foresaw nothing of what happened later on, the explosion of production in Japan and in Europe, our own long boom. He did not foresee the fundamental fact that the mixed economies would begin to grow so rapidly; I'd have to give him 'C minus', as if to a student who was brilliant but completely off the rails.

"But Schumpeter used to talk about one thing that seems to me today more important than it did, and that has come back into my mind after years when I never thought of it. I remember a famous debate at Harvard in 1940, with Wassily Leontief in the chair, between Schumpeter and Paul Sweezy. Sweezy was then Schumpeter's favourite pupil, he was young and good-looking and brilliant. Schumpeter, who must have been about 57 then, admired him greatly. The subject of the debate was 'Is capitalism dying?' At the end of the debate Leontief summed up. He said: 'You both agree in thinking that capitalism is dying. But Sweezy says it is dying of cancer, the cancer of the

internal contradictions of capitalism, in a Marxist sense.
Schumpeter, on the other hand, thinks it is dying of a psychosomatic disease. It's dying because it lacks the will to live. It's
dying of neurosis.' This is what Schumpeter thought. Well,
some years ago I would not have found that true. But today?
Look at the disorders at Harvard and in so many universities.
Is there perhaps a sickness of wealth? Are we sick of the Swedish
malady, of suicidal mania? No, I don't say that is so. I only
say that I found myself meditating about these things. Perhaps
Schumpeter, more or less by chance, foresaw this phenomenon."

I had telephoned to Samuelson from New York as soon as I
got there. "I'm here to start in America on an enquiry into
economics and the world today, and I'd like to begin with
Cambridge and with you." He replied, "Come the day after
tomorrow at three o'clock", but once in Boston he asked me to
put off the appointment until an hour later: on that particular
day the head of MIT, Howard Johnson, had suspended all
lectures and invited everyone, both students and teachers, to a
two-day discussion on the spreading unrest in the universities.
"We want to be ready for the protests that haven't yet happened
here", Samuelson told me later. And during the days I spent
there every single professor talked to me about this in amazement or distress or perturbation. But my subject is not the
situation of the American universities but that of economy and
the world today.

Travelling to Boston on the hourly jet shuttle service, full of
the usual businessmen in dark suits with briefcases (the middle-
class American dresses today as soberly as a Swede; in quiet and
orderly fashion they handed their credit cards—no one paid
cash—to the air hostess for their tickets), I had gone over in
my mind the little introductory speech that I was to make to
Samuelson. It went something like this: "When I last met you,
in May 1966, sitting in the sun on the steps of MIT on a finer
day than this, the long boom in the American economy had
gone on for five years, and you were very satisfied about it.
The boom went on for three years more; for eight years your
economy has expanded as never before, at an annual rate of
over 5 per cent; unemployment has virtually vanished, and

there have been no crises. Throughout eight fat years the 'new economics' has functioned, and this is partly thanks to you and the other economists who have educated the politicians well. Between the 'dismal science' of economics, that Carlyle spoke of in the days of Malthus, and the 'new economics' there is a great gulf. But America today is more disturbed and confused than it was eight years ago, and the 'new economics' are criticised by the young together with everything else. In the world at large, tumultuous economic growth destroys while it creates, it accentuates the differences between rich and poor countries, between the North and South that every country harbours within itself. Finally, at a certain point even the long American boom has come to an end and a recession has set in, a less acute recession than in the past, but nevertheless difficult to liquidate rapidly. The miracle of the permanent, eternal boom has not happened. Now I want to ask you, what, in your view, is the real balance-sheet of present-day economy? Is the economic approach inadequate for the economic problems it has to meet? Where is the economy going, if to be the 'science of growth' no longer suffices to satisfy people?"

This was the speech to which Samuelson replied with the sort of apologue I recounted earlier. I had chosen to make this speech to him first on my list because Paul Anthony Samuelson, who was then 55 (though he looked ten years younger), is perhaps the most representative personality of the post Keynesian-generation of economists who today guide the economic life of our world. Samuelson is also the man who in the whole of history has sold most copies of a book on economics: more than two million copies of *Economics*, the text in which he expounded his "neoclassical synthesis" of economy and which has given unity of language and concepts to economists throughout the world. Samuelson is a theoretician, a populariser, a practical man; a report of his on the state of the American economy in 1960, done for John Kennedy, is at the root of the innovations in economic policy of the subsequent decade.

Samuelson, who is small and lean with reddish hair, in conversation is not only highly lucid but often brilliant and witty, as in his column in *Newsweek*. He considers himself "the last general economist in an age of specialists". A great mathematical economist, he once defined the language of the non-mathematical economists as "depraved mental gymnastics". But besides using equations to express himself he can also do so in a scintillating English, a pretty rare gift among economists.

Our conversation was to a large extent dominated by a sober and realistic evaluation of the eight years of "new economics" and boom and by a balanced but impassioned summing-up of the great debate going on in the United States between "Keynesians" and "monetarists" on the techniques to be adopted, whether fiscal or monetary, to control economic cycles. These are the problems of the so-called "macroeconomics", which still occupy the greatest American economists. It is impossible to report the details of Samuelson's arguments, often elucidated by a graph or by figures written on the great green board that covered one wall of his study. The following is a summary of his views.

"The 'new economics' has shown that it is better able to resolve depressions than to function in a regime of full employment. The new economics has not yet discovered how to make an incomes policy work, and no other system of economics, from the Middle Ages to today, has ever been able to do this. In other words, no mixed economy has so far succeeded in having simultaneously, within a free market, full employment and stable prices. When there is full employment prices rise, and I know no simple method of solving this situation. Ever since we have had full employment, that is to say since 1965, we have never been free from the danger of inflation. Today we are all in agreement about a large part of economic science. But there are some things that we don't yet know: for instance, how to control inflation without creating unemployment, how to put on the brakes without throwing the passengers' heads against the windscreen."

Samuelson's frame of mind after the complex experiences of the 1960s is reflective—not pessimistic (as the father of six children he is a constitutional optimist), for the critical views I have mentioned take into account as a matter of course that side by side with the problems there is a great success-story;

the problems arise out of the success. But a scientist is not interested in looking back on solved problems or past successes: he wants to concentrate on the obscure and unsolved questions, on the failures and difficulties. This is the spirit of economic research today. Anyone embarking on this conversation with Samuelson in a mood of confident optimism would have soon found himself recalled to a more realistic frame of mind by this scholar's own self-criticism. Economics has made great strides, but it is reckoned that half of all the economic research accomplished in the whole of history has been done in the last ten years. And, as Samuelson says, "unfortunately we have only one history to work on, with no possibility of turning back to make experiments".

Samuelson is also particularly conscious of the fact that economic researches are expanding today into many new and different fields; this is a fact to be stressed. One of the most important economists at MIT, Franco Modigliani, a great friend of Samuelson, said much the same thing to me: "This is an interesting transition period in economics. But I must warn you: we, Samuelson, Heller and so on, are the old ones now, and there are many interesting young people coming on. We concern ourselves with the control of cycles and crises, with overhauling our cognitive instruments, such as econometric models and the fiscal or monetary means of intervention; but the young concern themselves with town-planning, transport, the economics of poverty or of education. But our problems still seem to me important, especially because no one is really convinced that the instruments we possess are entirely adequate to control the cycle."

The economic evolution of the past twenty years, which in general represents a success in almost the whole world, viewed objectively by the great economists can be broken down into a series of episodes, some happy some sad, into a series of problems some of which have been satisfactorily solved while others have found no solution. There is a conviction that economic knowledge is advancing, and into new fields as well—but with much unknown ground ahead of it, and many mistakes and uncertainties behind it.

Samuelson says to me: "Looking at the central problem of macroeconomics, that of control of the economic cycle and of growth, I would say that, as economists, we are in a good state of health; there has been a gradual and continuous advance. But there has been no Copernican revolution in economic science. We are not magicians, and we have not found the panacea, the remedy for all ills. We are just scholars."

So there has been no "Copernican revolution" in the market economy of the West. As we shall see later on in this journey among the economists, there has been no revolution capable of ensuring perpetual economic progress even in the centrally planned Communist economies. But on both sides there have been considerable advances and changes. The eight years of American boom undoubtedly owe much to the "new economics", and although they were followed by a "mini-recession", with a fall in the GNP to an annual rate of 1·5 per cent in the first six months of 1970,* nevertheless this check in development cannot be compared with the great and tragic economic crises of the past. Samuelson once wrote: "The insulin of budgetary deficits plus the penicillin of Federal Reserve policy increased the life expectancy of economic expansions by much more than medicine has been able to improve the life expectancy of man. But even Keynes could not guarantee that mankind would live happily ever after. He left us with an unsolved problem: how can we have full employment and also price stability? The truth is, we can't." Samuelson does not believe that the permanent answer to the problems of a full-employment economy lies in the control of wages and prices as recommended by Galbraith: "Wage and price controls are a powerful weapon in emergency situations", Samuelson says. "But with the passage of time, experience shows they develop leaks and inequities. Most experts think they should be husbanded for serious crises and not frittered away on creeping inflation." His conclusion is that in future there will always be "a bit of inflation and a bit of unemployment"; he likens

---

* And, according to some GDP calculations, to virtual nil growth (in common with Britain) during the course of the full year 1971 and the early months of 1972.

economists to dermatologists, who are said to be "the luckiest of medical men: they never cure their patients, but they also never kill them".

This may not be a heroic view of contemporary economic science, but it is certainly a realistic one, and not pessimistic at that. Realism, restlessness, even dissatisfaction with the results achieved, however brilliant, promise a stronger stimulus to further progress than would come from self-satisfiedness, ideological orthodoxy, or the weary repetition of stereotyped formulae. The restless spirit, tinged with scepticism, of Paul Anthony Samuelson is representative of what is the most authentically creative attitude in economic science in the world today.

Cambridge, Mass.

2. Heller: The Father of the Boom

At Cambridge, Paul Samuelson had said to me: "Walter Heller departed at the right moment, like Moses before reaching the Promised Land. He left the chairmanship of the President's Council of Economic Advisers in 1964, just when we were reaching full employment. Since then it has become much more difficult to regulate the economy." At Minneapolis, I began my talk with Heller by mentioning this view: what did he think of it? And was he worried about the criticisms of the "new economics" that had arisen in several quarters in these days of inflation?

Of all the "new economists", Walter W. Heller is the one most definitely identified with the golden age of the boom, from 1960 to 1964: "It was the highest point of our economic policy", Samuelson always says. At that time the newspapers spoke of "Heller's boom", and when we met some years ago, immediately after his return to Minneapolis, I asked him, "Is it true that you are the father of the boom?" He answered: "It has been my privilege to instruct two Presidents in modern economics, and it is modern economics that has led to the boom." There then followed a dialogue which I report because it serves better than anything else to explain what is commonly meant by "new economics". "The point of departure for us", Heller said, "was the theory of J. M. Keynes, as he expounded it thirty years ago in his *General Theory of Employment, Interest and Money*. To this theory", he went on, "we made some additions, especially in its practical applications. But, essentially, we took steps to realise the Keynesian revolution: we took Keynes's ideas and put them into practice in the contemporary political and economic setting. In fact, it amounted to an exercise in political economy."

I then asked him what were the fundamental principles of Keynes's theory. He answered with that synthesising clarity which is one of his great gifts: "The principles are as follows: in an economy there is no automatic machinery to bring it into a balance of full employment; consequently to bring an economy into full employment and maintain a process of development, the Government must intervene with its fiscal instruments, taxes and the Budget, with its monetary instruments, with a wages and prices policy and so on, in such a way as to ensure that the whole potential of the economy is utilised; but avoiding excesses and inflation, or vice versa stimulating the economy by means of reduction in duties or increases in expenditure. This is the essence of Keynes's theory: namely, that the Government must contribute towards regulating the economy in its development and in full employment, in the confidence that it can do so without allowing (and this is very important) public decisions to take the place of private decisions: in other words, protecting individual liberty even though the Government intervenes in the economy."

This, then, was the "new economics" of Walter Heller, possibly the most representative figure of our age, which he himself once defined as "the age of the economists". But now the "new economics" is under criticism: so if there was anyone to whom to put searching questions on the subject it was he, with his serene, Olympian certainty; and this is what I proposed to do.

But it was by no means easy, because Heller is one of the most agreeable people I know; not even his academic colleagues and rivals dislike him. For one thing, he has the great virtue of admitting his limitations as himself a practical economist and a politician of economy; he makes no secret, for instance, of the fact that he understands little of mathematical economics, and this wins him the sympathy of all those—and they are many—who don't understand it themselves but daren't say so. Heller is tall and good looking, with delicate long hands which he moves gracefully, and he looks rather like James Stewart. (He was as bronzed as an actor the day we met, having just come back from a trout-fishing trip.) He is a very nice man, and a man who believes in what he says and can convince others; it was really he who educated Kennedy in the "new economics".

He received me in his study, a small room full of books and photographs of Presidents on the eleventh floor of the tower in the School of Business. Here too, as in Cambridge, a river runs beneath the windows; not the modest Charles River but the fabulous Mississippi, already a colossal river even though it still has to cover hundreds of miles before it reaches the Gulf of Mexico. Minneapolis is a real American provincial city in which whole blocks have been cleared away, making room for parking-places. It is the city of Hubert Humphrey, who was its mayor and who is a great friend of Heller's. It is provincial, but it has an excellent university (and a big airport, as everywhere else: there is much in common in style between the airport and the university, a particular atmosphere of quiet efficiency and functionalism, and an intense rhythm of activity, which are typically American). So, I asked Heller, was it true that he had come back to Minneapolis at the right moment? And did he believe that the "age of the economists" was still going on, or had it lasted only eight years? "Those who are fond of biblical comparisons", Heller said, "threaten us, after the eight lean years of Eisenhower and the eight fat years of Kennedy and Johnson, with a fresh eight-year famine. But there's no reason for that fear." So his confidence in an active, conscientious, planned economic policy, as he called it, was not shaken? "No, for various reasons."

The main reason is that there is too obvious and striking a relationship of cause and effect between that policy and the state of the economy. In the eight years of Eisenhower there were three recessions and an economic growth-rate of 2·5 per cent per annum. In the eight years of Kennedy and Johnson, the "new economics" years, there was no recession and an annual growth-rate of 5·2 per cent. When Eisenhower gave place to Kennedy, America had an unemployment rate of 7 per cent; when Johnson handed over to Nixon, it had gone down to 3·2 per cent. In 1961 the "poor" families—families with an income of less than $3,000—numbered 42 per cent of all black

families, 16·2 per cent of white; in 1967 they were, respectively
27·1 and 12·5 per cent. "All that", Heller said, "didn't happen
by chance."

But the boom, I asked him, was it Heller's boom or the boom
of Vietnam? He answered: "When the big expenditure on
Vietnam began in May 1965, the boom had already been going
on for 50 months and had beaten all records [the previous
average duration of phases of expansion was 29 months]. The
war was not a help but rather a factor of serious disturbance.
In any case, there had never before been eight years of boom
without crises in the whole history of America, wars or no wars."

But, I observed, after the eight years the boom ended in
inflation: and the only sure way of curbing inflation is to
provoke unemployment and slow down productive development. This has in fact happened in America: indeed some fear
that they may end up by having stagnation and inflation together. How, I asked him, had this come about? Why was the
inflation not checked in time? Where did things go wrong?
"I admit", Heller answered, "that I did not think we should
be so bad at dealing with it. But at least we know where and
why we went wrong."

Heller's analysis of the economic policy of the last two years
of the Johnson régime, the inflation years, is detailed, and it
coincides, in fact, with that of the great majority of experts.
Both the politicians and the economists made some mistakes.
In 1966, when the first risk of excess of "aggregate demand"
appeared, Johnson did not follow the unanimous opinion of
his economic advisers that Congress should at once be asked to
increase taxation; he wanted to avoid a fiscal debate which
would have made all too apparent the high cost of the South
East Asian conflict. Two-and-a-half years went by, and between
Johnson's delays and the reluctance of Congress it was July
1968 before taxation was increased. Meanwhile the Pentagon
had regularly underestimated its forecasts of expenditure for
Vietnam. Thus the measures to control inflation were both
late and inadequate.

At a certain point the monetary authorities went wrong in
advocating an over-generous monetary and credit policy; and

in 1968 the economists too went wrong. Their forecast was that the 10 per cent supertax, when finally approved, would rapidly check global demand and inflation. But instead, said Heller with the figures in his hand, it checked, if more slowly than expected, the demand for private consumer goods; but it failed to check, throughout 1968 and early 1969, the demand for capital goods. Consumers and entrepreneurs reacted in only a limited way to the supertax, because today people are no longer afraid of economic crises: consequently, Heller explained, the propensity to spend and invest is much stronger than formerly. And then inflation already existed, people were expecting prices to rise higher, and so they reacted to the supertax not by saving but by spending more; it was not until a good deal later, so Heller said, that the anti-inflationary measures began to function.

Such is Heller's analysis of the mistakes, both practical and theoretical, of the last two years of Johnsonian boom and inflation: the years leading up to the subsequent recession. His analysis is critical but not disastrous. Mistakes were made, but they were not irreparable, and lessons were learned from them. Consequently Heller's faith remains intact in the Keynesian principle that active government intervention is necessary in order to maintain a "balance of full employment" in the economy. The medicine he recommends has not changed; but he thinks it should be administered in more careful doses (with "fine tuning", as they say in America). In future, Heller says, they will always be moving within the difficult "narrow band" of full employment and they will have problems that no country has so far solved completely; they will have to learn. In particular, three things must be done. First, an attempt must be made to introduce an incomes policy ("if Humphrey had been elected", Heller said, "triangular conferences would at once have been initiated with the industrialists and the trade unions to arrive at an agreed policy on prices and wages"). Secondly, the instruments for governmental monetary and fiscal policies must be improved. Thirdly, the structures must be tackled, by training the less fully qualified workers so as to eliminate structural unemployment without having to incur excess of demand and inflation in order to reach that result.

Heller talked at length on the second point, referring to the recommendations made to all Western Governments by an OECD committee of experts of which he himself was the chairman. The final report of this committee *(Fiscal Policy for a Balanced Economy)* is an important document, very optimistic in its general assessments ("The post-war economic performance of most Western countries . . . has been vastly superior to that of pre-war years. This, in our view, has not been accidental. . . . The more conscious use of economic policies undoubtedly played a crucial role") but minutely critical in its technical conclusions, full of detailed advice to governments on how to exercise a more subtle and precise influence on economic cycles, aggregate demand, and investments. Heller fully realises that there is no simple and easy answer to the problems of the "narrow bands" of welfare and full employment; but he thinks there is no need to be too frightened of a little inflation or to fight it by provoking unemployment. Looking to the 1970s, he was optimistic: the US Budget would have an annual "fiscal dividend", or natural increase in revenue from taxes, of 15 billion dollars, and only half that colossal figure (almost equal to the whole Italian Budget) would be absorbed, according to him, by the "natural increase" in expenditure. The other half can finance new social programmes or go into savings, In future, therefore, to "curb" the economy there will be no need to increase taxes, always a difficult thing to do; it will suffice to save on the fiscal dividend by not spending it—which is much easier.

Heller is not a programmatical optimist but an analytical economist who is convinced that he has a number of good reasons for his optimism. For one thing, he believes that Nixon and his advisers will pursue in their own way the "active policy" of the previous eight years: "Nixon", he says, "will be much more like Kennedy than like Eisenhower." But Heller is also of the opinion that it will be necessary henceforth to "look ahead, beyond the 'new economics', to social-economics". He has much faith in the young economists, fortified with a formidable scientific training and a profound social sense of involvement: "The young say, all right, we've got growth and full

33

employment; but let's go on from there." Heller's eldest son, Walter P. Heller, is also an economist; he was studying with Ken Arrow at Cambridge and was just about to start teaching, and he writes essays "that are pages and pages of formulae with a headline here and there". Heller *père*, at 53, was a trifle disconcerted by this: "My son's great joy", he said, "is to solve a theorem; my own is to solve the housing problem." The young, to him, are "a bit too mathematical"; but they will do much, especially in clarifying the functioning of the "non-market" sectors of the economy such as education, public health, town-planning, and natural resources.

"The young", Heller says, "will try to quantify these human and social values, to make possible precise and effective decisions, the fruit of knowledge rather than of the emotions. Economics is a science that satisfies the two fundamental characteristics of young people: their analytical spirit and their social involvement. It is a fine generation which will do a great deal, above and beyond the 'new economics'."

Minneapolis

3. Friedman and the Chicago School

The most widely discussed economist in America is called Milton Friedman; he is in the late fifties and lectures at Chicago University. He is the champion of economic free trade in the world and contests on a practically world scale the post-Keynesian theories which today dominate the economic policies of the Western States. The great majority of economists are convinced that the rapid development and absence of crises under "neo-capitalism" are due to these policies, based on the principle that the State must regulate world demand by its interventions in order to maintain economic activity at a level of full employment. Friedman, on the other hand, believes, so he told me in Chicago, that "State intervention is a luxury that only the rich countries can permit themselves: no policy of intervention has ever succeeded". Friedman has written: "The Keynesian economy does not function", and the ever-increasing numbers of his followers and "Friedmaniac" enthusiasts repeat these words of his at the top of their voices.

Friedman, who was economic adviser to Goldwater in the 1964 elections when the extreme right-wing Republican candidate was defeated by Johnson, not only wants the State to refrain from intervening in the economy for fear of doing harm; he would also like to see dismantled many of the institutions and policies that differentiate the twentieth century from the nineteenth: agricultural supports programmes, rent controls, minimum wage levels, any control of industry, social security and pensions, State housing, national parks, State monopoly of postal communications, licences for doctors. Friedman is convinced that the existence of trade unions has harmed the economy, and in particular the workers, by increasing the wages of a small minority and reducing those of the great majority. He also thinks military service should be abolished, and assistance to the poor should be carried out by means of a "negative tax" (the revenue should take money from the rich and give it to the poor).

I realise that this summary of Friedman's ideas makes him appear an almost grotesque and possibly unattractive character. Such a portrait is by no means true to life, for Friedman may be exasperating like anyone who fights against the general tide of ideas, but he is one of the nicest and most genuine people in America, and his intentions are good; his one real aim is to guarantee universal happiness and wellbeing by means of the return of the freest possible market. But if the synthetic portrait of Friedman is a bit disconcerting, this is his own fault—simply because it amuses him to "épater les économistes". He likes to "differentiate his products" (this is how he puts it)—in other words, to go blatantly against the current.

But let us begin by saying that he is an extremely serious scholar. His *A Monetary History of the United States* is not only the Bible of the "Friedmaniac" monetarists; it is also the definitive text on the subject for his opponents. The latter in speaking of Friedman oscillate between sympathy and exasperation. Heller, after many encounters with him (in the latest, a now historic public debate in New York, he had vainly tried to bring him to a theoretical reconciliation), spoke to me of him with real affection, recalling the days when Heller himself, as a young lecturer at the University of Wisconsin, led the revolt against the old professors in an effort to get a chair for Friedman. In Samuelson's talk with me Friedman's name came up in every sentence, recognising his acuteness and learning or recalling his phrase: "The economic Right, like the Bourbons, has learnt nothing and forgotten nothing".

Here we must add, too, that Friedman of Chicago, the pupil of Friedrich von Hayek and heir of the great liberalising tradition of von Mises and Einaudi ("Italy's monetary policy of 1948", he said to me, "was the beginning of the revolt against classic economics"), is also one of the Western economists most interesting to those Communist scholars who favour "market socialism". The theories of the Chicago free-trade school have filtered, via the great dispute of thirty years ago between Hayek and the Polish economist Oskar Lange, into the "new economics" of Communist Europe. It is from the East, in addition to Chicago, that the most vigorous apologetics for a market economy and against State intervention are heard today: the ways of economic thought are infinite.

So I came to meet Friedman in Chicago full of curiosity and expectancy. Everyone, his opponents included, had told me, "Friedman will conquer you". Friedman is a little bald man overflowing with gaiety. His study in one of the immense neo-Gothic buildings of the campus is in an incredible state of disorder, packed with books, papers and boxes. He sits half-hidden in the midst of all this, sunk deep in an armchair with his feet just touching the edge of the desk. To get to the University one has a drive of several miles along the vast shores of Lake Michigan. Chicago is immense, a vigorously vulgar city, with some of the most fabulous sky-scrapers of the "belle époque", all pinnacles, and some of the most bizarre and original ones of the 'sixties, pyramids or cylinders of fantastic dimensions: as far removed as can be imagined from the severe elegance of the lucid glass and metal parallelepipeds of New York.

In the taxi, the negro driver talked to me nostalgically of the Prohibition years, when the gangsters bumped off each other "but left ordinary people in peace". Everyone has his own ideas, and the negro with his nostalgia for the roaring years may have something to be said on his side. This is the city where the Democratic Convention of 1968 produced the "battle of Chicago" between Mayor Daley's police and the pacifists. It is also the city in which Daley, a magnificent demagogue, has realised grandiose plans for slum clearance. Two thousand new houses have been built on the site of a squalid slum around the University. Among the founders of the University in 1892 was John D. Rockefeller, the richest man in the world. The students sang: "John D. Rockefeller, Wonderful man is he, Gives all his spare change To the U. of C." At that time a strange man called Thorstein Veblen lectured in economics at Chicago, who regarded the Rockefellers and Morgans as "barbarian freebooters", slaves of their own "savage human nature". Rudyard Kipling after a visit to Chicago left it saying: "Having seen it, I urgently desire never to see it again. It is inhabited by savages."

Friedman too talked to me about that era. When I asked him what was his favourite period of history from the economic point of view he answered: "America from 1870 to 1914". It was a period of productive explosion in which huge masses of desperate, ignorant immigrants were absorbed. Friedman himself comes of a family of impoverished Jews from Ruthenia, who when they first arrived in New York worked for hunger-wages for some robber-capitalist of the day: "If there'd been a guaranteed minimum wage then", he said, "I'd be a Soviet citizen today".

We came to his ideas, and not those of a "political dilettante", as he describes himself (the Goldwater episode left a good deal of bitterness: "never again anything of that kind", says his wife, Rose, herself an economist), but his ideas as a professional economist. He began by reminding me that in 1942 he was joint author of a book called *Taxing to Prevent Inflation*. "At that time", he said, "I believed that fiscal policy was very important. Now I don't think so any more. In a certain sense, we are all Keynesians; in another sense, no one is a Keynesian now. We all use his bottles, but we put different wines in them. The differences of opinion about the usefulness of fiscal and monetary policy are not, fundamentally, a question of theory. It has to do with the empirical judgement about certain essential links between economic facts. My theory has changed since 1942, but what has changed much more is my understanding of the facts, or at least what I think are the facts, though I may be wrong. The fundamental divergence is about the facts". But then it is easier to agree? "Yes, and that's what's happening."

In Friedman's view, budgetary measures to control the economy have no effect of themselves, or only a "small, irregular, uncertain effect". Governments in the various countries increase taxes when they want to curb a too rapid or inflationary development; and they increase expenditure, or reduce taxes (as Heller and Johnson did in 1964, with great success) when they want to stimulate the economy. But Friedman maintains, on a basis of theoretical arguments and practical observations, that this does not work, and he also criticises credit manoeuvres (the increase or reduction of bank interest rates, with a view to restricting or encouraging expenditure by the public) and affirms that the stimulus or the curb come only from the rate of increase or reduction in the volume of monetary liquidity (money in circulation, bank drafts, etc.). In point of fact, his subtle arguments have convinced hardly anyone of the uselessness of fiscal and credit policy.

But Friedman has convinced many people of the fact that the policy of monetary liquidity is important: the amount of data that he has collected in support of his thesis is impressive. The "orthodox" Keynesian thesis, expounded for example in Great Britain in 1959 in $3\frac{1}{2}$ million words by the Radcliffe Committee and summed up by Harry G. Johnson in *The Times* (29 October 1968), was that "the quality of money is unimportant", and that only credit conditions mattered, because "they can influence spending, which can be more directly and reliably controlled by budgetary policy". Today, thanks partly to Friedman, partly to many Keynesians (beginning perhaps with a famous essay on liquidity by Modigliani in 1944), this oversimplified view has been abandoned. Samuelson himself cheerfully recognises the importance of the "rediscovery of money" ("there are fashions even in the sciences") and criticises the Radcliffe Committee just as Friedman does. "Friedman's studies", he told me in Cambridge, "show that money is important; but not that it is the only important thing, as he claims."

This seems to me to be the conclusion of the great majority of professional economists. As Guido Carli said to me some time ago, this is not a "querelle des anciens et des modernes" but a *querelle* purely between the moderns, the post-Keynesians themselves. Carli and many other scholars in any case think the dispute is not yet finally settled on the theoretical and practical plane.

Friedman has certainly contributed towards enriching the patrimony of economic ideas. theoretical concepts, and economic practice. But the paradox is that this partial technical success of his is producing results opposed to the aims of Friedman the economic philosopher. To explain how that comes about, we must go back to the ideas of Friedman the monetary technician. As we have said, he rejects the thesis that fiscal policy can be of use, and at the same time he maintains (I am reporting what he told me himself) that "on an average there is a close correspondence between changes in the volume of money and changes in economic activity". But this correspondence is not complete: "In certain cases", Friedman admits, "there are considerable discrepancies and delays. Changes in the volume of liquidity explain about half the variations in the gross product; the other half cannot be explained in this way but arise from a great variety of psychological, technological or other forces." From this cautious premise he draws the conclusion that "we simply do not know enough about it to use either fiscal or monetary policy as flexible instruments of control for the economy". Therefore, according to him, the only thing to do is to confine oneself to regularly increasing monetary liquidity by 4–5 per cent per annum and do nothing else in the way of an economic policy; in short, the State should disinterest itself from the economy.

This conclusion, however, which satisfies Friedman as the philosopher and apologist of a liberalising economy, has convinced no one. Friedman's opponents admit that money is important, but then they incorporate his technical ideas into their own ideological and practical pattern. In other words, they make use of his ideas not in order to eliminate State action, as he would like, but to make it more positive and vigorous.*
Thus Friedman as a monetary expert ends up by providing new weapons to the detested "statists": the spirit of the times is too strong.

He seems to me a victim of a "trick of Reason". His subtle talmudic dialectic, his immense erudition, end paradoxically by

* Perhaps the most forceful example of State action being increased and made "more positive and vigorous" has come from the United States itself. This was the Nixon Administration's singular abandonment of Republican tradition through the adoption of something looking very like a European-style prices and incomes policy.

turning against him. I raised these objections with him at the end of our conversation. His answer struck me as both clever and noble: "Certainly my theories can be made use of by the Keynesians. But one must distinguish between economics as a science and as an economic policy. We must discover what the facts are. Even if acquired knowledge can be used for wrong ends, that does not mean that we must abandon the search for truth."

And he went on: "You asked me if I had 'converted' many economists to monetarism. I don't like that word. Conversion has to do with faith. We economists are concerned with persuading, which is a very different matter. Our conclusions are always hypotheses; my own conclusions may be wrong, and someone else will find the true explanation. Recently I have several times found myself forced to warn people against exaggerating the importance of my theses. Naturally, economists don't discuss the things they agree about but the things about which they disagree. The only interesting thing in intellectual activity is to add something to what we know already, and how can one do that if one confines oneself to repeating what all the others say? When the day comes that I'm in agreement with the majority, it will mean that I've stopped working: and then someone else will have to go forward."

Chicago

4. McCracken: The Man with the Rule

Talking with Milton Friedman in Chicago, I had asked him whether he was satisfied with Nixon's economic policy. I'd said: "The Republicans have used Keynesian methods against inflation, maintaining the supertax, abolishing tax facilities for investment, and increasing rates of interest. The influence of your ideas is not apparent here." He'd answered: "It is important that there should be continuity in federal policy; and then, too, the President has to take into account public opinion. I don't think Nixon is wrong if he says to me: 'You may be right, but a lot of people think otherwise, and I have to do both things, what you advise and what other people suggest.' So I did not expect any revolutionary changes. But I think Nixon may change the fundamental direction of economic policy, as Roosevelt did. At the beginning he changed very little, but thirty years later everything had changed."

I was much struck by these comments of Friedman's. At Cambridge I had taken down something that Paul Samuelson said: "If Friedman's ideas had prevailed, this would have been the moment for the anti-New Deal. Nixon might have marked the beginning of the reaction, and thirty years later the workers would be back in 1929. But fortunately the Friedmanites are still in a minority." I copied this word for word from my notes: it gave one to think.

A comparison of these two comments gives rise to many doubts and questions: is the new economic policy of the 'sixties destined to last, or will it be overthrown? Are the apparent structural changes in the economy, the absence of crises, the more rapid development, merely ephemeral things? Are we perhaps victims of the same illusion that in 1929, on the eve of the great depression, caused the same sort of things to be said as are widely said today, namely that capitalism has changed its character, that there will be no more crises, and so on? Or, was, for example, *The Economist* right when it said (10 May 1969): "The great achievements of the 1960s are that the governmental mechanism has been reformed, and that the country has been set on the course . . . to semi-automatic economic expansion . . . American economic policy is now much more nearly idiot-proof"?

I sought an answer to these doubts in Washington in the course of a conversation with Paul McCracken, who at that time was Chairman of Nixon's Council of Economic Advisers (previously he had been a professor at the University of Michigan). His predecessors as Chairman were Okun, Ackley and Heller, in the Democratic years when the Council acquired great influence, becoming a sort of planning committee endowed with almost regal powers. Everyone I talked to spoke well of McCracken, from Samuelson ("he was my choice, though I didn't say so for fear of damaging his chances") to Heller and Friedman. McCracken owes this unusual consensus of approval to his rare gifts, which are obvious even in a single encounter: great precision and lucidity of exposition; balance and impartiality; and the vocation of a conciliator (in our conversation he two or three times used the typical phrase, "I would choose the middle way").

He is in his early fifties, small, thin, and kindly, and I would have liked to have him for an economics professor. He listens attentively and before speaking he stops to think for a moment; then he answers clearly and directly, speaking with the verbs and complements in their right place. And he gives you the great satisfaction of saying, in a precisely expressed and authoritative way, things that common sense had made you think yourself. He likes to hold a slide-rule in his hand; he even has a tie-pin in the form of a rule.

His big study in the Executive Building beside the White House (this is certainly one of the most horrific buildings in the world, a mass of pillars, architraves, capitals and porticoes in battleship grey) is impeccably tidy: black-and-white curtains drawn at mid-day, very bright lights, a green carpet, tables and desks in the Swedish style; and the stars-and-stripes flag beside his desk, as befits one of the great federal officials.

My first question was: "You are the President's chief economic adviser. What real prospects have you of carrying out an effective economic policy, as compared, let us say, with twenty years ago?" He answered: "The prospects are much better, for several reasons. Our system of economic information has greatly improved. Economic theories have been developed which enable us to make better use of our analyses. And what counts even more is that the public has a better understanding of economic affairs. Lastly, economists play a much more important part than they did twenty years ago."

"But there is sharp disagreement between the monetarists and the Keynesians. Does this worry you?"

"Not in the least. We are witnessing today a gradual convergence of the opposing standpoints. In the Hegelian sense, a synthesis is emerging, and I see no theoretical difficulty in arriving at it, even though I don't claim to have solved all the theoretical problems; but there are no reasons of principle to prevent our reaching a synthesis, and this is the direction in which we are moving. Ten years ago an economist who attached importance to the volume of monetary liquidity would simply have been laughed at; but not today. The development of Friedman's monetary school has been an excellent thing. Macroeconomics had virtually ignored monetary phenomena, with seriously harmful results: as in the second half of 1968, when a deflationary fiscal policy was pursued at the same time as an inflationary monetary policy."

"Friedman hopes (and Samuelson fears) that the advent of Nixon as President may represent a historic turn in the economy."

"Ours will be a more liberal approach—in the European sense of the word. We are also more conscious of the difficulties arising from government intervention in the economy. The great strength of the American system is the continuity between the successive Administrations. We shall pay more attention than our predecessors to monetary policy. But above all we shall be less inclined to have recourse to making big changes in economic policy for anticyclical reasons. The strategy of frequent and subtle interventions ignored the fact that the effects of economic measures make themselves felt only after a long delay. It was a policy that derived from an excess of ingenuousness and enthusiasm, and it has proved disappointing. We shall follow a more gentle, gradual method."

McCracken's dispute with his Keynesian predecessors does not concern the principle of whether or not the State should intervene. "If we are to have a fiscal policy, and obviously we must, and if we are to have a monetary policy, and that too we must", McCracken said, "then we need a strategy that will include both the Budget and the currency." The dispute is about what is known as "fine tuning", the Hellerian ambition of correcting economic policy almost from day to day by means of "subtle adjustments". This is the trend that caused one of the chief men in Congress, Wylbur Mills, to say in exasperation: "It's not a good thing for taxes to go up and down every six months like women's skirts."

Today quite a number of people think there was an excess of technocratic zeal in the ambitious "fine-tuning" programme. One of the critics of this technique, Peter Drucker, has observed that the difficulties of macroeconomic policy arise from the absence of a "theory of macroeconomics"; in other words, there is a wide margin of unpredictability in the reactions of the "economic molecules" (industrialists, consumers) to the indirect macroeconomic interventions, whether fiscal or credit, of the central authority. These interventions do not impinge directly on the big economic factors: they impinge merely on the heads of those who take the real decisions. This is why macroeconomics remains not only a science but also an art, to be applied in moderation.

From this point of view there is a good deal of sense in the greater caution with which McCracken approaches the problem of macroeconomic policy. But McCracken certainly stands beside Nixon in seeking an active economic policy. Another of Nixon's economic advisers, Herbert Stein, has brought out a book in which he condemns Eisenhower's economic policy in terms similar to those of the "new economists", and vindicates Nixon and various Republican economists for having fought for a Keynesian policy ever since the 'fifties. Ideas such as that of the "full employment Budget" (a technique which consists of evaluating the State Budget not according to the current figures but on a basis of what the credit or deficit would be if there were full employment; this technique leads, in countries where there is unemployment, to courageously deficitary Budgets) are now the common property of everyone, Friedman included. In short, the revolution represented by the "new economics" seems to be to a great extent irreversible; Friedmanist hopes of an anti-Roosevelt swing were dependent on uncertainties.

But if economic policy has radically changed, has the actual structure of "neo-capitalist" economy changed too, and for the better? This is a popular thesis of the journalists, and it is also widely shared by ordinary people: in almost all countries the fear of crises and mass unemployment which was a constant preoccupation during the first thirty years of this century has virtually disappeared. But the economists are more cautious: at the most they admit what Kenneth Galbraith said to me some years ago: "We are facing a solid evolution of the economic order". And the economists have good reason to be prudent: we need only recall to what extent this general boom rests on the immense growth of international trade to realise that a generalised monetary crisis or a "trade war" between America and Europe could have disastrous consequences.

It is always dangerous to generalise. Not so many years have gone by since an important economist, Jevons, seriously maintained that economic cycles lasted 10·45 years and were the result of spots on the sun; and even more recently no less important economists such as Simon Kuznets and Arthur Lewis put forward the theory of "long cycles", lasting twenty years, and on the basis of it predicted a world crisis in the 'sixties. Economists today confine themselves to thinking serious crises unlikely, without advancing counter-theories about the "progressive future" of the economy. My job, in any case, is not to theorise but to record. And it is interesting to note that the thesis of the "qualitative as well as quantitative" change in cycles and in the capitalist economy is beginning to be accepted also in the USSR. I have seen the text of a good lecture given at Philadelphia by Professor Stanislav Menshikov, of the Institute of World Economy in Moscow: it represents a real revolution in Soviet economic ideas.

Menshikov spoke of "drastic changes in industrial organisation" in the West as a result of the development of long-term planning in the big concerns. He noted the tremendous increase in "governmental functioning" for anti-cyclical purposes. He observed that "some of the changes in governmental and industrial planning, and in the economic cycle, bring the capitalist economy nearer to a socialist type of organisation". Menshikov recalled the pre-revolutionary writings of Lenin (those in which he praised German "State capitalism") as proof that a certain "similarity between the two systems" can arise, and he concluded by saying that today "the repetition of a crisis like that of 1929–33 is very unlikely".

How far away we are from the catastrophic predictions of Karl Marx, who envisaged capitalism being overthrown by a dramatic crescendo of crises and the desperate spread of poverty! It is no mere chance that our reading of Marx, even in the USSR, has become increasingly metaphorical and symbolical, like that of the Holy Scriptures: but for Marx violent revolution was a concrete thing, like, in the world of Genesis, Jacob's wrestling with the angel of God in the thicket of fire.

Thus everyone seemed to be agreed that there would be no more dramatic upheavals in our economic life—everyone including the Communists, the Keynesians, and even Milton Friedman, who told me in Chicago that Western economy was now "depression-proof". The reason, he said, was because "It cannot experience an economic collapse without first having a monetary collapse; and that is impossible today, given the wealth of data available to us. No monetary authority could repeat the mistakes of the 'thirties".

* * *

Some time has gone by since my meeting with Paul McCracken, who is now no longer Chairman of the Council of

Economic Advisers to the President. The "mini-recession" of the winter of 1969–70 showed that the control of present-day economy through the regulation of "global demand" by means of fiscal and monetary interventions was less easy than the optimists had hoped: expansion is not "semi-automatic".* True, the "mini-recession" is not a serious phenomenon like certain disastrous crises in the past. If the perspective is extended from America to the whole Western world, the crisis of the US economy in 1970 should not prevent the real economic growth of the OECD countries from reaching around 3 per cent; and forecasts suggest that in 1971 growth in those countries will rise again to about 4·5 per cent.

It is not, in fact, to be excluded that by the end of the 'seventies, looking back on the difficult outset of the decade, the American "mini-recession" of 1970 may come to be seen as an economic fact of secondary importance, a mere brief interruption in the rising curve of present-day economy. Already in 1971 real growth went back, in the USA, to about 3 per cent; 1972, according to preliminary calculations, was expected to be once more a boom year, with a real growth of between 5 and 6 per cent.

Nevertheless, the "high-level check" of 1970 is a phenomenon no less significant than the previous eight years of boom (and growing inflation). The history of American (and Western) economy in the 'sixties is, on the whole, a history to inspire confidence and even optimism. But the final chapter of this history, at the opening of the new decade, has a sobering effect and induces greater caution in expressing a judgement

* Or, to put it another way, how to have an effective counter-inflationary policy without removing the environment for economic expansion altogether. As an example of both the dilemma and the different approaches of the professional economists and the political managers of the economy, one has only to examine the British situation in late 1972–early 1973. Following the introduction of counter-inflation legislation in November 1971, economists of the National Institute of Economic and Social Research and others of equal prestige protested that the Heath Government could not possibly keep all the balls of its economic policy in the air at once. These included a prices and incomes "standstill", calculated to reduce annual increases in this sector to around 5 per cent as against 10–11 per cent in the previous two or three years; a 5 per cent overall growth rate from 1973 onwards; and, not least, a proposed 10 per cent value-added tax rate from April 1973.

on modern economics; its merits are indubitable but not unlimited. We can certainly be confident that some disastrous mistakes of the past will be avoided; but it may still happen, in the present state of knowledge, that a complex machinery like the economy of a great country, conditioned by a vast number of different factors, whether technological, psychological or political, may come to grief at some point and encounter difficult periods when it cannot function up to its highest potential.

Modern economic science will obviously devote ever-increasing efforts in the coming years to problems of this kind. But to solve them it will not suffice to operate within the traditional spheres of macroeconomics and around the question of regulation of global demand. In order to confront these problems it will be necessary to enlarge the scope of our reliable knowledge to many different fields. Avant-garde economic research has certainly more than one "new frontier".

Washington D.C.

49

D

5. Modigliani, Klein, Fromm: The Adventures of Econometry

Like every science that is concerned with human affairs, economics oscillates between reality and Utopia. Within the framework of contemporary economic studies, dominated largely by practical and immediate needs, the researches of econometry open up wider horizons to utopian tendencies. On the problems of econometry I have interviewed three great dreamers: Modigliani, Klein and Fromm. Each of them will probably be annoyed at that description, for all three are convinced that they are firmly anchored in reality. And they are right too, for their mathematical models of the economy have practical applications and can even be useful in business; moreover these models are complex but realistic representations of that highly intricate system of human relationships that constitutes a country's economy.

The theoretical systems of the great economists of the past were abstract. In econometric models mathematical abstraction represents merely a form of language; but behind the millions of figures, the hundreds of variables, the systems of dozens of simultaneous equations that constitute the model, there is reality with all its contradictions and variations. No, the utopian spirit of the econometricians lies not in their use of numerals (the motto of the Platonic Academy, "Let none enter who does not know mathematics", is valid for the whole of modern economies) but in the human impulse that moves and inspires them.

Theirs is a modern Utopia, nourished on statistics and matured in electronic calculators, but it is nevertheless Utopia: it is the image, that is to say, of a perfect world modelled by Reason armed by Knowledge. Modigliani, Klein and Fromm are visionaries, who have, indeed, an eye to business and to everyday problems, but who in their heart of hearts look far off to a future economy freed from every trace of anarchy and unpredictability. Their ideal is the forecast, therefore Prophecy ("If it would help me to make correct forecasts I'd hang myself by the heels from the ceiling," Samuelson told me). The perfect forecast—when it is achieved—should enable us to make logical choices and decisions. Schumpeter in the 'thirties was already saying that economic development was becoming increasingly a "question of calculation." Econometry was to transform Utopia into reality.

Modigliani, Klein and Fromm are all three men with clear eyes, rather remote, typical somewhat absent-minded professors. I have seen all three of them absorbed and caught up in the examination of great sheets filled with minute figures, and the saying about Robert McNamara could apply to any of them: "He reads balance sheets at home in the evening by way of relaxation, just as Brahms used to read musical scores: behind the figures he sees human beings." This does not mean that the three have any illusions about the difficulties of their adventure: econometry is still in its first infancy, and it has given its devotees as many disappointments as satisfactions.

The most self-critical of the three is Franco Modigliani, a Roman by birth but American by economic training. We talked at length in his house at Belmont, near Cambridge, after we had been together to a remarkable poetry-reading given in the public library by Ungaretti, then in his last years but doing an American tour. Modigliani told me: "At the moment I can't honestly say that the results are anything to be enthusiastic about. Unfortunately we have not yet reached the point where we can say: here we are, we have a model which is a solid basis for work, it only remains to perfect it thus and thus. We are still at the experimental stage." The other two are more optimistic. Gary Fromm, whom I met at that great research centre, the Brookings Institution in Washington, explained to me that we are on the eve of a real technological breakthrough, represented by the imminent entry into operation of public central "data banks", connected to electronic terminals in every research centre, which will enable any scholar or student to work on econometric models, experimenting with new ones and comparing them with each other. Lawrence Klein told me that his model, at the Wharton School of the University of Pennsylvania (where he received me in a study so minute that what with the two of us and the books you could hardly open the door), "has passed the most difficult test, that of the market." Today, forty-two of the biggest industrial companies and banks in America are collaborating on the three-monthly elaboration of the forecasts of the Wharton model, making practical use of it and financing it.

But both Fromm and Klein recognise the truth of what Samuelson said to me: "Economic models are still in their infancy. They do good work, but they can't yet take the place of judgement." "We shall never have the perfect model", said Klein, "but we are doing better all the time. The important thing is that in our forecasts we hit the mark in most cases." In fact, comparing the Wharton forecasts from the summer of 1963 to 1970 with those of practical economists, the balance is decidedly in favour of the model, even though in 1968 it and many others were widely off the mark in their premature forecasts of an end to inflation and the boom. Now they are analysing the reasons for the mistake (the models of the Friedmanian "monetarists" were less far out), and apart from "inflationary psychology, an element difficult to quantify", future forecasts will avoid the earlier mistakes. Or at least they hope so.

An econometric model is the representation, by means of a system of equations, of the whole range of economic activity. That is to say, it establishes mathematical relationships, based on theoretical analysis and on statistical elaboration of the data, between the main "variables" in the economy. The first model was constructed by the Dutch economist Jan Tinbergen in the 'thirties, for the American economy: thirty years later it won him the first Nobel prize for economics. Tinbergen's model of the Dutch economy in 1955 was very simple: it assembled together in eleven equations 55 "variables", such as the volume of exports, of goods and services, and of imports, the index of prices of State expenditure, wage rates, etc. Klein's model for Great Britain, in 1958, had the same number of equations. The present Wharton model, which is the most famous, has 47 equations. The models constantly tend to become bigger and more "disaggregated" in the effort to get closer to the extreme complexity of the original, which is the economy of a country.

The largest model is that of the Brookings Institution, on which work has been going on since 1962, with the collaboration of all the American universities, but which is still in the experimental stage ("we shall make regular forecasts in a few years", Fromm told me). It involves over 300 equations and seven economic "sectors", and is based on over 2,000 "temporal series of data". It will eventually become, so Klein told me, a model of 1,000 equations and 35 sectors, capable, that is to say, of making "disaggregated" forecasts for 35 branches of production, incorporating what is known as an "Input–Output model". Brookings, Fromm says, "stands in relation to the other models in the same way that the atom of today, subdivided into innumerable particles, stands to the simple atom of Niels Bohr".

In a system of simultaneous equations, it only needs a change in one variable for all the others to change. Only the infinite capacity of computers to make calculations, and the progress of mathematics, can enable such complex problems to be solved. But the chief difficulty in constructing a functioning model lies perhaps less in this than in the problem of interpreting rightly, and with a correct theoretical analysis, the assembled data, and of establishing the correct "parameters" which can be arrived at only by experiment.

"Things which we regard as stable parameters", observed Klein, "can be subject to cycles, trends, or casual shocks. Econometry is a bit like meteorology", also in the sense that it cannot do laboratory experiments. Physicists are the lucky ones because "they have to deal with stationary processes, since the structure of the universe changes very slowly", whereas "government institutions, banking practice, laws, and social life cannot be simplified for the benefit of the economists". Systems must be "continuously changed and disaggregated to make room for new factors that have only just been discovered".

A recent revision of the American statistical series has made it necessary to "recalculate" the Brookings model from top to bottom. New problems have been raised by the evolution of monetary theories. The econometry seminar at Philadelphia in the summer of 1969 was largely devoted to an extensive econometric analysis of monetary problems, mainly on the basis of work carried out at MIT by Modigliani and his colleagues on the MIT—Federal Reserve model, which contains, so Klein says, "the finest treatment so far of the monetary sector".

Klein also says: "You can't construct a model that is valid for always, and then leave it to the accountants. This isn't a job for armchair theoreticians. To construct a realistic model of the American economy, you need a year to collect the data, a year for estimates and experiments, and then years of tests before applying the model to practical problems; and every two or three years the model has to be brought up to date."

A labour of Sisyphus? Or will it be possible in the end to reach the goal of an economy that is explained, understood and forecast down to its most intimate and unpredictable developments? And if perfect, or almost perfect, models are achieved, what will be left of market economy? Shall we not be on the threshold of perfect planning, as Fedorovic and the other Soviet believers in "planométrika" dream? As far back as 1920 Trotsky visualised the day when planning would be able to count on "an ideal accounting apparatus, with the kind of keyboard where, by pressing a button, a certain quantity of coal, firewood, or manpower can be transferred to wherever it is needed". Trotsky lamented the non-existence of an "ideal keyboard of this kind", and in fact it does not exist even today. But in the electronic era this Utopia seems less remote than it did in the Russia of war Communism.

Meanwhile American econometry strives to absorb and synthesise all the experiences of modern economies. The three great models of Wharton, MIT and Brookings have been joined by many others ("some of them not without a touch of black magic", says Fromm). The United Nations is preparing a model based on the econometric analysis of thirty developing countries, which should be capable of providing a perfect recipe for economic progress. "All the simple explanations of economic life are destined to failure", Klein says. Reality is multi-equational and "non-linear", in other words there is not always proportionality in the relations between variable magnitudes.

While awaiting the perfect models, we have to "go on doing accounts on the back of an envelope", using the simple theoretical methods of economic tradition, from Adam Smith to Keynes. This is still the economics of today. That of tomorrow will be something very different.

Philadelphia

6. Leontief: What "Input—Output" Is

Wassily Leontief has a favourite quotation from Balzacs'
Cousin Pons: "Foreseeing future events is no more difficult than
discovering the past. If past events have left their traces, those
of the future have their roots." Leontief is interested in detailed
rather than general forecasts. In the market, he says, thousands
of concerns are involved in the "costly and delusive game" of
foreseeing the future. How? "I am a Darwinian", Leontief
tells me. "Read Darwin, see how he collected his data patiently
over many years; when he brought out a theory, it was a
terribly powerful theory." Wassily Leontief was born in St.
Petersburg in 1906, studied in Leningrad and Berlin, emigrated
from Russia in 1925, came to America in 1930, and has been a
Harvard professor since 1931. He, like Darwin has worked over
a long period on collecting data—in his case, the data needed to
construct that part of the edifice of modern economics that
bears his name: the input-output analysis.

Leontief does not much care for theoretical economists, who
"don't like dirtying their hands with data. They are like people
who are used to a hunger diet", he says. "Their stomachs have
contracted, too many facts give them indigestion." Leontief
has an iron stomach, and in the 'thirties he fed it on millions
of figures. At that time he had only one assistant at Harvard.
His bible was the economic census figures for 1919 and 1929;
his ambition, to arrange these myriads of figures in a logical,
reasonable way and discover their hidden order. Subdividing the
economy into its main productive sectors, he set about showing
what each of those sectors took from and supplied to each other
sector: what each sector put in (input) and gave out (output).

Leontief attacked the mountain of data, like a sculptor a
block of marble, with the scalpel of mathematical analysis.

"Economic theory", he said to me, "has to fly very high, and mathematics is a powerful engine that enables us to reach spheres to which we could not otherwise attain. But mathematics must set out from and land on the solid ground of facts" ("whereas", he added, "modern mathematical economics is often too abstract, like an aeroplane that cannot land"). Setting out from the statistical data, Leontief succeeded in constructing by means of mathematics a matrix, a picture of the whole economy which showed the flow of resources from one sector to another. From the concrete figures relating to a given year, a system emerges of coefficients which fix the relations of exchange between the various sectors; this system is none other than the image of economic society at a certain stage of technological development.

It is obvious that any change in the production of a single sector will be reflected in all the others, and the primary effects are followed by secondary and tertiary effects, in an interweaving of "reverberations" which in theory is inexhaustible. But modern mathematics can resolve these problems. It can also calculate the effects of the birth of a new technology or a new industry, and foresee, on the basis of technical data, how that new factor will transform, perhaps ten years later, the whole matrix of the national economy. Thus the "forecasts game" can acquire rationality.

To create a system of input-output tables is a most laborious undertaking today; but it was much more so in 1931 when Leontief came to Harvard, for there were no computers then. "I began by doing my reckonings by hand", Leontief told me. "By good fortune, an engineer at MIT, John Wilbur, was constructing a colossal calculating machine weighing 20 tons. He solved the mechanical problem and I the theoretical." Even with Wilbur's calculating machine, the first inter-sector tables of the American economy, covering the years 1919 to 1929, were ready only in 1936. The matrix that was subsequently prepared, with support from the Government (under the stimulus of wartime problems), concerned the year 1939; it had 95 sectors and was ready in 1944. In the matrix for 1947 "disaggregation" was carried to a maximum of 200 sectors.

Such detailed analyses are made possible only by means of modern computers and the practical and theoretical advances in statistics. Only in such minutely detailed pictures of past events can the roots of future events be discerned.

Within the framework of modern economics, Leontief by reason both of his personal role and his achievements has a key place. The input-output analysis is a meeting-point between theoretical and practical economics: "The deductive and aprioristic method of traditional economics, accustomed to describing the economy as a system of at most four or five great variables", Leontief says, "has now been replaced by the inductive and empirical method based on analyses of data."

Into this process is inserted the technique of input-output, which interests Soviet planners no less than American big business men. The more advanced countries use it to estimate the consequences of technological revolution; but the developing countries also make use of it to fill the voids in their productive structures.

Recently input-output has become allied with macroeconomics and with econometry. I have already mentioned that the great Brookings econometric model includes an input-output table covering 35 sectors. At Philadelphia the econometrician Klein told me: "It is the industrialists who are constantly urging us in the direction of 'disaggregated' forecasts: they are more interested in learning what will happen to their own particular industry than in knowing what the Gross National Product will be next year or five years hence." Thus forecasts range from "aggregate" predictions of the GNP to take in, via input-output analyses (one of the sectors of the matrix is that of aggregate demand), sector forecasts as well.

Leontief is pleased about these developments, but when we spoke of the Brookings model and the marriage between econometry and input-output he reacted by telling me a Russian anecdote. "A man says, 'I can make a splendid *bortsch* with a pound of nails'. All the peasants say this is impossible, but the man insists that he can do it. He takes a saucepan, puts water in it, thrusts in the pound of nails and a big piece of meat, some sausages, red cabbage, and beetroot, and produces a splendid *bortsch*. If you put an input-output analysis into econometric models they turn out all right. But why put in the nails?"

Leontief is a robust, lively, contentious person. His eyes and expression are very mobile, sometimes he wears his hair in an arrogant forelock, sometimes he smooths it back and his face takes on a mild gentle look. I saw him at Cambridge in his room in Littauer Building, a fine neo-classical edifice which forms the background to Harvard Square, where Galbraith, Gerschenkron, Kuznets, Eckstein, Duesenberry and goodness knows how many other famous people work. One might be tempted to conclude that the place contains the highest concentration of economic intelligence in the world, but for the splendid Georgian edifices on the other bank of the Charles River, of the Graduate School of Business and a bit further on the Sloan Building of MIT . . . and but for Cambridge, England. When you read this list of names on the ground floor of Littauer Building, you are struck at once by their different national origins, and you find yourself reflecting that economy is still, all the same, a single science, in which each school is linked to the others by invisible but strong threads.

Leontief is the most typical example of this situation. His first article appeared in 1925, originally in Berlin and then in Russia in *Planovoe Khozaistvo* (Planned Economy). At that time he was much influenced by the Soviet economists, a remarkable collection of talented men. But many of his Russian teachers or contemporaries vanished in the great purges: Stalin had no love for objectivity in science. The Soviet economic school was destroyed and rose again only thirty years later when it opened up to Western influences which sometimes, as in Leontief's case, had their roots in Russian soil.

It is indeed a remarkable fact that input-output analysis was not invented by the Soviets, as an indispensable instrument of rational planning. Instead the Gosplan always made use of "materials budgets", or tables of the use of essential resources, which were a crude and simplified form of input-output analyses. It was not until the 'fifties that Leontief's techniques were introduced into Russia through the Polish economist

Oskar Lange, who had spent many years in America (he lived in Leontief's house when he first arrived at Harvard), and the elderly academician Nemchinov. In the 1920s Nemchinov had prepared a famous analytical table of cereals consumption in Russia which, whether as a result of Stalin's misunderstanding or his deliberate distortion of it, provided the theoretical justification for the collectivisation of agriculture. Nemchinov, who died in 1964, spent the last years of his life in a courageous fight for the reform of Soviet planning, and Leontief was invited to the USSR in 1959. He was shown the very first Soviet input-output table, for the year 1925, which had been finished just in time for his arrival. A similar cross-fertilisation of research between Leningrad and Harvard, between Leontief's school and the work of the great Leningrad mathematician Kantorovich, now at the Akademgorodok of Novosibirsk, occurred in the field of linear programming, discovered by Kantorovich in 1939 and rediscovered and perfected at Harvard by Koopmans and Dantzig some years later. The strange thing is that the Russians only realised the importance of this discovery (linear programming is a highly refined mathematical technique for the solution of problems of choice) after a time-lag of twenty years, when it rebounded in Russia from America.

Input-output analysis is an essential instrument for a reasoned planning of economic activity, whether for the Russian type of centralised national planning or for the development planning of concerns operating in a market economy. It is in the latter field that the input-output technique is showing its full results in a country like America, where out of the incredible multiplicity of data and the constant comparison of forecasts a sort of pluralistic "planning by mutual consensus" is emerging. Leontief told me: "My work in recent years is mainly for private industry. I don't like business, but a scientist can't confine himself to solving theoretical questions."

Leontief collaborates with the big company of business consultants A. B. Little of Boston in the solution of practical problems. For example, from an input-output analysis done by Little of the American economy projected up to the year 1980 the financial and industrial operation emerged which led to the formation of North American Rockwell Aviation, one of the key concerns in the space field.

"Today", Leontief says, "many private companies use these techniques to organise their own development", placing it within the framework of calculated projection of the "disaggregated" sector-by-sector development of the whole economy. Federal organisations are also making increasing use of input-output: a vast sum is to be spent on an inquiry into the hydrological resources of the watershed area of the Rocky Mountains, by means of an input-output analysis for the development of the whole region up to 2000 A.D. Thus even without central planning the "rationalising" effect is achieved; and this without destroying the market or annulling its function as a mechanism of control of costs and efficiency and as a channel through which the consumer expresses his judgement about the quality and trends of production.

From my talk with Leontief, one of the recurrent themes of this inquiry into the state of economic science in America seemed to me to emerge very clearly: namely, the universal preoccupation with the marriage between theory and practice. Another of the Harvard economists, Hollis Chenery, who after the war was one of the originators of the first input-output tables for the Italian economy, said to me: "Economics is going through a modernisation crisis. Theoretical and practical work is no longer separable, but at last a scientific procedure is being followed. A theory is worked out, statistical tests are made, we go back to the theory to refine and amplify it, and compare it once more with the facts, and so on through more and more improvements until we end by arriving at a theory which will explain the greater part of the facts observed and will satisfy both the theoreticians and the practicians. Thus economics is laboriously becoming a science."

Cambridge, Massachusetts

7. Ford: "Business" and Market

Flying between Washington and Detroit on a sunny morning, America seen from above seems like a gigantic "op" picture: the anti-erosion ploughing draws circles, spirals, and black and white scrolls upon the hillsides. An hour of silent flight in the jet, half-an-hour rushing along the motorway, and I find myself at Dearborn, the headquarters of Ford. Detroit is still a long way off, and from here you cannot see the procession of skyscrapers along the Detroit River, where steamers go by even though we are right in the middle of the continent. All round the Ford industrial complex there are great open spaces with grasslands and woods. Dimensions in America are boundless. There is no problem of building areas here.

My appointment with Henry Ford II is for the afternoon, so there is time to meet some of the managers. We talk about the "Maverick", the new "utility" 2000 cmc which costs only a few dollars more than the Volkswagen, the "beetle" that the new Ford model wants to squeeze out. Ten per cent of the American market has been won by foreigners, especially the Volkswagen and the Japanese; a possible offensive by other European giants could create serious problems.

It is odd that Fords should be the people to lead the counter-offensive against the Volkswagen, for the first "beetle" in the history of motorcar manufacture was Henry Ford I's "Tin Lizzie", the famous T model that you could get "in any colour so long as it was black". The "Tin Lizzie", like the Volkswagen, had a long life, and when it suddenly went out of fashion Fords very nearly went down with it. But all that is ancient history; today there are so many Ford models, and so many choices of colour and accessories, that by mixing up all the possible combinations the factory could produce two million cars each different from the other.

I had come here to talk to Ford because among the subjects of economic research one of the most important is the big concern. How far does giant size in industry modify the market? Is it a good or a bad thing? And what are the relations today between big business and the State? I wanted to check at the source some fashionable economic ideas. Henry Ford II received me in his shirt sleeves in a well-lit modern study. He is a big bronzed man with grey hair and side-whiskers. His manner is direct and businesslike. They tell me he is an excellent organiser. During the conversation I suspect that some of my references to economic theory struck him as rather odd; but he listened to me politely.

I began with a subject that Ford, an "engagé" industrialist, had dealt with in many speeches: the social responsibilities of the modern industrialist. I had in mind a recent comment of Gunnar Myrdal: "We are witnessing today a remarkable and rapid increase in the number of enlightened entrepreneurs. This trend may be among the main reasons for continuous rapid development and reforms to eradicate poverty." What had he to say about this?

"The first thing industry has done and is doing is to organise itself so as to provide work for the hard-core unemployed who are regarded as unemployable. Here we have done some good things. But what we can do depends on the state of the economy. The boom has made it possible to absorb the hard core of unemployed, but they are the last to be taken on. If there were a decline in the economy as a result of the struggle against inflation, those people would unfortunately be the first to be sacked, on the basis of our contracts with the trade unions on the subject of seniority."

"What does business think of the economic policy of these recent years?"

"It is very important that the Government should provide for a situation of full employment. This is what it has been trying to do, at least since Kennedy. The economic climate created by government policy in recent years has been advantageous to business too. We have all shared in the country's growth."

What did he think about control of investments, wages and prices? "I am against it. Market forces are a better guide than any government directive. The Government's wage guidelines have not been much use and have been abandoned. As for price control, whether by law or by the arm-twisting technique (used by Kennedy with the steel industrialists), it is unfair. Only a few arms can be twisted. Mine was." This is the view of Ford and many others. But the prospect of some anti-inflationary control over wages, prices and profits won some approval at a meeting in the summer of 1969 of the Business Council, a governmental consultative organisation to which the hundred biggest concerns in the country belong. (Later on, Nixon's new policy of controls was supported by most businessmen.)

I went on: "Galbraith, in *The New Industrial State*, says that today the market is dominated by the big oligopolistic firm which, 'far from being controlled by the market, has made the market subordinate to the goals of its planning'. And thus 'prices, costs, production and resulting revenues are established not by the market but . . . by the planning decisions of the firm'. Is it true that the market counts for so little today?"

"If Galbraith came here to see how work functions, he wouldn't hold those theories. Have you read today's papers? The General Motors 'Corvair', the car with the engine at the back, is dead. The reason is because people wouldn't buy it. The market decides what it wants; if it doesn't want it, it doesn't buy and that's the end of it. We need to have competitive prices and an attractive product, otherwise the consumer says no. There used to be two thousand makes of car in the United States; today there are four. What has happened to the others? They failed to survive because they had not the right prices or products for the market. People always have standards of comparison between all our models and the foreign ones. The truth is, there's a great deal of competition even between our own models, let alone the others."

The English economist D. H. Robertson has defined the great concerns as examples of rationality in the midst of the anarchy of the market, as islands of conscious power in an ocean of unconscious cooperation, like clots of butter coagulating in the whey of milk. This, according to some, is a good thing; to others it seems as if the islands were becoming continents and getting too much power. I asked, "Has the word 'capitalism' still got an unreservedly good meaning in America as it once had? How does the public regard the business world?"

"The country has differing views about business. There's a lot of social unrest, and some people criticise everything, business included. But without business the country wouldn't exist. People work either for us or for the Government; and the Government looks to our pockets to find the money for its dependents. Some people attack us for publicity, or because they think it's necessary in order to defend the consumer. But I don't think that is the view of the public in general."

Adam Smith used to say that the majority of factory owners "seldom take a direct interest in their business and are quite satisfied with getting that interest on capital which their directors deem convenient to allow them". Today many economists, beginning with Galbraith, maintain that the real power has definitely moved into the hands of the managers, the technical establishment. Did Ford think this true?

"The question doesn't interest me."

"Has the Government's ability to manage the economy improved?"

"Answering as an amateur, I would say yes. They have done a great deal, especially in recent years, for the good management of the economy. We try to keep ourselves abreast of what the Government is doing; even if we can't always see the entire scope of its problems and certain things may seem wrong to us, what has been done should in general help the economy as a whole."

Such is modern economy as seen from Dearborn. The judgement of the radical Swede Gunnar Myrdal seems to me correct. The task entrusted by Kennedy to Heller in 1960 ("I want you to educate the country in modern economics") has been carried out pretty well.

I will end this chapter with a comment on Galbraith's thesis on large concerns and the market (I was unable to meet Galbraith himself then since he was abroad). The trend

65

E

towards giant size in industry goes back a long way. Before Galbraith, Berle and Means pointed to it in the 'thirties, Rudolf Hilferding referred to it in his *Finanzkapital* (which was closely imitated by Lenin) at the beginning of the century; and so did Engels in *Antidühring* in 1877. This trend is both criticised and extolled, even by Engels and Lenin: extolled because, in large concerns, "the unplanned production of capitalist society yields to production according to a plan of the upsurging socialist society", says Engels.

These critics-cum-extollers always believed that the trend towards concentration was on the point of triumphing, and that the big concerns were about to twist the market's neck like a chicken. Paraphrasing Churchill, I would say, "Some chicken! Some neck!" If this is a death-agony, it is certainly a very lively and long-drawn-out one, so much so, indeed, as to make one wonder whether what was taken for a rising trend is not a more or less constant feature of a market set-up which may be "imperfect" in relation to theoretical patterns but which nevertheless works—and possibly works better just because it is imperfect.

The doubt arises whether Galbraith may not have discovered old things and ignored the new. For example: the increase of inter-sector competition, "between steel and aluminium, aluminium and plastics, plastics and cement, cement and steel", as Robert Heilbroner instances; the formation, in the last twenty years, of a world market and a genuine international competition; the emergence of the tertiary sector of the economy, of services, schools, hospitals, tourism, transport, trades. Victor Fuchs, a theoretician of "services economy", considers that Galbraith "overlooked" the fact that the predominance of big industry is really drawing to a close, perhaps is already over. The United States is the first "services economy".

Since the day when Colin Clark wrote in 1940 that "the economics of tertiary industry remains to be written", the studies of Fuchs and many others have illuminated the strange rules of this new supporting sector of the economy. It is a sector in which the small and medium-sized concern predominates; where owner and manager are often one and the same person; where non-profit-making undertakings feature widely (such as schools, universities, hospitals, all kinds of social and public services, transport etc.); where levels of production are stable and economic cycles tenuous or non-existent; where work is not alienating but highly personal. The exact opposite, in fact, of big industry. Fuchs has demonstrated that in America the biggest concerns "reached the apex of their growth in 1956"; thereafter, their share in the GNP became stabilised or declined.

Thus, judged alike by the big industrialist concerned with the inconvenient realities of competition and by the economists involved in *avant-garde* researches, the picture of an industrial society where the market is killed by the sheer gigantic size of big business seems, to say the least, roughly drawn and incomplete. This is, moreover, the thesis of Robert Solow's famous answer to Galbraith. The market, even if it is no longer that of the sacred tests of Adam Smith and Ricardo, is slow to die.

Detroit

8. Denison: The Factors of Development

With Edward Denison, at the Brookings Institute in Washington, I talked about one of the new fields of research: the economics of development. Why does an economic system grow? What are the development factors? The classic analyses mention two main ones: capital and labour. The third factor, technological progress, had already interested Ricardo, but we had to wait for Schumpeter and the first decade of this century to find the formulation of an economic theory that gave just weight to that innovation. Then a gap of nearly fifty years ensued before an American economist, Robert Solow, in an eight-page essay of 1957 established the theoretical bases for a quantitative inquiry into development.

In the intervening years since that essay was written a great deal of work has been done on the subject. But Hollis Chenery was right when he said to me at Harvard: "This is only the beginning: we are scratching the surface". Denison's inquiries into the causes of development in the United States and Europe also retain an almost experimental character. "We still have to devote 80 per cent of the time to collecting information and only 20 per cent to analysis", he told me. Economics is a young science. It will be many years before the efforts to disaggregate and quantify the Schumpeterian concept of the innovation can give precise results. There are many difficulties in a field like this, on the new frontiers of economics. Traditional macro-economics, including the post-Keynesian "new economics", aimed, and still aims, as its main goal at realising, by means of manipulating aggregate demand, the full use of the human and physical resources available at a given moment, thus bringing actual production close to the "rising ceiling" of possible production. This new branch of the "new economics", the economics of development, aims instead at discovering the means to raise the ceiling, or its slope; it deals, that is to say, with structural rather than functional problems, although both are closely linked in many ways. For in an exhausted and depressed economy technological progress is much slower, whereas in an economy stimulated by strong demand the structures become spontaneously transformed to productive ends.

There is immense interest in these studies, especially among young people, even though a less mythical significance is attached to the actual concept of economic development than was the case fifty years ago: "In addition to growth", Franco Modigliani told me, "the accent today lies on the kind of social investments which are not registered as an increase in the GNP, but which improve living conditions. The GNP only registers certain aspects of the economy—not happiness or good living." Despite this evolution in the dominant economic philosophy, most economists would certainly agree with the view expressed to me by Paul McCracken: "The problem of development cannot be set aside—America is the richest country in the world, the average American family in the year 2000 will have an annual income of 25,000 dollars, but for the time being there are many families whose material needs cannot be satisfied. The only answer to their problems still lies in productive development."

People today have a much clearer and more precise idea than even a few years ago of the phenomenon of economic growth. A volume such as Walt Rostow's *The Stages of Economic Growth,* of 1960, important though it is for certain ideas it contains, is out of date by now on the plane of technical analysis. To find out what stage research has reached I came to Denison, whom *The Economist* has described as America's master-economist in those problems.

Denison has never been a university professor, and he says himself that he regards himself as a "lone wolf". But he worked for fifteen years, from 1941 to 1956, in the Department of Commerce, and was a member of the team that evolved the national system of economic accountancy adopted by the

United States at the end of the war and later by all other countries (we don't realise how new certain familiar terms are: Keynes in the 1930s never made use of the idea of a "Gross National Product"). Denison has been at Brookings since 1962, and I wish I had the room to talk about that splendid research centre, for it is one of the most important things in America today; it has no equivalent in Europe. But I haven't the space for that, or even to spread myself about the personality of Ed Denison—a kindly giant who slowly, with deliberation and a sense of humour expresses precise and deeply-thought-out ideas—or about his methods of work: I will only mention that other scholars use different techniques, for the methodology of this type of research is still a matter for debate.

Denison's two great inquiries, the first (1962) on the United States and the second (1967) on the comparative development of the United States and Europe, represent in substance an intensive effort to "disaggregate" the concept of productivity. His American study *(The Sources of Economic Growth in the United States and the Alternatives Before Us)* reached a fundamental conclusion: that the increase in manpower productivity, or in the product of each individual worker, in America was to be attributed only to the extent of 10 per cent to increase in the capital utilised; 90 per cent of it was due to advances in knowledge, education and organisation, according to Denison's precise reckonings. This 90 per cent, in short, represented technological progress, which had become the main factor of development in the world of today. Other investigators have arrived at similar results. Much is being done, and much more remains to be done, to define these ideas more precisely.

I come now to his comparative study on America and Europe *(Why Growth Rates Differ)*. In writing it Denison had to overcome immense difficulties; European statistics, "especially the Italian", he told me, were not always of the same level as the American. But all the same great progress has been made; a study of this kind would have been unthinkable twenty years ago. Take, for example, from among the mass of data, tables and statistics that Denison provides, the figures relating to development in Italy, Federal Germany, and

Great Britain in the period 1955–62: as will be seen, they permit of significant comparisons. During those years national income in Italy increased by 5·78 per cent per annum, and in Germany by 5·39 per cent. Denison's analysis shows how these similar rates of development were achieved in profoundly different ways, and how the rate of growth in Britain, which was much lower (2·27 per cent), might have been increased. But we will concentrate here on the comparison between Germany and Italy.

Denison analyses the rates of growth by dividing them into two main categories: the percentage of increase due to a rise in input, or in the physical factors of production, capital and labour; and the percentage due to rise in production per input unit, or the increase in productivity of the factors mentioned above. Some substantial differences emerge. The increase in the volume of manpower contributes to the rise in national income to the extent of 0·20 per cent in Italy and 1·13 per cent in Germany. Improvement in the level of workers' education, on the other hand, provides a greater contribution in Italy than in Germany: 0·40 per cent as against 0·11. Increase in capital gives a contribution of 0·80 per cent in Italy, 1·57 per cent in Germany (the Germans save and invest a higher proportion of the national income). Taking into account the fact that during the period in question shorter hours of work per worker were introduced in Germany but not in Italy, the total of the "physical" factors, capital and labour, contributed to the increase in the Italian income to the extent of 1·48 per cent per annum, in the German income to the extent of 2·51 per cent.

In compensation, the "better use of resources", or in particular the transfer of workers from backward sectors like agriculture to more productive sectors like industry, caused an annual increase in income equal to 1·44 per cent in Italy and 0·66 per cent in Germany. "Economies of scale" are also greater in Italy than in Germany; 1·40 per cent as against 1·25. In conclusion, the increase of production per unit of physical input is 4·30 per cent in Italy, 2·88 per cent in Germany.

Sources of increase in the national income in Italy, Germany, and the U.K. 1955–62

(Contributions to the annual rate of increase, in percentages)

Factors of production (input)	Italy	Germany	U.K.
Manpower:			
Employment	0·20	1·13	0·37
Work-hours per worker	0·03	−0·45	−0·30
Age-Sex	0·05	0·15	−0·02
Workers' Education	0·40	0·11	0·30
Capital	0·80	1·57	0·80
(a) Total of factors of production	1·48	2·51	1·15

Increase in production per unit of input	Italy	Germany	U.K.
Advances in knowledge	0·76	0·76	0·76
Better use of resources:			
Reduction in agricultural and crafts uses	1·44	0·66	0·09
Lowering of international trade barriers	0·16	0·10	0·02
Economies of scale	1·40	1·25	0·43
Irregularities in pressure of demand	0·00	0·00	−0·29
Other causes	0·54	0·11	0·11
(b) Total productive increase per unit of input	4·30	2·88	1·12
Total annual increase of production	5·78	5·39	2·27

What do these figures mean? They mean that development in Italy was rapid, but it would have been much more so if the increase in capital invested and in manpower employed, two closely related factors, had been quicker, as was the case in Germany. I calculate that had that been so, the rate of development in Italy—other things being equal—would have been 7·48 per cent per annum instead of 5·78 per cent.

Making use of Denison's data, another American scholar, Michael Boretski, has compared Italy and the Soviet Union for the period 1950–1962. During those twelve years the two countries had almost identical annual rates of development: Italy 6·1 per cent, the USSR 6·3 per cent. The USSR obtained this result thanks to an annual increase in "physical inputs", capital and labour, of 4·48 per cent, and in productivity of

1·82 per cent; Italy thanks to an increase in "physical inputs" of 2·13 per cent, and in productivity of 3·97 per cent.

The Italians can, if they wish, congratulate themselves on this analysis: it shows that, thanks to greater efficiency, they obtained the same advances as the USSR with fewer sacrifices. Boretski calculates, in fact, that if the Soviet economy had had the same increase in productivity as the Italian, it could have devoted nearly 190 billion dollars more to consumer goods between 1950 and 1962; this explains why people live better in Italy than in Russia.

But I don't know whether we Italians should really congratulate ourselves on this comparison. The fact is that if Italy had increased the "physical factors" of production at the same rate as the Germans and Russians, by saving and investing more, its economy would have grown by $7\frac{1}{2}$–8 per cent per annum rather than $5\frac{1}{2}$–6, thus definitely approaching the Japanese "phenomenon". These analyses give particular pertinence today to the question, is Italian society really so advanced as to be able to permit itself to invest less than Germany and the USSR? Is it not absurd that Italy today should be exporting both capital and labour, instead of using them at home?

Naturally Denison's analysis does not say why this underemployment of capital and labour exists in Italy, whether because of absence of aggregate demand, or entrepreneurial shortcomings, or for psychological or other similar reasons: "I have tried to calculate", Denison says, "the contributions of use of manpower and capital, and of the reduction in wastage of resources in agriculture; but I could be asked, in respect of each of these sources, why has it changed in the way described? There is no room in my classification for the final and more determining influences on growth such as birth control, physical structures, spirit of initiative, labour intensity, or planning; their effect is not analysed here."

Denison does not, therefore, suggest remedies: his analysis merely shows that the "traditional" factors of development, capital and labour, are those that offer, in Italy's case, the most immediate and easiest possibilities to accelerate the rate of growth. Another of the fundamental factors in Italy's rapid development of the past twenty years, the large-scale absorption of underemployed manpower from the agricultural sector, will, as Denison pointed out, eventually become exhausted. In compensation, the marked improvements in the sphere of education and training, which are greater than in any other European country, are "a very important factor in future growth".

Denison's analysis shows its versatility if, on the basis of these data, a quite different comparison is made, that between Western Germany and Britain. Here we have two economies which are very similar in respect of size, level of development, per capita product, and national product. Nevertheless Western Germany's economy during the period 1955–62 grew at an annual rate of 5·39 per cent, more than double the growth rate in Britain, which over the same period was 2·27 per cent. How is it that two similar economies reached such very different results?

The first striking difference lies in the increase in employment, which contributed to the growth of the German economy to the extent of 1·13 per cent, and to that of the British economy to the extent of only 0·37 per cent. Leaving aside other minor differences which had a favourable effect on one or other of the two economies, the second conspicuous difference lies in the increase of capital: the German economy, devoting a much higher percentage of its resources to investments, increased its stock of capital much more rapidly. The annual contribution made by this increase to the growth of Germany's GNP was 1·57 per cent, as against 0·80 per cent in Britain. The third fundamental difference concerns the reduction in agricultural and handicrafts employment, in other words the transfer of labour from those branches to industry: in Germany this contributed to growth to the extent of 0·66 per cent per annum, whereas the corresponding figure in Britain was only 0·09 per cent. The fourth factor, "economies of scale" (made possible by the greater speed with which, for the other reasons indicated, the German market expanded), contributed to growth to the extent in Germany of 1·25 per cent, in Britain of 0·43 per cent. Lastly, attention is drawn to the negative effect of irregular pressure of demand in Britain (–0·29) and the lesser advantage (0·02, as against 0·10) derived by the British economy from the lowering of international trade barriers.

Now, it is obvious that some of the reasons for the swifter growth of the German economy (for example, the more rapid increase in employment and the transfer of manpower from agriculture to industry) would not apply to the same extent in Britain. But if Britain's economy had invested more and increased its stock of capital more quickly, if it had taken greater advantage of the lowering of international trade barriers, had maintained high internal demand, and had created more favourable conditions for securing economies of scale, its rate of growth, though still less than that of Germany, might have been much higher. An English economist, Alan Day, reckons that it might have reached 3·70 per cent per annum instead of 2·27 per cent. The lessons in economic policy to be drawn from such an analysis are clear. The difficulties, naturally, lie in carrying out the desired policy, and here political and social factors enter in which fall outside the strict scope of the economist. Economic problems, as we know, concern not only economists but businessmen, workers and politicians as well.

One of the fundamental lessons of Denison's analysis of growth to emerge particularly clearly from the comparison between American and European economic development is not to overestimate the effectiveness of anticyclical measures towards achieving a higher rate of growth in the long term. Whatever economic policy America might have adopted in the 'fifties, the rate of growth of the economy would still have been lower than that of the European countries, for the simple reason that America lacks certain structural growth-factors which are present in most European countries because of their relative backwardness. In particular, the high growth-rates of the European economies benefit from the transfer of manpower from the less productive sectors (agriculture) to the more productive (industry); and they also benefit from being able to imitate the American model and the techniques of

75

work evolved in the United States. On the other hand, capital formation is lower in the United States, and this factor is, in theory at least, susceptible of modification. The conclusion to which these comparative international examinations lead is clearly that every country must, above all, compare its own achievements with its possibilities; this is the most productive analysis with a view to drawing up an effective economic policy for more rapid growth.

I have given only a very impressionistic and sketchy picture of the work being done in the sphere of development economics. It should be emphasised that research in this field is still mainly in the pioneering stage, and as such it is sometimes unsatisfactory even to those who are carrying it out. This is inevitable when working in one of the more advanced fields of economic research.

Washington, D.C.

9. Mesthene's Technology

Of the five million parts of the Saturn-Apollo system in one of the journeys to the moon, only five failed to function properly. The index of efficiency was 99·9999 per cent. This result, without precedent in the history of technology, represents, so to speak, the technological apex of human evolution, although it was the fruit of barely ten years of study of space problems. The speed of progress achieved is less amazing when we recall that 90 per cent of all the scientists in history are alive today.

Facts and considerations of this kind, Emmanuel Mesthene would say, are manifestations of that optimistic vision of technical progress which in simplified fashion regards technology as "a providential thing for humanity, the motive power of all progress, the solution of all our problems, the source of permanent prosperity, the Utopia of our times". Mesthene indicates at the origin of this technocentric ideology great thinkers from Marx to Comte, and he numbers among his followers not only politicians and industrialists concerned with space matters but also authoritative scientists. He nevertheless considers this triumphalistic vision of progress just as mistaken as the opposite, wholly pessimistic, view that produces "paranoid literature".

To the pessimists, Mesthene says, "technology is a calamity; it deprives people of work, of a private life, of participation in democratic government; it generates materialism and destroys religion, it annihilates the individual in a technocratic society and a bureaucratic State; it threatens to poison Nature and blow up the world". The list of pessimists, from Marcuse to Jacques Ellul, from Lewis Mumford to Hannah Arendt, is illustrious; this view has conquered scores of publicists and is highly popular with the young. But what is the real nature, apart from myths, of this central fact of our times, technological progress? Where is technology going, and humanity with it?

It is fairly typical of American culture today to tackle subjects of this kind, which we would be more inclined to leave to the intuition of poets and philosophers or the rhetoric of politicians, by means of a research programme entrusted to a band of specialists. There is certainly something ingenuous about this attitude. But the great myths, always contradicted by opposite myths, are of little help as a guide to understanding such phenomena as the technological revolution. A certain degree of scepticism should not, therefore, prevent us from appreciating the organised efforts of research teams to detach facts of this kind from the surrounding fog of myth and commonplace.

Emmanuel Mesthene, director of the ten-year study programme on "Technology and Society" which is being carried out at Harvard and financed by the IBM (the International Business Machines corporation), cherishes no absurd ambitions. "Our aim", he says, "is to raise the level of public discussion on this subject, to try to understand and explain more clearly the effects of technology, and to diffuse the results of our researches by making them known among the leaders of thought in the Government and the Universities."

The headquarters of this research programme is a nineteenth-century house in one of the residential quarters behind Harvard University, in that area between the University and the Charles River where brick-built houses covered with red American creepers create the illusion of some corner of England. This particular house was once a rectory; today, in what used to be the kitchen, with a black iron stove adorned with the heads of Roman emperors, the secretaries work. Mesthene's office is in the sitting-room. Mesthene himself is not an economist but a philosopher; he is around fifty years old and has behind him years of work for the Rand corporation and for OEEC; he also used to play the flute as a professional soloist. He speaks several languages and is a very attractive person; the *New York Times* in an article about him mentioned his "fine Mediterranean profile". He is a Greek-American. Above his fireplace is the motto in Greek ,"Think" (a publicity gadget of the IBM), and he is convinced that the Athenian citizen was much less individualistic and more conscious of his civic responsibilities than the modern American. As we talk we drink thick Greek or rather Turkish coffee—or, to be quite honest, an American imitation thereof. The Programme's permanent staff is quite small—just three researchers and their secretaries. But the research plan mobilises, at a total cost of five million dollars, the efforts of dozens of scholars. Now in its fifth year of work, the large number of short essays that have appeared so far are being incorporated in the first big volumes.

I have thought it right to talk about this research here, even though it is only on the fringes of economics, because it is one of the typical aspects of present-day economics that the boundaries between it and the other human sciences tend to overlap and become blurred. The great virtue of a programme of studies like this, Mesthene tells me, is to be inspired by "the ideal of inter-disciplinary work". In this way economics acquires a non-economic approach to economic problems; sociology and politics imbibe the analytical and factual strictness of economics; the foundations are laid for a new human science. All this "comes about more easily on the fringes of the university atmosphere"; in universities—American universities included—the disciplines are more separated and jealous of each other.

It is not possible to sum up briefly a vast complex of studies like that directed from the suburban house in Cambridge, Mass. "One of our main themes", Mesthene tells me, "is the transference of the demand for private consumer goods to public, social goods, such as air, the countryside, education [this trend, still widely prevalent, derives from Galbraith's criticism of the opulent society]. In America private business was especially equipped to produce goods for private consumption, which used to represent 90 per cent of total consumption. But today the ratio is half and half. Who is to produce public goods? Who is interested in producing them? Can the private concern be modified so as to satisfy the new demands? Or will new organisations have to be created?"

Mesthene often uses the word "externalities", which has become almost a slogan today: it means the benefits, and more frequently the *external* social costs, of the private individual's search for well-being or for profit. A large part of the drawbacks of technology are "externalities" and fall outside the normal economic accountability of the market or the State. In order to evaluate them better, Daniel Bell, a theoretician of the post-industrial society, would like to see set up a national "social budget" instead of the usual financial budgets: the idea has some affinity with that of "global" (and not purely economic) planning which is gaining ground in some European countries. But to arrive at such a budget it will be necessary first to penetrate and illuminate widely differing spheres of economic and social life, and to destroy mountains of commonplace acceptances. The problem is arduous.

Let me give an example. A study in progress of Edward Shils on "Technology and the individual", whose conclusions I give in advance, dismantles the facile myth of the "destruction of individuality" in a technological society. "This", Mesthene says, "is perhaps the first era in history in which so high a proportion of men regard themselves as individuals." The fields of choice, whether of consumer or ideological choice, are wider than ever before. By comparison, the Victorian era may seem "the golden age of privacy" only in the sense that then "no one bothered about what happened to the average individual, who was free to remain ignorant, suffer hunger, grow ill and die in the most complete privacy".

The present-day trend towards collective and State initiatives, far from reducing man to mass level, permits him "very much wider individual aspirations than before". But the tensions of our time also derive from this. "When technology makes a social and human ideal theoretically attainable but society shows itself incapable of realising it", says Mesthene, "the conflict between ideal and real becomes acute, and tremendous tensions are born." Within this framework, "the

traditional American system, individualist rather than socie-
tarian in its orientation, is no longer adequate for the needs
of our society. . . . It becomes necessary to invent a system of
values and a social, economic and political organisation adapted
to a society so strongly dominated by technology. This problem
will have a foremost place in our research programme for the
coming years".

I would describe this as a scientific-revolutionary trend in
studies. The methodology, which includes within it medicine,
economics, education, town planning and transport, lies in the
non-acceptance of any cultural idol without first discussing
and checking it. The America of the "technetronic" era, as
Brzezinski describes it, shuns alike traditional patterns and new
mythologies. Global ideologies, such as the Marcusian theory
of "single-dimensional man", survive only half a day.

The studies in the Harvard programme are mainly social.
Elsewhere they are striving to analyse the sources and productive aspects of the technological phenomenon; researches
are multiplying, and here too some myths have collapsed. The
belief has been confirmed that the growing speed, measured in
every detail by some experts, with which scientific discoveries
are being assimilated into the productive process is one of the
mainsprings of economic evolution. But the view of Schumpeter
and Galbraith, that the big concern is the privileged seat of
scientific, technical and economic progress, is no longer held valid.

At the University of Pennsylvania the thirty-eight-year-old
economist Edwin Mansfield, a sort of blond cowboy who is
one of the most brilliant scholars in this field, summarised for
me the results of dozens of specialised pieces of research: "For
a long time it was believed that large-scale production was the
main source of technical and scientific progress. With certain
exceptions, this is not so. The majority of the important
discoveries of this century have come not from the great corporations but from the universities, or from small and medium-
sized concerns or government initiatives." The big concern,
on the other hand, maintains an essential function in the subsequent phase, that of "innovation" or the "practical application of the inventions".

F

This conclusion, undisputed today among the specialists, represents a powerful argument in favour of a non-bureaucratised and widely differentiated market, in which small and medium-sized concerns can continue to exist side by side with the colossi of industry. The American experience seems to show that even where the colossi exist, ambitious small concerns can live and prosper. We must leave room, Mansfield says, for the "unpredictability of invention". Scientific discovery naturally flourishes well in the framework of a society that can mobilise vast forces and allocate huge sums for public and private research. But there is always an element of surprise and unpredictability about it, and it develops better in a pluralistic and differentiated economic atmosphere. Then the fall-out of scientific discovery, which is quickly exploited by the big productive organisations, "irrigates the system, giving it vitality": that is a simile I have borrowed from Guido Carli.

Cambridge, Massachusetts

10. Forrester: The World is a Complex System

"The problem is not to foresee the future but to create the future. My mentality is not like that of the mathematical economists, who aspire to understand; it is like that of the engineers and politicians, who aspire to change and project." So Jay Forrester said to me in Cambridge, where he is professor of management at the Massachusetts Institute of Technology, creator of a new discipline called Industrial Dynamics, inventor of the "magnetic memory" used in computers, and projector (in the 'fifties) of the Aviation's system of continental defence, SAGE (the semi-automatic ground environment system). Forrester is a great electronic engineer who has become an economist, and he is one of the most unusual people I have met in this enquiry. Not a few of the great economists of the past had, in conjunction with their genius, a grain of craziness, a certain strain of the visionary. In the course of this journey of mine I have met many brilliant men with a very high intelligence quota: but all or nearly all of them seemed to me eminently practical and reasonable people. This, whether rightly or wrongly, is slightly disappointing. But Forrester did not disappoint me, and he is certainly a highly stimulating thinker. Someone described him to me as the most brilliant brain in the whole of Cambridge. Someone else considered him an eccentric with original methods of research, but of doubtful value.

Forrester is concerned with "complex systems". Examples of such systems: a city; a business concern; international trade; a government. The most complex system of all is human society on earth. "Complex systems", Forrester says, "are counter-intuitive, non-linear." In other words: the number of variables is so great, and the interactions of factors and the

83

multiplicity of reactive circuits, or "feed-back loops", are so complicated, that the intuitive interpretations of a normal person accustomed to the physical, homogeneous and "linear" world are "more often wrong than right". All the mistakes of man throughout history are born, fundamentally "from the inability of the human mind, accustomed to linear reasonings, to understand a social world that is non-linear". One of the scholars in this subject, Ladis Kovach, has said: "We have overcome the sound barrier, we are about to conquer the thermic barrier, but we are only on the threshold of the non-linear barrier. Of the three, this seems the most insurmountable. It is strange that non-linear phenomena should be so intractable. It is as if man was denied complete knowledge of the universe, unless he can make a superhuman effort to solve its non-linearities."

In Forrester's view, traditional economics is linear; that is to say, it reduces economic phenomena, which are features of a complex system, to schematic processes. It distinguishes, it simplifies, and it goes wrong. "Economic science", Forrester says, "has artificially restricted its point of view and interests. It talks of *homo oeconomicus,* but men's motivations are not solely economic. It is necessary to include in a single science, a single discipline, everything that happens. It is necessary to include psychology, technology, sociology, economics, geography—and to try to find the relationships between all these things."

Forrester—who is in his early fifties, fair-haired going grey, and of an unusual appearance, very tall and thin and with a penetrating look—has created special methodologies to try to understand the dynamics of complex systems. In constructing his models, which are finally elaborated by means of computers, Forrester sets out not from a series of statistical data, as the econometrists do, but from a preliminary inquiry of an almost journalistic kind. He gathers together a certain number of experts in the system under examination, and in lengthy sittings extracts from their experience the analytical picture of the essential factors. He rationalises, that is to say, not abstract data but an integral practical and human experience;

thus he can include in his "simulation" psychological and moral as well as economic factors.

The final complexity of his equations, diagrams and patterns, in which a network of lines connects, as in an abstract picture, circles, squares, and signs symbolising the variables of the system, is incomprehensible to the layman. But the point of departure and the conclusions are perfectly accessible, even if sometimes the results are "counter-intuitive" and therefore surprising. Forrester has studied in depth two complex systems: the industrial concern and the city. His *Industrial Dynamics* is regarded by many as a very important work; there are also scholars in Japan and Russia who are concerned with this subject. His volume on *Urban Dynamics* is controversial (it does not cite a single recognised text on town-planning!) because of certain "counter-intuitive" conclusions. For example, Forrester "demonstrates" that plans for low-cost housing, to all appearances necessary in order to rehabilitate a town in decline, are useful only in the short term but disastrously aggravate the urban crisis in the long run. And Forrester's long run is really long: a normal econometric model makes forecasts for a year ahead; Forrester's urban model embraces a cycle of 250 years.

"My methodology", Forrester says, "can be applied to every imaginable thing." He considers that it would be "relatively simple" for an expert in industrial dynamics to use the same technique to deal with such questions as the problem of the Federal Bank, or to "structurise in a formal model the general theory of Keynes", which is something he would like to do. The result, he says, would probably be to discover that "a large part of the decisions taken by the Federal Reserve are harmful" and that "much of Keynes and of his conclusions and those of his followers is wrong, as in the majority of the social sciences". Now Forrester is working on problems of theory: he showed me the first ten chapters of a new book on *Principles of Systems*: "The principles that are valid for any complex system", he says, "are not yet properly understood".

I asked him what he thought of the ideas of a "world planning" which were put forward recently in America in a book by Aurelio Peccei, *The Chasm Ahead,* which has aroused much interest there (for instance at the Ford Foundation) and in Russia. Did he consider a plan for world development realistic? He answered: "The complexity of a model is independent of the geographical dimensions of the system. Probably the model of world development would not be much more complex than the development model of a city. My urban model has twenty variables; the adequate representation of a social system can have anything from ten to a hundred." Forrester does not consider it difficult to combine different values—whether economic, technological, or psychological—quantitatively: "When man thinks", he says, "that is exactly what he does—he quantifies and compares different magnitudes. If I decide something, it means that I have a scale of values, that I establish proportions. This is what we do in our models; we can include in them factors like courage and honesty."

Despite the originality of his methodology and his "eccentric" position in the profession, Forrester is in fact operating in one of the most extensive and important fields of modern economics, a field in which it is not easy to orientate oneself just because it is developing so rapidly. Thousands of scholars are working in it today. It is the field of the new analytical, decisional, operative methodologies, which are being applied on an ever-increasing scale to all the economic, technical and social problems of productive concerns and State organisations.

The various schools and methods of work are distinguished from each other by names that are sometimes clear, sometimes fantastic: operative research; network analysis and theories of the "critical path" (these are techniques for working out the rational plan of execution for a project); theory of decisions; "tree of decisions"; queuing theory; theory of games; linear programming; cost-benefit analysis; PPBS (planning, programming and budgeting system); PERT (project evaluation research technique); "Delphi" method (for forecasting the future); systems analysis; systems engineering; social engineering; and the list could be continued.

Economists, engineers, mathematicians and managers have all contributed to the elaboration of these methods. The immense logistical problems of the war period were perhaps the first trial-ground for these new branches of economics. The disciplines I have listed above differ widely among themselves; but they all aspire to introduce rationality and efficiency into the proliferating activity of the State outside the market, just as they also aim to reduce or eliminate the chaos and difficulty of decision-making processes in firms operating within the market—what the chairman of Unilever, Lord Heyworth, described as "the creative fog of managerial choices".

To such a combination of disciplines the Pentagon turns to decide on the characteristics and the timing and methods of construction of a new defensive or offensive system; or a public department which has to plan the development of a town, carry out an educational reform, or evolve an organic system of transport; or a big firm which has to decide in which city or continent to establish a new factory and how it should be built; and so on. Similar methods were used by Nasa (the US National Aeronautics and Space Administration), which solved the most complex problem of all time in scientific industrial planning when it created from scratch a new technology and a colossal system of industries with the object of putting two men on the moon, all within a period of nine years.

Many experts consider that the superior efficiency of American management and productive machinery is largely due to the extensive use of these techniques. Certain chaotic situations which have arisen in Russia in the field of industrial investments ("dispersion of resources", time-lag and delays in the building of plants, etc.) undoubtedly derive not only from the non-existence of the market but also from backwardness in the methods of programming and operative techniques. And computers alone are no help: the first 120 computers bought by Yugoslavia were disastrously underemployed for lack of experts.

In England it was foreseen that 10,000 systems analysts, or computer programmers, would be needed by 1970, but in 1967 only some dozen were being trained. In the Budget department in Washington the officials at the head of PPBS, in other words the men charged with disseminating throughout the vast machine of the American State the most modern techniques of analysis and programming brought by McNamara to the Pentagon, admit that only modest results have so far been obtained, and they explain this partial failure by the shortage of experts. The picture given me of the PPBS (an activity which is followed with intense interest by the Italian and French departments in charge of programming) is somewhat disappointing. But notwithstanding the disappointments these new fields of economic research are growing at an impressive rate. In particular, the number of "think-tanks", public organisations or private societies carrying out research, project-planning and advisory functions, is increasing rapidly and can now be reckoned in thousands instead of hundreds. Some of them are like big universities, though the majority are small but highly specialised organisations of from ten to twenty researchers. Some people foresee that the "thought industry" may be destined to become one of the mainsprings of future productive development. Already it often fulfils the function of brain of the State in its new undertakings.

The new fact of recent years is that the work of the "think-tanks" is becoming increasingly transferred from military to civil sectors, from the problems of the Pentagon to those of society. This development has speeded up a lot in recent times, and may produce surprising results for American life; certain problems might become tractable which at present seem well-nigh insoluble despite the country's immense resources. Where some purely economic techniques have failed, the new "interdisciplinary" techniques might succeed.

Jay Forrester told me: "Complex systems are extremely subtle and can lead man into error. So industrial concerns fail, developing countries plunge into crises, and American cities degenerate. But man can react without having to wait until he can command perfect knowledge." Meanwhile man can "organise the available data". But to that end, Forrester says, the essential thing is to "knock down the barriers due to freaks of history which have arisen between the various disciplines and which divide our thought".

Cambridge, Massachusetts

11. Ecology, The Unknown Quantity in Our Future

This Ephemeral Golden Age

Men have no love for prophets of disaster: it needs an effort to listen carefully to their arguments and judge them with the necessary equanimity. I mention this in order to indicate the state of mind with which most people have received the results of the research into the future of the "world system" undertaken by Jay Forrester.

In the United States I had the opportunity of attending a conference at which Forrester expounded and defended in his own brilliant and provocative style the conclusions he had reached in his research, which are fully set out in his volume *World Dynamics* (1971). I was also able to consult some of the vast documentation drawn up during the preparation of the book published in 1972 under the title *Limits to Growth,* brought out by a group of MIT research workers under Professor Dennis Meadows. This piece of ecological research, carried out under the auspices of the Club of Rome, aroused violent and worldwide debate on publication. Meadows's views are only slightly less catastrophic than Forrester's.

I will confine myself here to Forrester's views. The first American reactions to *World Dynamics* were a mixture of enthusiastic praise and sharp criticism. Some defects in Forrester's world model seem obvious even to me; but all the same I consider the thesis and the method of work he puts forward to be a pioneering effort of great importance. It will lead to a debate that will involve statesmen and scientists, even if Forrester's cry of alarm is not accepted in its full dramatic urgency.

Forrester's theses come within the framework of those neo-Malthusian and pessimistic views which within a short space of time have come to the fore even among the general public. Every magazine-reader or television-viewer today is aware of the great dangers of world starvation, population explosion, atmospheric pollution, and exhaustion of resources. Thus the hypothesis that the industrial revolution, and consequently "progress', may end by making the earth uninhabitable is no novelty, and it is indeed remarkable how quickly the awareness of these dangers has become widespread. A well-known book of only a few years ago, Herman Kahn's *The Year 2000* (1967), hardly mentioned the subject, and discerned only one threat, that of atomic war, to the unlimited growth of production and prosperity in the world.

That awareness now exists; but it is still only a partial awareness. In actual fact, both in general opinion and in the dominating political ideologies and practice of governments, with no exception, the idea still prevails that everything possible must be done to create ever newer and more colossal industries as the symbol and condition of progress.

Everyone, Europeans and Asians, capitalists and Communists alike, bows down before the "myth of the GNP"—the Gross National Product. True, people realise that some shadows overhang the future of progress; but at bottom they believe that science and technical advance will disperse them, and that all peoples will become richer: in fifty or a hundred years they will all be Americans.

Forrester's view, advanced in uncompromising terms, is, instead, that growth is nearing its end, and that our era is the "golden age" of mankind, the time in which the quality of life is higher than it has ever been in the past or can ever be in the future. "This period of explosive growth of industrial production and population", says another American scholar, M. King Hubbert, "is one of the most abnormal phases of human history . . . a short period of transition between two immensely longer periods characterised by changes so slow as to be regarded as periods of non-growth."

"Exponential growth", Forrester says, "cannot continue for ever"; on the contrary, it is coming to an end, because "very disagreeable mechanisms" are about to be set in motion which will cut it short; a "state of equilibrium" will follow, and the only thing we can do is to make the transition from growth to equilibrium as painless as possible. If we do nothing, "dormant and fundamental forces of nature and of the social system" will gain the upper hand.

It is unnecessary to explain in detail Forrester's methodology, which is not in fact particularly complicated; there is nothing incomprehensible to common sense about his systems of equations and his graphs, however repellent they may seem at first sight. Suffice it to say that he assembles, in a mathematical simulation or schematic model of the world system, some fundamental variables: population, capital investments (industrialisation), pollution, natural resources, agricultural production, "quality of life". Then he examines "what happens when an exponential growth (of population and production) clashes with a fixed environment".

The causal relationships which he establishes between these values are all obvious to the ordinary understanding. But the play of reciprocal influences provokes disconcerting and unexpected results. "Forrester's law", as Harry Schwartz of the *New York Times* calls it, is that the "complex systems" (which include all social systems) cannot be comprehended by the usual methods of analysis of the human mind; and this means that the greater part of the measures adopted to remedy different situations generally make them worse, at any rate in the long term, even if in the short term they provide some relief. It is a sceptical and bitter view of man and society.

Forrester tells us, in fact, that Forrester's models alone allow us to understand the world; this presumption of his is irritating, but it is as well to overcome our irritation and listen to what he has to tell us, however absurd some of his "counter-intuitive" conclusions may seem at first sight.

The most counter-intuitive of all is that it is no use developing industrial production in order to improve men's living conditions, as all governments and peoples wish and try to do. That only aggravates the situation, and in the end—an end not far off—modern human society will be destroyed by one or other of four different possible threats: exhaustion of resources, pollution, starvation, or the terrifying social tensions caused by overpopulation of the world.

To summarise Forrester's analyses in this way does not do them justice; they seem crude, but in fact they are extremely lucidly reasoned, even if in the end they may appear excessively catastrophic.

Forrester sets out from a "standard model", which is the projection of present trends into the future. In this model (presuming his facts and arguments to be correct) the "catastrophic" crisis would happen soon, around 2020, through exhaustion of natural resources. Then the author manipulates his standard model and offers various alternatives.

He supposes (second model) that technological progress may make it possible to economise in the use of existing resources, thus avoiding their exhaustion in the short term; but in that case industrial society will continue to advance only for a few decades, then a pollution crisis will explode which, around 2050, will halve the population and put an end to industrial society. In the third model the author assumes the hypothesis that science can also avoid pollution: but in that case alarming overpopulation of the earth would soon explode and make existence intolerable. In short, we would have no means of escaping ecological catastrophe.

The only way to avoid it is, in a certain sense, to anticipate it: in other words, it is not enough to establish birth-control, in the efficacy of which Forrester refuses to believe (as long as there are resources, the population will inexorably continue to increase beyond the tolerable limit). The only way to defuse the "demographic bomb" is to instal "pressures" which will prevent man, "the wild animal", from continuing to multiply. In other words (and here are the final, "counter-intuitive" and clamorous conclusions), industrial production must be reduced, not developed; agricultural productivity must diminish, not increase.

"Compensatory pressures" must be "intentionally created" with a view to bringing nearer the day when the population will be stabilised—i.e., "reduce production of food, reduce medical services, reduce industrialisation". In the long run this will not worsen the quality of life too much: and it will prevent a catastrophe that would destroy civilisation.

Among other things, this means (here is Forrester's second "scandalous" thesis) that the underdeveloped nations would do well not to develop: let them be content as they are, since they are nearer to the final equilibrium than the richer nations are. In any case, they have no possibility of reaching the productive levels of America: if they tried to do so, long before they could succeed they would become involved and submerged in the universal ecological cataclysm.

How far are these theses plausible and credible? It is useless to embark on an abstract or theological discussion. The studies must be thoroughly gone into and the data and arguments checked: Forrester himself says quite clearly that he does not claim to make precise forecasts but merely wishes to indicate trends, propound hypotheses, and provoke a discussion. Nevertheless after a first study of his "world system" some criticisms seem to me fairly obvious—and in particular two main ones.

The first is that Forrester regards the volume of natural resources as a finite quantity, about which it is only possible to economise, but which will inexorably become exhausted. This conception contains, to my mind, an error which is reflected in the construction of the model. It lacks a "circuit" or feed-back loop which takes account of the historically proven fact that "the use of resources itself creates resources", since such use sustains and nourishes the scientific and technical progress which will render utilisable new and hitherto inactive resources (such as uranium). There is thus a positive loop which Forrester neglects, and which is highly important. It is possible, indeed certain, that other newly-created "resources" may be added to the fund now existing, and such an acquisition will modify all Forrester's projections.

The second objection concerns the problem of population increase. Forrester projects into the future the average world rate of increase of the past seventy years: but this aggregate rate derives from a mixture of, in some cases, opposite trends, which are anyway quite exceptional in human history. There is no reason to doubt that once a certain level of progress has been achieved the explosive birthrates of the "underdeveloped" nations will decline sharply and the "demographic bomb" may therefore be defused long before it explodes.

Other objections are certainly possible. But I would like to put it another way. If the efforts of science and technology are not directed towards the discovery of "non-exhaustible" resources, and if the present still dominant trend towards population explosion is not reversed, then I have very little doubt that Forrester's catastrophic forecasts will, give or take a decade, be realised. But this means radically putting in question the "philosophy of growth" on the basis of which we are all living: it is a fantastic cultural revolution that Jay Forrester suggests.

The Less Opulent Morrow

The fundamental thesis of the Boston neo-Malthusian school is that mankind must change its ideology: it must cease to believe in productive growth as the supreme good, and aspire instead to realise a "state of equilibrium", in which the only activities to continue to grow will be those that do not consume limited resources—such as the arts, culture, religious thought, or scientific research. Progress yes, growth no: this is the new ideal; and it opens up prospects so revolutionary and disconcerting as to make it difficult to grasp them in concrete form. But, so the neo-Malthusians say, there are no other prospects, because "exponential" growth leads only to ecological catastrophe.

The "World 3" model, the latest to be set up by the MIT study group under Professor Dennis Meadows in continuation of Jay Forrester's researches, indicates an annual per capita income of 1,500 dollars (the figure for Italy today, or three times the present world average) as the maximum permissible to mankind on earth if a state of equilibrium is to be maintained.

At that level, Meadows says, we should in fact be rich enough to live well provided these resources are fairly and intelligently distributed; it will also be easier to realise equality between social classes and between nations once the ideal of growth loses force, with its illusory promises of an opulent future for all.

But is it then certain that growth cannot continue without bringing us to disaster? Is it not conceivable that the population might be stabilised by means of a change in habits and principles and that, as a result of scientific progress, new resources might be created more rapidly than existing resources are consumed, at the same time reducing pollution to tolerable levels? The neo-Malthusians' theories do not, I must say, totally reject this "optimistic" hypothesis: they admit that, in the abstract, everything is possible.

Even the ecological catastrophe, Meadows says, "is not inevitable, but only possible". What matters, however, is the admittedly very convincing demonstration that the "optimistic" hypothesis demands a radical ideological and political revolution. Without this—if, that is to say, the whole world continues in the blind pursuit of development—it will end by coming up inexorably against insurmountable and destructive obstacles.

The fact is that any "exponential" growth (such as occurs when a given quantity grows by a constant percentage in equal periods of time) produces surprising and sudden results which have always impressed and fascinated mankind. The classic example which Meadows likes to adduce is that of the legendary courtier who invented chess, who as a reward asked the King of Persia for only one grain of corn on the first square, two on the second, four on the third, eight on the fourth, and so on. The King rashly accepted, not realising that long before reaching the sixty-fourth square the whole past and future production of the kingdom of Persia and the world would have been in pawn.

Meadows also cites a French children's game. A water-lily grows in a big pool and doubles in size every day; if it were allowed to grow freely, by the thirtieth day it would cover the whole pool. The question is, supposing it were decided to cut it when it had covered only half the pool, which day would it be cut? The answer is, the last day but one. Here we have the typical and disconcerting condition of any "exponential growth": during almost all the time that precedes the moment when this growth comes up against an insurmountable "limit", the limit itself appears totally remote; only in the last stages (and in human affairs it may be too late) is the very existence of a limit perceived.

This reasoning is truly disquieting if applied to the relationship between the exponential growth of the human population and of production (population doubles every 32 years, per capita production every 14), and the "finite" character of the globe. It may be claimed, and rightly, that science and technology will succeed in expanding the "ecological sphere", by creating new resources or better still by making hitherto inactive resources utilisable; but it is nevertheless difficult to escape the feeling that one day a limit will be reached in our "finite" world.

The chief merit of Jay Forrester's and Dennis Meadows's "world models" lies in the demonstration that this limit is much nearer than is realised by ordinary common sense, once the present trends of "exponential" population growth and production are projected into the future ($3\frac{1}{2}$ thousand million people today, 14 thousand million in 2030). We are near the final stage: when the water-lily we thought so lovely achieves monstrous growth and occupies the entire pool.

The technical data upon which these estimates depend are certainly open to debate; but they remain disquieting. Meadows puts forward the following figures: the iron ore deposits utilisable today, which would suffice for 400 years at the present rate of annual consumption, will in fact suffice for only 73 years when we take into account the rate of increase of population and production and hence of consumption. In the same way, natural gas will suffice for 14 years instead of 35; oil for 20 years instead of 70; nickel for 30 years instead of 140; and so on.

True, the atomic revolution will make it possible to replace coal, now nearing exhaustion, by practically "inexhaustible" sources of energy; and the "green revolution" has in recent years multiplied the world's agricultural productivity; but neither of these revolutionary changes offers an easy way out of future straitened circumstances.

In fact, any temporary alleviation in the problem of resources, whether industrial or agricultural, or in the threat of pollution will automatically provoke another leap forward in productive development and in population growth. Every space gained will be immediately occupied, every ten-year breathing-space used up, unless a way is found to arrest the two fundamental exponential growths that threaten the future of mankind.

This emerges from Forrester's and Meadows's models more clearly than had appeared till now from the separate analyses carried out by agricultural, industrial, or demographic experts: in fact, the Boston school's "world systems" bring together for the first time all the main variable factors. The fact comes out more clearly that certain remedies, which at first sight might seem efficacious in a particular sector, are really likely to create future and greater difficulties in other sectors. Only a "global" programme, which impinges on the whole system, can give us the hope of controlling and avoiding the "ecological catastrophe" that threatens us.

The first condition for the success of any programme, Meadows maintains, is that world opinion should become convinced that exponential growth to all eternity is impossible: if we allow natural forces a free run, the result will be a catastrophic crisis, probably within a hundred years. So what is to be done?

Meadows's recipe, a provisional one based on still unfinished research, is slightly less unpalatable than that of Forrester, for whom the only remedy would be a drastic voluntary reduction of industrial and agricultural investments in order to "defuse" the demographic bomb. Meadows, it seems to me, has more faith in mankind's capacity for self-control.

His plan can be summarised as follows. First of all, the rich countries must undertake to restrain the exponential growth of their production, and the underdeveloped countries must arrest the exponential growth of their population. There should then be a massive transfer of investments from the traditional productive sectors to other sectors which consume fewer resources (social services, education, and also production of food). It will also be necessary to further technical advances

97

which will increase the average duration of every form of capital and reduce both consumption of natural resources and pollution of the environment—in other words, to develop both the recycling or recovery of resources and "closed-cycle" productions.

Lastly, it will be necessary (this point is not in Meadows's plan, but it seems to me obvious) to initiate large-scale international projects for directing scientific research towards the "creation" of new resources which will be inexhaustible on our earth (e.g., nuclear fusion).

In order to do all this, even though a real "world government" may not be indispensable, something very like it will be needed, at any rate an authority which will have the effective power to assign to the various nations the right to consume a given quantity of resources and diffuse into the world a given quantity of pollution and no more.

Is it a Utopia? Maybe; indeed I am sure Forrester himself would regard Meadows's proposed solutions as illusory. Forrester states explicitly that in his models he bases himself on the way in which man has behaved up till now, projecting into the future the behaviours and principles of the past and not other more rational or idealistic standards—on which Meadows, for his part, reckons. It is unnecessary to repeat that all these calculations and forecasts have to be checked, and it may be that the pessimism of the Boston school will prove excessive. What strikes me in particular about these schemes is that they underestimate, not man's idealism, but his ingenuity.

All the same, when one goes deeply into the study of Forrester's and Meadows's models, one ends up by finding one's initial scepticism shaken; and at the end one is almost convinced that, failing a revolution in the whole order of human society, the most catastrophic possibilities run the risk of being realised within a period that will affect us personally, on the supposition that we have some concern for what will happen to our children or grandchildren. There may be some postponement; but is there a way out?

It is to be hoped that other research centres, using other

methods of inquiry, will soon devote themselves to the study of the "world system". The great merit of the "dynamic of systems" invented by Forrester is that it permits of experimental conjectures about human society, using mathematical simulations and models, since we cannot conduct live experiments. Today the method is imperfect; perhaps tomorrow we shall be able with greater precision to try to foresee for a ten-, fifty-, or a hundred-year term the consequences of the most important political or economic decisions adopted today.

Cambridge, Massachusetts

12. The Professors of the "New Wave"

I was taken to Harvard from my Boston hotel for my meeting with Kenneth Arrow by a crazy old driver with strange mad eyes. He began by displaying an almost aggressive joviality, but bit by bit his manner became more and more angry and apoplectic as he talked to me about the bearded youths who had invaded the little town of Zap, in North Dakota, a few days earlier and devastated it. He only wished they'd come and try it on with him—he'd be ready for them, good heavens, he'd shoot and kill them all, it was the only thing to do; Hitler knew how to treat those beastly bearded Jews, the gas oven was the only place for them. Bad luck that when the judgement day came in America good Jews would be taken as well, and he knew some—but it was their fault, after all, wasn't it? And the crazy old man hurled some fierce insults at a couple of young fellows with beards who were standing staring at him in astonishment on the edge of the pavement.

Then the taxi began cruising along the bank of the Charles River, and in the distance the sharp spires and green, gold and blue cupolas of the Cambridge university buildings came into sight half-hidden among the trees: an idyllic picture of harmony and architectural equilibrium, expressive of a whole humanistic and rational way of living. The old wretch's cursing had an almost unbearably sickening effect on me, and I longed to get to Cambridge and find myself once more in the world of mature, rational intellectuals in which I had been living ever since I began my inquiry among the American economists.

Afterwards I reflected that this disconcerting episode had its uses because it served to remind me that there was not only another America but another form of humanity. From the half-crazed old racialist to Ken Arrow the gulf was immense.

The taxi-ride ended and the interview began. My feeling of nausea died away and I calmed down. Arrow had come to Harvard from Stanford only that year, and his arrival, so an eminent local professor told me over dinner at the Ritz Carlton in Boston, "sufficed to turn the faculty into the best in America". His intellectual powers are legendary, though the ordinary public knows little about him. The story is told of a student who, when assigned to him for an examination, said: "What a tremendous honour! But I'm sorry to arrest the progress of economics for half-an-hour." I arrested it for more than an hour and feel even more guilty.

Arrow, who is in the mid-forties, looks like any ordinary official in shirtsleeves; simple and cordial, he said nothing that I couldn't understand; then he presented me with a pile of slim offprints of his essays, each one of them a mine of figures and equations. Thus I am not in a position to do full justice to the scintillating mind of Kenneth J. Arrow. I report here on the central theme of our conversation.

We were talking about the "new economics", and Arrow said: "The difficulty about the new economics is that it has had too much success. It aimed to bring about full employment and it succeeded, and that is a big result. Now I agree there's inflation, but I don't think it's anything particularly serious; we can live with inflation. The problem is a different one. The problem which is becoming acute is that the market, as it is, does not produce a distribution of income and power which satisfies the ideals of modern justice. We ask ourselves: what kind of economic policy can produce a more equitable distribution? To increase production helps the poor, but not enough. These problems call for new ideas. With methods like PPBS we ought to be in a position to choose precisely which is worth more, a dollar spent on a school or a dollar spent on a motorway. We must arrive at more rational choices, and calculate the externalities, the advantages or the external costs of every economic initiative. These are the problems that interest young people."

On the same subject, on the other side of the river at the Graduate School, another top-ranking economist, Raymond

Vernon, provided me with a thought-provoking parable. "If an economist on Mars, the corresponding member of some academy, were to receive only our technical literature but not our newspapers, he would say, 'In the country of America, on the planet Earth, everything is going well. All the problems are being solved. The negroes today have an income equal to what the white Americans had around the middle 'fifties, when the United States was already the richest country in the world. There is immense social mobility, and the rates of growth are very high. This is certainly a happy society.' But the Martian economist would fall out of the clouds in amazement (supposing there are clouds on Mars) when he learnt that the harmonious symphony of economic data was accompanied by agitations, difficulties and unrest on a growing rather than diminishing scale."

I have cited the parable of the Martian economist because it is symptomatic of a phenomenon about which I have already had something to say: the discomfort of the "terrestrial" economists at finding that purely economic, productive advances do not seem to solve any problem; and the consequent transference of much of their efforts from the field of pure economics to that of "social" economics. I would like to stress the fact that this is the sector of American economics to which the greatest number of young scholars are turning. The fifty-year-olds concern themselves with cycles, the thirty-year-olds with the poor, the negroes, and social matters.

There are a great many young economists—perhaps ten times as many as in the preceding generation. In 1969 students at the Graduate Business Schools numbered 75,000 or 65 per cent more than in 1964. The dominant interest of these hordes of young economists is social economics. I talked about it with a lot of people, both the young and the not so young. I quote what was said to me by a thirty-year-old associate professor at MIT, Lester Thurow, a tall, fair, cheerful young man from Montana, the land of bison and good milk. His first two books were due out that year. One was to be called *The Economics of Poverty and Discrimination*, the other *Investments in Human Capital*. He studied at a minor university and then went to Oxford as a Rhodes scholar. Now he has the room next to Modigliani's at MIT. He talks enthusiastically, almost as fast as Modigliani, who, as is well known, competes with Arrow as the fastest speaker in America (judging by my shorthand efforts they are both around 250 words a minute).

I asked Thurow, "What does the generation of young economists want?" He answered: "Most of us younger people think that the macroeconomic problem has been solved by the generation of Samuelson, Modigliani and Arrow. Our students have never seen a cycle. If there are cycles, it's because the governments are stupid enough not to follow the advice of the economists. In fact, the problem of control of cycles is political rather than economic. Even inflation doesn't worry us. I and others have analysed the problem sufficiently to convince ourselves that inflation doesn't harm either economic development or the poor; and so it doesn't interest us."

Does theory interest them? "Today there are no revolutionary contributions to theory. Theory, as an abstraction, as an abstract scheme of economic facts, is exhausting its usefulness. Perhaps some genius may come along who will invent quite new theories and discover new hidden relationships between the facts. But for the present there isn't one. We aren't against theory, though—indeed we use it as the basis for our researches. We all know about theory. All you have to do is to find an interesting field and use your own inventive power to set out your chosen problem properly. All the young are excellent econometrists, with statistics as their weapon. Theory by itself doesn't tell you how to solve the problem of poverty, for example, with the 'negative tax': you have to do experiments (they're doing them on a big scale in New Jersey) and then work out the data. The same is true for the effect of education on people's incomes."

And he went on to say: "There are so many interesting problems: how to reduce poverty quickly and radically; how to reduce the difference of incomes between blacks and whites; how to ensure that the Government spends its dollars wisely; what suggestions can be obtained from economic analysis about such problems as town-planning or the conservation of natural resources. These are all vital problems, but practically nothing has been done on the economic plane; theory gives valuable suggestions, but these are never applied. Young economists are looking for answers that are precise and realistic, not merely generic or intuitive. The more precise the answers, the more effective government intervention will be."

I asked him if they were interested in planning. He answered: "In the field of analysis of costs and benefits a lot of work is being done by young economists. But we are working on the instruments of planning, not the theory. We are interested in evolving a technique and a methodology, and applying them to concrete questions." (The answer is revelatory of the pragmatic spirit of American economics today: there is little interest in big ideological questions, and structures are accepted as a fact—the most important thing is to solve concrete problems more efficiently.)

"Isn't there a generation gap, or some rivalry, between you young people and the fifty-year-olds in the new economics?", I asked him. "No", he said "the generation gap is between us and some of the very young, who read Marx according to Galbraith and would like to blow up big business. But they don't really know what to put in its place. They don't want state bureaucracy or Russian-type planning. They talk about participatory democracy, but that's no answer. They haven't really decided who ought to be in command. But such young people are a minority; the majority have a pragmatic orientation, like us. As for our relations with the preceding generation, they are excellent. I don't discuss Samuelson's theories, I make use of what he has done and go in a different direction. There's no reason for us not to get on perfectly well."

Modern economics is advancing on a very wide front: there is room for all the young people of good will who want to make decisions more rational and society more just. Another typical meeting I had was with Gary Becker, a professor at Columbia University, New York. He was 38 years old and was one of the main experts on educational economics. The central economic problem in this sector is to evaluate the cost and benefits of expenditure on State education, comparing them with other possible productive or social investments and estimating the existing alternatives in the field of education. Many people are working on these problems both in the universities and the Department of Education, using up-to-date techniques like PPBS.

"Studies on the subject", said Becker, "have already had an important effect on the policy of the Government and the local authorities. For example, the concrete demonstration that education is a good thing not only from the moral but also from the productive point of view has facilitated large allocations in this sector. On the other hand, our studies have reduced to size the myth of education as the panacea for all our ills. It isn't so: we have shown that education is less profitable to negroes than to whites in relation to social promotion. In other words, education does not suffice to provide an answer to the problem of social improvement or racial equality. It isn't enough just to give a man a degree. The planning of wellbeing is something more complex."

Further research and more studies are needed. "Today the majority of economists are working in this field. And there is the feeling that economics can make a great contribution. Problems such as education, poverty, and racial discrimination used traditionally to be the preserve of the sociologists. Today they are coming increasingly into the field of the economists. I am an imperialist economist, in other words, I believe that economics offers a strict theoretical framework which enables it to make a decisive analytical contribution. Economists are more rigorously trained to deal with facts, figures and statistics. This, for me, is the trend of the future in modern economics."

Cambridge, Massachusetts

13. Ackley: Success and Usefulness of the "Professors"

Economists today enjoy great prestige. Like successful business men in the past, they can even become ambassadors. Gardner Ackley, Heller's successor as chairman of Johnson's Council of Economic Advisers from 1964 to 1968, was Ambassador in Rome in 1968-9. Ackley and Heller: the same policy but different methods; Heller an extrovert with the vocation of a preacher of the "new economics", Ackley a "quiet American", a typical university professor and son of a professor (of mathematics). He is author of an important book on *Macroeconomic Theory* and of several other works, including his *Econometric Model of Italian Post-War Development*, the fruit of two study periods in Italy.

He was in Rome in 1962 when a telephone call from Kennedy summoned him to Washington to become a member of the three-man committee of economists which advises the President on what should be done to generate "maximum employment and production" in America. In practice, the Council of Economic Advisers is a planning organ, though the word is not used in America. But the reality is not very different. The American economy and that of the "planned" European countries, such as Italy, resemble each other: "It is the same animal, the same species", says Ackley, "and the differences are diminishing."

This is not a new development. In 1933 one of Roosevelt's advisers, Raymond Moley, asked the President if he was really convinced of the virtue of planning, which had been inaugurated with the first measures of the New Deal. Roosevelt replied, "I have never been more certain of anything in my life." Between Roosevelt's day and now a great many things have happened, Democrats and Republicans have alternated in power, but the "public sector" in America has continued to grow. The State does not itself conduct productive concerns, as in Italy, but it controls a sufficiently large portion of the national income to be in a position to guide the economy. There are many concerns in America that are known as "the captives", or prisoners of the State, which is their chief or only client. The State finances the scientific research on which the direction of economic development largely depends. The State has the power and therefore the responsibility for successes and failures. With the State, the economists share in power and responsibility. Let us see what the economists and their "marginal usefulness" amount to.

The first thing I asked Ackley was how the immense expansion of economic research came about. He answered: "When I began, in the 'thirties, there wasn't any money. The universities hadn't the funds to pay for assistants. It wasn't until after the war that the general prosperity began to flow into the research institutes as well. The chief reason for the expansion of economic studies is undoubtedly money."

Before the State began its large-scale intervention, a key role was played by the Ford Foundation, the biggest in the world, with a capital of about $4 billion and an annual expenditure of some $250 million. Today there are about 5,000 Foundations in America, at least 400 of which are important. Together they finance a little over 10 per cent of scientific research of all kinds (the State finances 75 per cent). But their importance is much greater than those figures would suggest. The fact counts that there are a great many centres which distribute funds and which compete with each other to secure the most valued prizes in the "brains market"; there is also competition between the agencies, the government departments and the government corporations. Thus there is money even for those who are outside the official orbit. And there is a lot of money.

Ackley cited the example of the Urban Institute in Washington. I have been there: it is a centre for social and economic research concerned especially with problems of town-planning. It was only opened in April 1968, but a year later it already had a staff of 50 professors and 25 other employees (observe the ratio). In another year the number of researchers was to be doubled. So swiftly has a centre of studies been established which is probably superior, in this field, to any university (and, incidentally, between 1955 and 1957 two hundred new four-year-course colleges were set up, and one new junior, two-year college a week). Simultaneously the Rand, the first and most famous of the "thought laboratories", opened a branch in New York for town-planning problems (the original establishment, in California, is still mainly concerned with military research). In short, the sheer volume of intelligence that had flowed in a couple of years into the key-sector of urban development—a sector involving all the crises of American society—was immense. In a few years this capital should begin to bear fruit.

An "interdisciplinary" multiplicity of study-centres corresponds to the multiplicity of problems. From among all the many research studies in progress at the Urban Institute I cite, for example, those of Charles Holt on the relation between inflation and employment (the "Phillips curve", as the economists call it). This is one of the central themes of economic research: the aim, Holt tells me, is to understand the mechanism on the basis of which, once full employment has been achieved, the inflationary process sets in, and to prepare instruments which will permit full employment to be maintained without inflation.

In addition to the universally recommended techniques, such as a good "incomes policy" which does not raise wages and profits beyond the limits tolerated by the dynamics of the system, efforts are being made to perfect the mechanism of the State's "structural" interventions for the training and re-education of manpower. The studies of Holt and others show that by improving the quality of the "human capital" and securing a highly-educated manpower, "the Phillips curve is improved" and the structural conditions may be created which will permit of full employment without inflation. Economic research makes it possible to move from general indications to precise practical suggestions, calculating in advance the cost and usefulness of the interventions. But it is only in an "inter-disciplinary" centre like the Urban Institute that all the approaches to a social problem such as that of cities can be studied contemporaneously: only from a complex of co-ordinated research studies can "global planning" develop. This is how the "thought laboratories" function and can be called on to solve any problem.

Let me give a concrete example. Aerojet, the concern which constructed the satellite "Gemini", realised a couple of years ago that the 200 human "great brains" and the numerous electronic brains that it had gathered together were under-employed. It offered its services to the State of California and initiated two investigations, one on the elimination of waste matter and rubbish, the other on the rehabilitation of 200,000 ex-prisoners (by means of electronic elaboration of their case-histories). The brain, whether human or electronic, is a highly flexible instrument: research conditions in America facilitate this flexibility.

Research is carried out in all sorts of places: in banks, government departments, firms, Foundations, or Universities. "When I first began as a professor", Ackley told me, "I used to teach for ten to twelve hours or more a week. Today a course envisages an average of three to five hours' teaching; that leaves time for research." It leaves time (a professor in Italy certainly does not teach more, often less), because "in almost all the American universities paid outside activities are restricted to the equivalent of one day a week".

The American university professor is an organised being. He is to be found in his office, like any business man, from 9 to 5; he has a secretary who arranges his appointments, and he is extremely punctual. His simple clear language bears the stamp of the pragmatic style that is typical of his country. It would hardly occur to you to call him an "intellectual"; he is more like the Russian idea of a "worker in thought". His manner is serene and relaxed, which may perhaps have something to do with his prestige and his good income. "Today economics professors earn more than physicists and chemists", Heller told me. When I asked him how much they earned,

Ackley said: "On an average 20,000 or 25,000 dollars a year, the best ones more; and perhaps the same amount for the weekly day of extra-university work." Fifty thousand dollars is £20,920: it's a lot of money, even in America.

University work is facilitated by the sensible ratio between the numbers of teachers and students—usually about one to ten or less. In 1969 at Harvard the teaching staff numbered 5,568, the students 24,917; at MIT, 950 as against 7,300. In many European universities the ratio is 1 to 30 or 1 to 50. The abundance of funds, the pluralistic organisation for their distribution, the multiplicity of study centres, the serious character of the regulations governing the universities, all these combine to form the structure which has made possible the great expansion in economic research. What results has it produced? Are they satisfactory or "disappointing", as Murray Rossant, director of an important institution, the Twentieth Century Fund, seemed to think when I talked to him in New York? Rossant maintained that economics in America lacks the sense of the unity of science; there is no systematicness about it. "Despite all the amount of research being done", he said, "I don't believe economics has made such great advances, and this is because it specialises too much. There is too much hair-splitting, too many restricted investigations which find no echo in other fields. There has been some useful research of a detailed kind, but it sometimes seems as if the economists can't see the wood for the trees, or even the leaves."

I asked Ackley what he thought of these views. He answered, "That is probably how things are, broadly speaking. But I don't know whether that isn't on the whole an advantage. There is a great variety in fields of study, techniques, and methodologies. To an outside observer our economics world may seem very disorganised. But my impression is that as long as we have adequate resources it's a system that works. I don't think we have yet discovered the perfect economic methodology. Until that happens, the multiplicity of study centres has its uses."

The science of economics in America is going through an explosive phase in respect of the volume of research being done and the variety of subjects treated. One gets the impression that even if there has been no "Copernican revolution", as Samuelson said, there is nevertheless so great an accumulation of data and analyses as to create in the course of time (a generation?) the necessary "critical mass" for a new leap forward on the part of economic theory itself.

Looking at the exponential growth of economic knowledge, one is tempted to think that while the great syntheses of the preceding generation, such as the Marxian or the Keynesian synthesis, still remain valid and important in their general lines, they were really only points of departure, marking, as it were, Year Zero of a new science. Perhaps Keynes was not so much the Einstein as the Newton of economics. Perhaps analytical and detailed knowledge will have to increase tremendously before a new synthesis becomes possible, a synthesis which will be much more complex and articulate and therefore profoundly different—as different as the theory of relativity or the atomic theories are from the laws of gravity.

This evolution of economic science, analogous to that of the physical sciences, will be the more difficult because the actual material to be explored, namely economic society, is changing so rapidly and radically, whereas earth and the universe underwent only imperceptible changes in the cosmic moment that separated Newton from Einstein. The ceaseless evolution of the economic situation is certainly an awkward factor. But in the meantime, it is reasonable to hope that the methodical and pragmatic application of the scientific economic mentality to the problems of contemporary society may bear concrete fruits.

"I have always thought," Ackley said to me, "that economics is interesting for its usefulness." In the world of the American economists today, social involvement is a decisive factor, together with their anti-dogmatic and critical spirit, in directing the researchers' efforts. These seem to me the dominant themes of the search for knowledge, and for its civil application, in which they are involved.

Rome

II

EASTERN EUROPE

14. Strumilin: The Doyen of Russian Economics

In his house in Moscow, Prospekt Lenina no. 13, in a study full of dark old furniture, old books, and big vases of pink and yellow peonies, the *doyen* of the Soviet economists, Stanislas Gustavovich Strumilin, talked to me about the great debate that was going on among the Soviet economists.

Strumilin is 92 years old, but his great age has not impaired his lively mind any more than it has bent his tall robust frame. He has a tremendously mobile face, a white beard and moustache, and an almost Cossack-like lock of hair falling across his forehead. His hearing is not good, and so he concentrates while listening to a question, then his face lights up as he brings out his answer explosively in a loud strong voice.

Old age has given him serenity and humour; it pleases him to have conquered the years. He took some trouble about composing a dedication for me to the *Strumilin Bibliography*, a 156-page volume that came out recently; but his latest article, published in *Voprosy Ekonomiki* of September 1969, is perfectly lucid, indeed brilliant, and he is now working on the sequel.

To me, Strumilin represents the Soviet economic past—more than half a century of fame and honours under Stalin and after—sitting in judgement on the present. I began with a general question: what did he think of Soviet economic science today?

We were sitting at a round table; his wife, much younger than he, who called him Stanislas Gustavovich and addressed him as "you" (not "thou"), sat behind him, occasionally drawing nearer as if to support him. Strumilin reflected and then replied: "We have reached a fairly high level, certainly higher than when we started planning. But at present—and this may be a sign of the advance in our economic knowledge—

the disagreements among our economists are greater and more significant than at any other time in our history."

This categorical statement aroused some doubts in me. I thought of the historic polemics of the 'twenties, the golden decade of Soviet economic culture, when all the hypotheses and utopias concerning the development of the "first socialist country" were being advanced and discussed, and I said, "Even more so than in the 'twenties?" "Certainly. At that time there was disagreement between Marxists and non-Marxists, but the Marxists were in agreement among themselves. Now, on the other hand, people are looking for a new course. Courses there are in plenty, and different ways of arriving at the truth. And there are many disputes—even if we call them, more politely, exchanges of view."

So after fifty years of Soviet history, disagreements among the economists about the different roads that lead to the truth (I imagine he means "to Communism") were more lively than ever before. From this categorical statement of Strumilin's my present swift incursion into the new frontiers of Soviet economics, from Moscow to Novosibirsk, took its starting point; and I may say at once that each fresh meeting, each new document I have come upon has merely served to confirm and illustrate this fact.

The great debate that began around 1955 after Stalin's death had relit the smouldering embers of an economic way of thinking that once sparkled with great intuitions and immense ambitions: the greatest ambition of all, the Marxist and Leninist ambition to introduce perfect rationality into economic affairs and ensure universal wellbeing for mankind. With the passage of time, the debate has acquired ever widening dimensions, independently of the evolutions or involutions of party policy (and this is a moment of serious involution in the relations between political authority and the intellectuals of more openminded and advanced views). But cultural economic renovation has gone ahead regardless, influenced by an illustrious past, by new Western ideas, or by original intuitions.

Returning to the USSR after seven years, I almost seem to feel the physical dimensions of this evolution, as if I were witnessing a natural fact. I do not, of course, ignore the restrictions, and not merely formal restrictions, that still accompany the economic debate; and I do not pretend to understand the logic of a policy that permits, all things considered, wide freedom of discussion among economists while at the same time bringing to bear an atmosphere of restrictions and repressions on writers, historians and poets. There is a serious inconsistency here, which according to some reflects genuine contradictions at the top, different political lines interacting and coming up against each other; only the future will clarify its significance. In any case, I register the fact that an economic debate exists, and a very lively one. As Strumilin wrote in an article in 1968: "During the years of bitter struggle against the counter-revolution, certain divergences seemed very dangerous and for that reason were implacably suppressed. But times are changing. We are no longer afraid of scientific divergences. We can welcome the fact that our scientific life is prolific in disagreements."

I shall try in this inquiry to illustrate some of the great ideas that are at odds with each other in the Soviet economic world. But, first of all, what is the reason for this search for something new? It is the result, obviously, of a state of crisis, of the economy's transition into a new and more difficult stage in its evolution. The Soviet economy is still growing, but it is nevertheless a fact that the rate of development almost halved within a decade: from 11·5 per cent per annum in 1951–55 to 6 per cent in 1961–65, according to the official data. Later the decline was faster: in 1972 the national income rose by only 4 per cent (official figure).

Above all, the Stalinist machinery of development has run down. The era of "shouted planning", as Naum Jasny called it, is over. The conditions, whether political or material, no longer exist for a growth which was based on the transfer and forced exploitation, by means of under-consumption, of vast masses of industrial and agricultural manpower. A crisis has developed in Bolshevik determinism, which scorned the objective logic of economic science (not a single general economic treatise was published between 1928 and 1954) and which in the 'twenties caused Stalin to say, and Strumilin to repeat, "There are no strongholds that the Bolsheviks cannot overthrow. Our task is not to study economy but to change it. The question of the rate of development is subject to the decisions of human beings."

I asked Strumilin why the rate of development had slowed down so radically. He answered that there were "many reasons": the main one was that the first two five-year plans, of 1928 to 1937, had been "a period of transition from capitalism to socialism; the new factor of planning proved particularly efficacious; there was an industrial revolution". Today, however, according to Strumilin, "the rate of development could be one-and-a-half times greater than it is". He is not alone in thinking this. Kantorovich, the greatest Soviet mathematical economist, in an important book in 1959 which was one of the points of departure of the "new economics" in the USSR, maintained that between a quarter and a third of the potential product was being lost through inefficient planning inherited from Stalinism (cf. pp. 72–3).

All are agreed, therefore, that something is wrong, and also that the past is irrecoverable: moreover, beyond the Soviet confines, post-Stalinist economy has everywhere entered on a stage of profound change. The problem is how to arrest the decline, and what new paths to follow. But to what extent do Strumilin and his followers understand the new ideas? What does Strumilin think of the thought-provoking optimal models of the economy that the mathematicians have evolved, or of the proposition advanced by many practical economists that renewed strength should be injected into the economy by granting autonomy and profit to business concerns? How does he view the more radical and daring ideas, of Yugoslav or Czechoslovak origin, of a real "socialist market", guided by indicative planning on wellnigh Western lines? What, lastly, does he think of the current economic reform in the USSR?

Strumilin answered by starting from what is the real crux of the disputes: "In the question of price formation and the role of the market to that end, I stick to the old beliefs. That is to say, I stick to the position of the Marxists. I believe that market socialism, as some people call it, is not the way for us. Naturally, the market has to be taken into account, but its dictates do not have to be followed; the plan must be orientated in the desired direction."

About the reform he said: "The reform is moving in various directions. The new directions do not all lead to an increase in the rate of development. I think decentralisation, the democratisation of economic control, will have a good effect. Some people have become enthusiastic about the idea of profit; but this does not always give good results."

In his 1968 article Strumilin described Liberman and the rest as "hotheads"; and he defined Kantorovich's ideas about "objectively determined" prices, and Fedorenko's ideas about "utility prices", as "foreign to us", being tinged with marginalism and remote from the Marxist – Leninist theory of workvalue. In the writings of Strumilin (who by no means represents the most dogmatic wing) and the other conservative economists like Ostrovitianov, Gatovski, Kronrod etc., technical arguments are constantly mixed up with polemical quotations and political warnings.

Strumilin is pleased that "in spite of all the divergences, party directives remain decisive for us" and that these directives do not ask that "profits should be maximised". He admits, in point of fact, that if concerns acquired all the net profit, paying the State only taxes and interest on capital, many important benefits would result, including an increase in the yield of investments and, "for a certain time", an accelerated rate of development. But he rejects this "deviation of socialism towards syndicalism" for a variety of reasons: as representing a danger of "chaos and imbalance in the economy", but also as "a decentralisation incompatible with the Leninist principle of democratic centralisation".

Political resistances (dictated by anxiety to defend the power of the Party) to the economic reforms are strong. The conservatives have strong positions of power. But today the ranks of the reformers occupy important positions, able to influence the direction of economic policy, and in their researches they sometimes show a high spirit of adventure. It seems impossible that only in 1957 a vice-president of Gosplan condemned econometry in Stalinist terms as a "statistical-arithmetical deviation of planning". Today Strumilin re-echoes this concept. But in this he is now completely isolated. Enriched by Western transplants, the soil of Soviet economic thinking, for decades so arid, has begun to produce important fruits.

Certainly, faced with the multiplicity of models, reform projects, and utopias, it is difficult to orientate oneself. I asked Strumilin, "Where are socialism and Communism going?" His answer held a barb of ancient guile: "For the present we have socialism, and it's going towards Communism". I insisted: "Towards what kind of Communism?" While in the background Mrs. Strumilina made an impatient movement ("But there's only one Communism") he found the phrase on which to escape: "Towards the Communism of Lenin".

So I know as much as I did before. But I can't blame that on the excessive diplomacy of the ninety-two-year old Strumilin. Our conversation was over, and he was delighted to be photographed by my cameraman, who expended two whole films on him. He only regretted that he was being photographed today when he was old: "You ought to have taken me when I was young!" The photographer had the last word: "But, Stanislas Gustavovich, I wasn't here then!"*

Moscow

---

* Stanislas Strumilin died in 1970.

15. Birman: Reforms Go Slowly in Russia

I asked Alexander Birman what he was working on. He answered: "I'm ruining my holidays staying in Moscow because I have to write another article for *Novy Mir*. The last one had a two-word title, *Sut' reformy*, the essence of reform. The title of the next will be only one word: guess what." I asked him what it would be about. "Economic reform, of course. For the next twenty years that will be the only topic."

I didn't guess the title, and given the atmosphere surrounding *Novy Mir*, the target of all the Soviet reactionaries, I can only hope that Birman's summer labours would not be wasted.* But in any case he will continue the battle for the reform, which he greeted in 1965 as the third great stage in the Soviet economy, after the NEP and planning under Stalin. But not everyone wanted so radical a change. In his previous article Birman said that there were two "absolutely different" ways of seeing the reform; some thought it might be said to have been completed in 1969, with the transition of almost all concerns to the new system; others, on the other hand, considered that these changes "by no means exhaust the essence of the reform". This is naturally Birman's view, and not his alone. Baibakov too, the chairman of Gosplan, said: "We are freeing ourselves extremely slowly from the old methods of management."

Even the official analyses show that Soviet concerns continue to manoeuvre to get easy plans assigned to them from above, and this, Baibakov says, "goes against the spirit and the letter of the reform". The new financial indices, like profit, have not replaced the old physical indices but have often merely been added to them: both of them weigh on the concern, which is still strictly controlled. The list of products *(nomenklatura)* still

* His article in fact never appeared.

comes from above. A concern's productive funds financed from profit, which should ensure autonomy of initiative for the concerns, are utilised only in part, because the Plan does not assign them machinery and materials. Workers' bonuses, which are also supposed to be based on profit, are too small, and most workers are not even aware of the innovation, as has been shown by some inquiries carried out in Soviet factories.

Going by the official statements, in short, what Birman calls "the essence of the reform" has not yet been achieved. The Soviet economy is still essentially an economy conducted from the centre by administrative methods: a "command" economy, as Stalin created it in the years of industrialisation by forced stages. Only the commands function badly, the plans are constantly modified, discrepancies arise between the ministerial–sectorial organisation of industry (abolished by Khrushchev in 1957 but reestablished in 1965 at the same time as the reform) and regional needs, and investments continue to be dispersed over too many new factories which take a long time to complete.

All this, in fact, is just as it was before. But perhaps there is nothing surprising in that. Birman is quite right when he says: "In an enormous country such as ours vast changes cannot be made in a hurry. A big ship cannot turn round quickly like a little boat." And some partial progress has in fact been made. I am not speaking of the annual rate of increase of industrial production, which is far from satisfactory, rising only from 8·6 per cent in 1961–65 to 9 per cent in 1966–68 and then falling to 7 per cent in 1969.* These fluctuations have really nothing to do with the reform but are to be explained by the existence of "productive cycles" (investment cycles) in the Soviet economy. Figures relating to the rate of development and productivity in the "reformed" concerns as compared with the "non-reformed" are also ambiguous and contradictory, and Strumilin was right when he told me he did not think such data significant. What is important, however, is that certain mechanisms postulated by

* It was 7·8 per cent in 1971, 6·5 per cent in 1972, always according to official, probably inflated, figures.

the reform are slowly coming into being: there is a gradual development in factory capital, non-central investments (which have risen from 5 to 10 billion roubles in four years), and in direct contracts between firms. Baibakov includes among the urgent tasks of the reform the further development of these new mechanisms and of mechanisms to provide incentives.

On the whole, I think Birman is right when he says that the reform will go ahead—partly because reforms occur when things are not going well, and the fundamental defects of the Soviet economic system are still the same. They include the very low yield of investments, the poor quality of production, the disastrous state of services, the workers' sense of alienation, and dissatisfaction on the part of consumers (the average wage of a Soviet worker in 1968, including all categories of factory workers and employees, was 112 roubles, or $125·4, a month, and it only rose to 130·3 roubles in 1972, whereas the minimum budget of a typical Soviet family living in a town was officially reckoned at 205 roubles; the average income of kolkhoz workers is certainly much lower). And there are some new threats to be reckoned with too.

The above-mentioned increase of 7 per cent in industrial production in 1969 was then the lowest in the whole history of the Soviet Union, equalled only by that of the worst year in the Khrushchev era, 1964. Can any improvement be obtained without radical reforms? The problem is that the material conditions of development are deteriorating. In particular, the once unlimited resources of manpower are becoming exhausted. In 1970, Baibakov said, the economy would be using 92 per cent of the population capable of working, as against 78 per cent in 1960 (and 72 per cent in America). This means that "the possibility of transferring to industry manpower at present employed in domestic or private economy will be completely exhausted in many parts of the country". As *Sotzialisticeskaia Industria* says: "Our economy has entered upon a stage in which further development will be possible only if production becomes more efficient, qualitative achievements improve, and manpower productivity increases." The "extensive" machinery for development that was characteristic of the underdeveloped Russia of Stalin's day needs to be replaced by a new "intensive" machinery suited to an industrialised country, and based on technological and organisational progress.

Another risk is that of the relative saturation of some particular sector of the market with goods that are still of poor quality but are more abundant than formerly. In the big stores in Moscow I have seen departments full of inferior goods which would be unsaleable in any other country, and perhaps even here too: the masses of insatiable purchasers of ten years ago have thinned out, at any rate in Moscow. Today, Y. Orlov says, "there are goods chasing purchasers", for the first time in Soviet history. What will happen if the quality of the goods does not improve, once the essential needs have been satisfied? There is the risk, if possibly not an immediate risk, of a drastic discrepancy (which has always existed on the theoretical plane) between the production plan and the *market* for consumer goods. Once the market ceases to be a "seller's market", conditioned to such an extent by the scarcity of goods that it can automatically absorb any product, a quite new kind of crisis may explode. Sooner or later, the planned productive machine is in danger of running down.

These problems worry the industrial leaders, and it is with complex matters of this kind that economic thinking is concerned today: the debate among the economists is one of the fundamental themes of life in the Soviet Union and in the other post-Stalinist countries of Eastern Europe. Great things are looked for from the reforms of the innovationary economists: "The fruits of the reform", said Birman, "will be beyond anything that anyone, either here or abroad, could have imagined". He has in mind, no doubt, a really radical reform which would embrace the whole economy from top to bottom. Like the other reformist "practical" economists (the group to which Liberman also belongs—he was then in disgrace, and I didn't manage to see him), Birman sees profit as the lever to revolutionise the system and resolve its contradictions. Profit will spur on the worker to behave towards the factory "like the owner of a flat", to take trouble to make everything "modern, fine and rational";

and it will spur on the economy to produce what the consumer wants.

Unlike the Czech and Yugoslav sociologists, Birman did not talk about alienation among workers and management, but this seems to me to be the fundamental *malaise* to be tackled. His reform concentrates on a psychological renewal on the part of Soviet economic man, produced by the mechanism of profit and a general "consumer-type" aspiration towards prosperity. This approach, in nature political-economic and sociological, is rich in important suggestions for any industrial economy or for any large-scale alienating productive structure. Participation in profits and competition between firms will seem, to anyone with experience of rigid administrative planning, the essential means to change a certain negative attitude congenital in the productive worker, an attitude intensified by the lack of an autonomous trade union, which is an instrument of struggle but also of participation. The much more acute economic crisis in Czechoslovakia was born of such conditions. This subject could obviously be taken much further.

During our conversation, Birman developed it rather cautiously. Our meeting took place at the office of the Novosty agency, the obligatory channel for conducting my inquiry: a foreign journalist is not allowed to get into direct touch himself with a Soviet personality. Birman arrived holding behind his back a bunch of flowers intended for the charming and pertinacious young woman, a journalist of the agency, who had organised this and all my other meetings: in Russian 'bourgeois' circles you often come across an appealing old-world courtesy. Birman, who is a Professor at the Plechanov Institute in Moscow, is in his early fifties, tall with grey hair, distinguished, witty and wide-awake: my conversation with him sometimes turned into a polite fencing-match.

In his article in *Novy Mir,* in arguing with the dogmatists (such as a colleague of his who said, "My Party conscience will never allow me to vote for profit") Birman had written: "As at the beginning of the 1930s the Party said that the main task of the Bolsheviks was to learn technology, so today it is necessary to teach economics, the scientific management of production and sociology to the economic leaders and the trade union and Party activists. This problem must be faced as a task of national importance."

I observed that this idea reminded me of what Kennedy said to Walter Heller in 1960 when he invited him to "educate the country in the new economics", and I asked whether the Soviet "new economists" also felt that they should become the educators of the politicians. Birman answered cautiously: "It is life itself, the only Marxist means of education, that will make people carry out the reform. Tchaikovsky used to say that music comes from the people, and the composer merely writes it. In the same way, life teaches, and economics merely transcribes the teachings."

"Life" is a concept that recurs constantly in Soviet phraseology; it can justify so many things: today, in economic affairs, "life" is pushing in the direction of reforms. In order to carry them out, Birman does not think it necessary to liberalise prices, nor does he believe in the Yugoslav type of "socialist market" ("that isn't a market but a socialist bazaar", he says); but he does think that some very substantial reforms are necessary. He would like to see a tax on average profits, similar throughout the economy, for all firms (today the taxes on profits exacted from firms under the Plan differ according to each particular case or category), except in areas where development is in progress. This would benefit the more efficient firms able to produce goods that are in demand on the market.

In the long run the Plan too would be influenced by it, including the structure of investments. "In future", Birman said, "only the new firms (and not all of them) will develop as a result of central investments." Existing firms will modernise themselves through their profits. "But in this field progress is very slow: the Gosplan, you see, is like the hand", and he opened his hand slowly and unwillingly and then closed it hard and fast; "it has a good clasp, but to open it is difficult, and the hand opens only little by little. It has to be forced. This is what I am writing articles about."

In fact, the reforming proposals of Birman and the "practical" economists, though they start at the bottom with the factory, end by involving the highest centres of economic power right up to the Gosplan. There are enough unknown quantities, political as well as economic, in these proposals (envisaged to cover a twenty-year term) to alarm the conservatives, both economists and administrators, who fear to find the Plan superseded. And the Party is jealous of its power. It is logical to suppose that because of such resistances, as well as because of objective difficulties, the progress of the reform will be slow: proof of this can be seen in the great debate on economic policy in 1970, in view of the launching of the new five-year Plan for 1971–75.

The reform, which from the outset has been very fluid and ambiguous, has still to be more precisely defined. "But", Birman said, "what does it really mean if the reform goes ahead slowly? Slowly as compared with what? A Moscow newspaper said the ice on the Volga melted this year later than the usually established date: established by whom? The reform goes on at its own pace. It's another thing to say that we might perhaps have wanted it to go ahead more quickly. But we want so many things, and that isn't to say that our wishes are objective. No, I see no reason for pessimism about the reform. Such pessimism, I think, is typical rather of those who don't want it."

Moscow

16. Fedorenko: The Simulated Market

I came to Moscow when the lime-trees were in flower. In some of the old streets in the centre and along the eighteenth-century "bulevari" the scent of the great trees was so strong that it overpowered the acid cabbage-soup smell of 70-octane petrol. It was in July, and the nights were short; at eleven o'clock a glimmer of light still gave the walls of the Kremlin a fabulous profile. By day the Muscovites went about puffing and panting and those who could rushed off to the banks of the Moskva shaded with pines and birch-trees. Some of the economic luminaries were already in their dachas, unreachable and unaware of my efforts to disturb their summer peace. I pursued Kantorovich, perhaps the most famous of all the Soviet economists, in the course of four trips, from Moscow to Novosibirsk, from Novosibirsk to Leningrad, and from Leningrad, after a journey of some hours by car along the pleasant shores of the Baltic, to his great wooden dacha in the forests of Karelia; we found the dacha, but there was only the "ekonomika", his housekeeper, who said she didn't know exactly where the great academician was—somewhere on holiday on the Black Sea.

In Moscow I met Fedorenko, Nikolai Prokofievich, head of the Institute of Mathematical Economics at the Academy, a few days before the Institute closed for the holidays. Fedorenko, a big jovial man, greeted me wearing a jacket and then told me the story of when he went to see Adriano Olivetti: "We were both wearing jackets and ties. It was frightfully hot like today, and we just looked at each other and decided to take off our jackets and talk in our shirtsleeves." Obviously, Nikolai Prokofievich and I did the same during the two hours' private lesson on the optimal management of the economy that he was good enough to give me.

Standing in front of a blackboard—only it was pink, and almost as big as Samuelson's green board at Cambridge—he explained his economic model with the help of drawings and an intensive Socratic technique of question and answer. At the end—it was three o'clock in the afternoon and I, at least, had gone without lunch—we were both exhausted by economics and the heat, and only some iced white wine produced from a hidden refrigerator saved me from collapse.

Fedorenko is in his early fifties. His Institute only came into being in 1963, and it is the rival establishment to the Institute of Economics, stronghold of the conservatives. Fedorenko was chosen by the old academician Nemchinov when the economico-mathematical laboratory which he directed became an institute. "Let's make way for the young", said Nemchinov; the average age at the new Institute is thirty. Fedorenko is a central personality in the great economic debate. He is constantly under attack by the conservatives, and even the reformers of the "practical" school are a bit jealous of him: "I'm not sure that I really understand all his theories", Birman said to me. "I sometimes wonder if he understands them himself." But criticisms do not seem to have impaired Fedorenko's vigorous enthusiasm for his project of a "System of optimal functioning of the economy"—Sofe, he calls it, using its initials in the American way. He certainly does nothing to placate his adversaries' irritation when he maintains that Soviet economic science is only now (with Fedorenko) becoming "constructive" instead of "descriptive".

The most controversial part of his optimal system concerns prices. Traditional Marxism maintains that prices should be fixed on a basis of work-value, in other words on the amount of work "socially necessary" for the production of each single piece of goods. Fedorenko's theory is that prices should express "the effective contribution of each resource to the satisfaction of the needs of society". He says: "The logical basis of the criterion of optimality consists in the premise that the consumer's demand effectively reflects his aspiration. The economists' job is to express and maximalise the choice of the collective consumer."

J

On the basis of this system, so Fedorenko's scandalised opponents object, planning "starts from the bottom". But this is what he wants. To the question, who decides the scale of values, he answers: "*Narod* (the people). We must study the population's demand and contribute towards educating them." Certainly, the "needs of society", so Fedorenko says, also include defence or foreign aid, and the State can regulate consumption on grounds of health or morality (e.g. consumption of alcohol). But the optimal system rests on the insistent affirmation that the dominant aim of socialist society is "to satisfy fully the preferences of its members".

This is the first important point of Sofe. The second, and central, point concerns the machinery for assigning resources. Fedorenko does not want to abolish the plan, or to set up a "socialist market" regulated by free prices, on Yugoslav lines. But his *optimal plan* is like an envelope that contains within it an *optimal market*, which conditions it. At the Institute of Mathematical Economics they call this market *rynok v kabinete* (the simulated market).

Let us suppose, Fedorenko says, that you and I have to make the plan for 1971–75. From the business concerns and the Ministries a series of production plans come in to us, and consequently a series of requests for essential resources. For example, the Ministries of Power, of Urban Economy, and of Chemicals ask us for a total of 700 million cubic metres of natural gas. But the gas industry informs us that it will produce only 500 million. Who are we to assign them to? The cost of gas production is one rouble per thousand cubic metres. But we know that by using gas instead of coal the chemical industry saves three roubles, domestic use two, and the power industry one rouble. If we fix the price of gas at 3·90 roubles, the chemical industry will be interested in buying it but the other two won't. So this will be the optimal price of gas which will permit of a rational distribution of this resource. But this, Fedorenko goes on, is only the first step. At a price of 3·90 roubles, the gas industry will probably offer to produce 600 instead of 500 million cubic metres. At the headquarters of the plan, therefore, the process of "iterations" will begin, of offers and counter-offers, made possible by means of the use of models and electronic computers; by successive approximations, we shall arrive at a balanced and optimal plan, and, simultaneously, at optimal prices. Both plan and prices will remain fixed at this point (as they would be fixed by a contract, in the capitalist market) until a change in technology or in demand leads them to change simultaneously.

Fedorenko's system is a synthesis of plan and market. He is opposed to the cybernetic extremists, who dream of an economy that will be "a single gigantic organism whose elements receive all orders from a single centre and execute them mechanically". He regards as "not interesting and very unattractive" the utopia of Trotsky (and of certain Soviet mathematicians today), of a planner who with a "magic keyboard" moves about men and materials at will. "There is no need", he says in a significant phrase, "to add the totalitarianism of machines to the totalitarianism of regimes." Besides, as he observes, even in the age of cybernetics such a system is impossible: "The model of a complete production plan of 50,000 concerns which produce two million articles (the Soviet economy is larger) would involve two million variables and a million identities. The number of operations necessary to work it out would be equal to 10 to the eighteenth power: even with a computer of a million operations to the second, it would take 30,000 years. Mathematics is a key to the economy, not a picklock."

In order to solve the problems of this "complex and increasingly vast and dynamic system" that is modern economics, therefore, Fedorenko would make an extensive use of the decentralisation and autonomy of the "productive cells". A single index of profit would be applied to all the concerns in the country, and they would be asked to maximalise this profit. If I understand Fedorenko rightly, this means that the concerns would be conditioned in a downward direction by the market demand and the wishes of the consumers, just as they themselves would condition in an upward direction, by means of the mechanism of marginal prices, the "simulated market", and therefore the plan.

This "hierarchical system" would take the place of the

billions of operations described above. Oskar Lange's answer to von Hayek, when the latter questioned the possibility of solving in a planned economy the millions of simultaneous equations necessary for rational choices, was: "I solve millions of equations every time I order a meal in a restaurant".

Various objections to Fedorenko's system can be raised. To the traditionalists' accusations of anti-Marxism and marginalism (still a hateful term in the USSR), Fedorenko, Novozhilov and Aganbegian answer with an elegant display of mathematical logic designed to demonstrate that their theories are reconcilable with Marx and Lenin. But this is not particularly interesting to us. The more valid objections concern the practical difficulties. Consider the billions of pieces of information, offers and counter-offers which would have to percolate through the vast structures of the Soviet economy, in innumerable iterations, during the frantic period when the plan was being drawn up: as if all the interminable bargaining of a market economy were to be concentrated in a single short but colossal annual fair. Given the bureaucratic rigidities of the Soviet economy, would not the real (or even "socialist") market be more efficacious than this "simulated" electronic market?

Fedorenko answered by maintaining the opposite: his electronic iterations, he said, would be superior to market bargainings because they would be quicker and would always take into account the whole framework of the economy. "The capitalist market", he said, "works with a time-lag and does not recognise global demands; therefore it can operate in a destructive sense. Our mechanism, on the other hand, works with an eye to the future and takes into account the interests of society as a whole." Coming into operation in a "just" society, this shadow-market would moreover express a more rational model of consumption, demand, and the use of resources. In short, Fedorenko's *rynok v kabinete* would be a super-market free from the imperfections of the actual market; by expressing itself in an optimal organic plan, it would guarantee an economy without cycles and without crises.

Obviously, many doubts and unknown quantities remain: the more so since this grand design is being put forward in an economy which, despite its advances, has not yet succeeded in satisfying some of the most elementary demands of the consumers. To move from a traditional administration burdened by bureaucracy (Nemchinov described it as "automation rigidified by chaotic processes") to Fedorenko's optimal utopia would signify a really fantastic leap. But the very inadequacy of present planning makes Fedorenko's ideas attractive: the Gosplan supports his researches, if with some reserves.

In June 1967, after long and bitter debates, a "Committee for the Study of Optimal Planning" was set up, with a directing council of 89 economists, including three academicians, Fedorenko, Kantorovich, and the conservative Kachiaturov. Five hundred institutes are collaborating in the project, and it was hoped to arrive in possibly five years at an *eskiznyi proekt*, a schematic project for optimal administration. All this is being carried out mainly within the orbit of the academic and university institutes. Fedorenko has proposed, so far without success, that the project should be sponsored by the Cabinet.

During the 1960s the process of organisation of the reforming economists made great advances. Today optimalism is the fashion. "When a new theory is born", Alexandr Lurie says, "at first it is denounced as absurd, then it is recognised to be partly true, and lastly people find that in reality its fundamental theses had always been recognised. The optimal idea is at present in the second stage." It cannot yet be foreseen when it will move into the third; but the fact must be admitted that Fedorenko and his colleagues, in formulating their idea of an optimal society of consumers and scientists (so different from the present-day party-cum-ideological Soviet society), are consciously attempting an ambitious new synthesis of modern economics.

"We are the first", says Fedorenko, "to pose systematically the problem of optimality." This design has an undeniable grandeur, and it tackles problems that are present in all the developed economies: such as the right balance between the autonomous initiative of concerns within the market and the rational and planned organisation of development; or the problem of the organic quantification of all economic and social values; or the methods of applying the new cybernetic techniques to the economy. These are matters that are being discussed today by economists throughout the world.

Moscow

17. From Bureaucracy to Technocracy

Vadim Aleksandrovich Trapeznikov, president of the Institute of Automation, vice-president of the Committee for Science and Technology, academician, Stalin Prize winner in 1951, is, at the age of sixty-three, one of the great personalities of the USSR. In appearance he is stiff and stern, and he speaks slowly and with authority. In August 1964 a celebrated article of his in *Pravda* marked the coming into line of the technicians with the ideas of the innovating economists and contributed towards convincing the Party that reform of the economy was necessary.

Trapeznikov's arguments were the arguments of scientific progress. He had realised, after a research visit to the West, that the scientific and technological gap between the USSR and the West was widening, and he had become convinced that the difference was due mainly to economic causes. Authoritarian planning was discouraging progress. The application of each new discovery involved long delays. Firms found no economic inducement to adopt innovations. In short, to ensure scientific progress reform was necessary.

"I am a technician who has had to take an interest in economics because without economics one cannot direct one's course", Trapeznikov said when I met him at the headquarters of the Committee, a huge building in Gorky Street (Ilya Ehrenburg lived almost opposite to it, in an ugly little two-roomed flat with the walls covered with marvellous pictures by Picasso). "Good management derives not only from technical but also from economic progress. Fortunately economics here is not what it was twenty years ago. In those days our economists did not concern themselves with concrete questions, but today they do."

On the morrow of Stalin's death, when Vladimir Dudintsev wrote his famous novel *Not by Bread Alone*, the problem of the inventor, the representative of the new technology, crushed by the gigantic and impersonal machine of the party bureaucracy, was a literary theme. With Trapeznikov the technicians' arguments have become a political fact; the slogan of the "technical-scientific revolution of our times" has come into fashion. In the name of this revolution many innovations can be adopted, many violations of the dogmatic tradition of Soviet society become permissible, and some liberties can even be taken with the overruling power of the Party.

Personalities like Trapeznikov are important in elucidating the circumstances in which the Soviet "new economics" is developing. What he says relates to the cultural rather than the economic situation. In estimating the reform, of which he takes a favourable view, he said, "It must be admitted that it could not be done all at once. It's not as simple as that. It's not a purely mechanical thing: people have to be prepared for it. They have to change their way of working and to understand more clearly the economic aspect of their activities."

In the new organisation of the economy, a central role will be played by specialists and scientists. Trapeznikov talked to me about the experiments that are being carried out to facilitate the manufacture of high-quality goods. In some ministries, committees of experts award certificates of quality to the various products; and their judgements reflect on a firm's rewards. "These measures," Trapeznikov said in answer to an obvious objection of mine, "are, of course, administrative measures, but they aren't bureaucratic, because it is the scientists who give the certificates of quality. This is something new. With you it is the consumer who expresses his judgement, but he does not know the world level of technique as our scientists do when giving their judgement on a product. This is, in fact, a scientific rather than an administrative method."

I don't really find this argument convincing. These measures strike me as expedients; they really show that the reform is not functioning yet, and that the economic incentives, which ought spontaneously to urge firms to produce good-quality articles, are inadequate. But it is significant that Trapeznikov regards such measures as important novelties demonstrating the change-over from bureaucracy to technocracy. A great deal has been written about the rise in prestige and power of the technicians and scientists and the relationship of the whole educated class to the party bureaucracy; and any opinion about this is bound to be empirical and uncertain. In general, I would say that while the Party has had, for practical reasons, to yield power to the technicians, economists and scientists, it has become correspondingly more repressive towards writers and historians, in other words towards the humanistic and political *intelli-ghenzija* which might have expressed on the political plane the demands advanced by the technicians. If Trapeznikov is allowed to go ahead, that cannot be permitted at the same time to Dudintsev. The Party wanted to split the intellectual "united front" that was developing, ranging from the physicist Sakharov to the historian Yakir and the writer Solzhenitsyn. This, perhaps, is the particular logic of power that explains both the great economic debate of the 'sixties and the series of writers' trials.

In these circumstances, one is tempted to conclude that, in any case, the Academy has strengthened its position vis-à-vis the Party. But even that formula is oversimplified: the real relations between political power and scientific power are extremely complex. Confining ourselves to the economy, the Party remains for the most part outside the economic debate (the "old engineers" who govern the country, from Kosygin to Brezhnev, have long kept silence on the subject); but it indicates certain insuperable limits in the discussion and in certain extreme cases supports the conservatives.

This explains the condemnation, referred to as a matter of routine, of Ghennadi Lisichkin, one of the most brilliant Soviet economic journalists, who had become identified with the "market socialism" trend on Yugoslav lines. According to Birman, who is a friend of his, his only fault was "to have evolved two or three unfortunate phrases around which a lot of demagogy has been built up." It is worth noting, however, that the attacks had so far not prevented Lisichkin from continuing to write in *Novy Mir*: a good article by him appeared in the May 1969 number of the "liberal" review of the Writers' Association.

The authorities do not always intervene openly against the innovators. More usually, a sort of contamination occurs between Party and Academy, so that it is difficult to decide "who makes use of whom". Take sociology, for example. In the 'sixties there was an explosion of sociology in the USSR. In a certain sense, the young sociologists are replacing the young writers as revealers of the "other Russia", even if their opposition is less radical, more integrated within the system, and not so sensational. Nevertheless, the boom in sociology is one of the central manifestations of that evolution from bureaucracy to technocracy (or, if we prefer it, of that process of modernisation of the ruling class) which is going on all the time, almost independently of the reactionary involutions or the contradictions at the summit.

The central personality of the sociological revolution is perhaps Aleksey Matveevich Rumiantsev. An academician and economist, then (and until July 1972) director of the Institute of Social Research in the Academy of Sciences, founded in May 1968, Rumiantsev was editor of *Pravda* in 1965, after the fall of Khrushchev, and at that time wrote some notable "liberal" articles about cultural aspects (they even contained echoes of Bukharin). This phase of relative tolerance in cultural policy unfortunately proved ephemeral. Rumiantsev was replaced as editor of *Pravda* in September 1965, ten days after the arrest of Sinyavsky and Daniel which marked the beginning of the reactionary turn that still goes on. But he did not fall into disgrace: he continued to be one of the great personages in the Academy, and threw himself into sociology. Rumiantsev received me in his study, a splendid room in the former royal villa which is the headquarters of the Praesidium of the Academy. I had great hopes of this meeting, but it proved the most disappointing of the whole trip.

Rumiantsev talked to me in the solemn language of officialdom. He eloquently proclaimed the importance, more than ever today, of elucidating the Marxist-Leninist doctrine of sociology. Why more than ever today? "Because", he answered portentously, "this year, 1970, we are preparing to celebrate the centenary of Lenin's birth. Not only that", he went on with growing enthusiasm, "but the 150th anniversary of Engels' birth also falls this year. Yes, this year, for us, lies under the auspices of Marxism-Leninism." I asked him if sociology in Soviet Russia, as in other East European countries, was coming up against the problem of alienation of the workers (as a matter of fact I already knew from official Soviet communications to the VIth World Congress of Sociology that this was a matter of concern). He answered me with a scholastic demonstration that alienation is impossible in socialism "where every man is both owner and worker! What room is there for alienation, tell me?"

He explained his continual references to the classics (he cited certain standard formulae all in one breath, with no pause between one word and the next, like a distrait believer reciting the Creed) by saying: "We are Marxists, and therefore we refer to Marx: though I don't mean (and he smiled to himself) that we behave like the Muslims who quote the Koran." He also contrived to slip into the interview a categorical denunciation of the "Maoist group", "who describe themselves as Marxist-Leninist but they are not and never have been: obviously (and he shook his head sadly) Mao has never read Marx or Engels or Lenin".

This disconcerting interview, with a man whom I know to possess a shrewd and lively mind, had been preceded by a valuable and stimulating talk with some of his closest collaborators whom he himself had chosen for his Institute. From this encounter Soviet sociology really emerged as a young science interested in everything ("anyone who doesn't believe in it is an *otstal*, a back number", said one of my interlocutors), including, naturally, the problems of the workers' situation, which arise from the fact that "the worker has a very abstract comprehension of the fact that he is theoretically the master and has a share in production: in actual practice he sees only his assembly line and his wage packet".

Problems like this which impinge on the efficiency of the economy are thoroughly studied in an unprejudiced way together with many others. Aleksandr Abramovich Galkin told me: "The Party, the State, and the industries are greatly interested in sociology. We get a mass of requests, letters and questions from firms, organisations, and *kolkhoz*, who want us to work a miracle and reply at once to all their problems."

Galkin is just beginning to study the question of social structures and mechanisms of power. His thesis is that social changes—advances in education, for example—provoke changes "in the form and substance of power, in the relations between authority and society, in the levers of which authority makes use: today the rational principle is beginning to prevail over the emotive principle". It is no mere chance that the new sociology describes itself as "concrete" (with a quite involuntary polemical emphasis, as opposed to the "abstract" or theoretical sociology of Marxism).

"Anyone who studies the problems from an overhead, theoretical standpoint will deny", I was told, "that there is any alienation in socialist society." But "if we had attained the ideal state, there'd be nothing left for us to do but to sit with a bottle of brandy and wait for them to bring us another one as soon as it was empty. The reality today is something different." In order to know that different reality, that other Russia which does not coincide with the official view, a new departure was planned for 1970 with the carrying-out of periodical soundings on Gallup-poll lines: "We shall sound the public on political questions, and try to ascertain the attitude of public opinion on our current problems."

The development of sociological studies in such countries as Yugoslavia or Czechoslovakia has led many students of affairs to adopt critical attitudes. In the more tightly controlled atmosphere of the Soviet Union too, the development of sociology, even under the guidance of trusted characters like Rumiantsev, is a harbinger of changes: changes that may strengthen the system but that should also make it in the long run more modern and open-minded.

What struck me most was the realisation that it is society itself that is pressing from below for the development of sociological studies. It is against the background of this society (still largely an unknown quantity, the real "x" of the Soviet system) that such phenomena as the development of the new sociology and the new economics are at work. Within this framework, the conception of Marxism itself is being brought up to date. Marxism, so one of the most brilliant young scholars of the Institute of World Economics, Stanislav Menshikov, said to me, "is very useful because it is a dynamic theory, which sees the economy as a changing reality; and because it is what we call today a kind of *sistemnyi analiz,* of systems analysis of the economy. This is important".

Moscow

18. Aganbegian, The Youthful Prodigy

I fancy that when this journey of mine into the economic world
is done Abel Gezevic Aganbegian will prove to have been the
youngest—and Strumilin the oldest—of all the economists I
have met. Aganbegian was born in 1932 and when I met him
he was not yet an academician but only corresponding member
of the Academy. But he is director of one of the most important
economic institutes. His team of 800 scholars, including 20
professors and 80 associate professors, is larger than all the three
main economic centres in Moscow, Fedorenko's Institute of
Mathematical Economics, Gatovski's Institute of Economics,
and the Gosplan Institute directed by Anatoly Efimov.

Two hundred mathematicians are working with Aganbegian,
more than Leonid Kantorovich has in the other research centre
of Akademgorodok, the economics section of the Institute of
Mathematics: "But the other institutes", Aganbegian says,
"have more academicians and professors, more big shots, who
are the people who count." I mention these figures to give an
idea of the immense forces that are mobilised for research, and
not only for economic research. Such concentrations of scholars
are rarely to be found anywhere else in the world. Akademgorodok, which is the site of the Siberian Section of the Academy
of Sciences, was then little more than ten years old, but some
fifty Academicians and more than a thousand professors and
associate professors had already been transferred to it; whereas
it had less than 5,000 university students, who in Siberia are
chosen by extremely stiff competitive examinations.

I find this planned effort really more interesting than the
rather over-popularised image of the "city of science in the
taiga". We are, it is true, in the midst of the Siberian forest,
but we are also less then twenty miles from Novosibirsk, a city

of over a million inhabitants, with important industries and a railway junction as big as Clapham: but here it's not a junction for millions of suburban commuters but for tens of millions of Siberians scattered over a territory of millions of square miles. Novosibirsk is approximately halfway between the Polish border and the Pacific Ocean: on either side there is roughly the equivalent of the whole of America.

I came to Akademgorodok to meet Aganbegian, travelling on the "Academy circuit" ("What circuit are you travelling on, *gospodin* Levi: Intourist? Academy? Novosty Agency? Are you a *turist* or a *spezialist*?"). There are great advantages in travelling on these privileged circuits; you find seats, you magically jump the queues, and in aeroplanes, where there is only one class, you are sometimes put in the little part in the front or the back reserved for *nachalniki* or VIPs, Aeroflot officials, or even drunkards (who are always regarded with indulgence and taken care of here). To be a foreigner has some disadvantages, however. For example, the direct airline from Novosibirsk to Leningrad was closed to me: a foreigner must fly to Moscow and then go on by train. There was another curious episode. I had booked on the Moscow–Novosibirsk flight of 23.30, but at Domodedovo airport, which is new and huge, I was told that the flight was delayed owing to bad weather and in fact I left at 3 in the morning. But the story wasn't true: on arrival at Novosibirsk I found that what had really happened was that I had been transferred to a later flight, while that on which I was booked had arrived two hours before, "but with no foreigners on board". I never discovered the key to this puzzle, which is just another among the many other small or larger signs of a certain persistent "diversity" (I don't know how else to put it) of this country. To give an example: here in Akademgorodok on the houses and laboratories you see the usual huge slogans written up, such as "Glory to our great Soviet people", "Glory to great chemistry", "Long live our country's government", "Party and people are united". Elsewhere you don't notice it. But in this capital of scientific thought it seems incongruous.

And another thing. Akademgorodok is a pretty place, well designed, with plenty of green spaces; but the houses, the shops, and even the Academy hotel where I stayed, and which was rather like a *Jugendheim* in the Bavarian Alps, all have the same Spartan and rather inferior character. In fact, only direct experience of this inferior quality in goods or services of any kind can make the foreigner understand what Soviet economists mean in practice when they talk about the need to spread "a new industrial culture" among the people and to change the psychology of the Soviet workers by means of radical structural reforms.

But let us get back to Aganbegian and his Institute of Economics and Industrial Organisation. The studies there are both theoretical and practical. The aim is to construct econometric models which will make efficient planning possible. The point of departure of these researches in the Soviet Union is probably indicated in the adoption of Wassily Leontief's "input–output" analysis, or, as they say here, of the "method of intersectorial budgets". Leontief, as we know, is a Russian who has lived in America for forty years, and a lively debate tinged with passionate partisanship has gone on about the Russian influences on his work. The Soviets claim Bolshevik precedents; Naum Jasny (another Russian émigré) has eulogised the importance of the work done by the Menshevik Groman; Leontief himself merely mentions quietly that he left Russia at the age of nineteen, and everyone in fact recognises the original character of his studies. It is a fact that the Soviets continued for decades to draw up their plans in accordance with a primitive and imperfect system known as the "material budgets system", which in fact never enabled them to produce balanced plans. It was not until 1956, as Aganbegian confirmed to me, that the Gosplan Research Institute began seriously to set about adopting Leontief's techniques. The first input–output model of the Soviet economy is for the year 1959 (Westerners know only some "pieces" of it, on the basis of which the American economist Vladimir Treml has reconstructed a complete picture of the matrices, like doing a gigantic puzzle; when the Soviets are sure that these tables no longer have a strategic value, we shall know whether Treml's reconstruction is right). More than a decade later, this work was now bearing fruit:

Efimov had recently made public that the "intersectorial budgets" were used to prepare the next five-year Plan (1971–75). Great practical importance is attributed to these techniques. Certainly the research developments now in progress, which Aganbegian talked to me about, are of considerable interest.

This great young economist is of Armenian origin and after being educated in the Moscow economic school came to Novosibirsk in 1960; he is a strange mixture of reserve and open self-assurance. He irritates his older colleagues when he calmly announces that he has demonstrated with two equations (which not all of them understand) the final solution of an economic problem that has always been at the centre of impassioned arguments. He offers proofs, not opinions. He talked to me in a slow, precise English which he learnt by a quite new experimental method, based on the exclusive study of one language for a short period of time; I found that he also expressed himself equally deliberately in Russian. In appearance, Aganbegian is a "sad Armenian", and resembles like a twin brother a Neapolitan economist friend of mine who, when we were students together in London (I was studying theology at that time), was constantly being taken for a Jew or a Persian: Mediterranean civilisation covers a vast area. His figure would benefit from a bit of sport, but I don't suppose he has the time for it.

Aganbegian's job is to make models. With his eight hundred scholars and a powerful BESM 6 electronic brain he constructs many models of different kinds. This is a fascinating undertaking, in Russia as in America, because the econometric model is science's most advanced attempt to discover the most intimate causal links between economic facts, the hidden laws of phenomena so variable and complex that they have so far challenged every attempt of human reason to elucidate them satisfactorily. The model is, indeed, something more: it is the effort to foresee and shape the future. When one thinks of the crudeness and violence of the methods with which Stalin's economic policy (much policy and very little economics) proposed to "change the economy" and "transform Nature", and then considers the refinement of the cognitive analyses of a team of scholars like Aganbegian's, one seems to be dealing with two totally different worlds—even though, in both cases, the aim is "planning" (for want of a better word).

In the construction of models Aganbegian's institute is in the forefront, together with a few other American and European centres. Here I had the almost physical feeling that my journey had really brought me to one of the "new frontiers" of economics, on the threshold of a vast unexplored country ("the Cosmos is easier", Fedorenko said). Contacts between Aganbegian's mathematical economics and Western econometry are very close. A first important series of models worked out here derives directly from those of Leontief: but those models, Aganbegian told me, "were not of use for planning because of their static and linear approach, and because they did not contemplate [macroeconomic] factors like capital investment, manpower and so on. We therefore had to move on from static to dynamic models, and this we have done. In 1965, when we began to work for the Gosplan, we achieved our first dynamic model, of thirty sectors, which is already in use. Now we are working on a model of 180 sectors, which will include about 15,000 indices: half a billion operations are needed to work out one variable."

According to Aganbegian, his models lend themselves to practical use better than the American, since the latter embrace few "sectors". To me it doesn't seem quite like that. The points of departure may be different, but the points of arrival seem to me very much the same. Western econometry, under Tinbergen, Klein etc., sets out from "macroeconomic" models with few variables, of Keynesian derivation, but it ends up by incorporating in them, so as to increase their practical use and meet the demands of industry, the intersectorial models evolved by Leontief (as we have seen at Brookings, in Philadelphia, etc.). In Russia they set out from static intersectorial models and transform them into dynamic forecasting econometric models, integrating them with macroeconomic variables. I don't know enough about it to grasp which is the more advanced; obviously the fundamental difference lies in the existence of State planning in Russia: only in those conditions, according to the Soviets, can the "planometric" model exercise its full usefulness.

Aganbegian regards as even more original the two other directions in which his team is working. The first aims at the creation of intersectorial-interregional models which, so he told me, "will reveal the relationships between the twenty-five great economic regions into which we have divided the USSR. This model is the most complicated of all, and in it a billion operations are needed to work out a single variable. It has important practical applications for planning." It too obviously derives from Leontief's analyses, but it seems that it represents an original development of the method.

The last sphere of the team's work is that of models for individual sectors of industry with which they are trying to establish the optimal lines of development for a particular industry. "I believe", Aganbegian told me, "that this is the best thing our team has done. More than a hundred researchers are at work in this field, divided up into 'laboratories' each of which is dealing with a particular branch of industry such as energy, mining, and so on. We are working under contract for the ministries, the planning institutes, etc. These bodies pay us a certain sum for our research and supply us with technical data. Then we prepare the models, work out the economico-mathematical analyses, and finally go to Moscow to discuss our final report with the Ministry."

Thus Aganbegian's institute carries out functions which, in America, are divided between the university institutes and the private or public advisory centres. Leontief at Harvard described to me in very similar terms some sectorial researches of this kind which he was directing, on behalf of big firms anxious to plan their development rationally, for A. D. Little of Boston, the biggest consultant company in America. In a certain sense, Aganbegian's institute aims to be Harvard plus A. D. Little. One cannot help being struck by certain similarities in the developments of economic theory and practice in such different circumstances.

Akademgorodok (Novosibirsk)

19. *Novozhilov's Optimal Plan*

An hour's run by car through a Scandinavian countryside of grey-green forests, lakes and shimmering views of the Gulf of Finland took me from Leningrad to Komarovo, where I was to see Viktor Valentinovich Novozhilov. We had left behind us in the pale morning sun that visionary city with its watercolour tints, Leningrad; we travelled along roads laden with Leninist memories of flights and revolutions; we went through villages that were unusually neat and clean—they had once been Finnish and were now holiday resorts for young "pioneers". Komarovo is the refuge of the Leningrad intellectuals, as Peredelkino is for the Muscovites. The houses are built in the woods. Distinguished-looking gentlemen were walking along the roads which had curious names like Artillery Road or Officers' Road; and there, after a good deal of searching, was Academicians' Road.

Under the great trees were some wooden buildings with their windows painted in red or green. This was Novozhilov's retreat, though he is not an academician: he has always been too anticonformist to become one, and in Stalin's day he used to be accused of marginalism and Keynesianism. Now the difficult years are past, and Viktor Valentinovich, at the age of seventy-seven, is regarded since Nemchinov's death as the doyen of the mathematical economists and perhaps of all the ranks of the reformers; some years ago he even got the Lenin Prize. He is a thin, cheerful old man with a delicate, handsome face; he divides his time between economics, music, and cinephotography. He plays the violin and the viol d'amore (he has two old Italian violins and a splendid Salzburg viol d'amore); he composes romantic trios and plays them himself, recording the three parts one after the other. His wife accompanies him at the piano. He also composes the accompanying music for his little films. At the end of our interview he asked me gaily what kind of music I would like to hear; out of loyalty to my wife, who is a Neapolitan, and because it seemed to fit in with the tastes of his day, I suggested a tarantella.

I spent two quite delightful hours with Novozhilov. He speaks an exquisite Russian, supplementing it when necessary with English spoken with an excellent accent and with some words which I took to be Italian but which instead proved to be Latin. He said, for example, that "planning is the *differentia specifica* of socialism," and added: "Do speak Italian; I understand it because I still know Latin quite well; I finished at the high school in 1911". We talked in a little study on the first floor; in the kitchen below his wife was picking off the stalks from some huge strawberries. We talked about prices, and about the two schools into which the mathematical economists are divided (though they are all reckoned as reformers): the Fedorenko school, regarded as more radical, and the school of Novozhilov and Aganbegian. In a debate in 1966 which lasted two days and in which practically all the major Soviet economists, both conservatives and innovators, took part, Aganbegian was one of the chief supporters of Fedorenko, who was the rapporteur, in his encounter with the traditionalists; but he made a point of explaining, citing his inevitable equations, what were the differences between the two mathematical schools. We have shown, he said, that there is no contradiction between the theoretical necessity (advanced by all the innovators) to satisfy the people's needs to the maximum, and the practical principle (dominant in Soviet Marxist tradition) of making maximum reductions in production costs or work input: "the optimal solution from the first point of view is optimal also from the second", and there is a proportional relationship between the values or prices attributed on the basis of the first and the second criterion. From that, he went on, some economists (Fedorenko) draw the conclusion that "the price should be established according to the social usefulness of the goods produced" measured by demand, and in practice by the market, and not on a basis of work-cost.

Others, on the contrary, among them Novozhilov and Aganbegian himself, consider that prices should be arrived at according to their work-cost, but that it should be calculated in a new way.

The new way, as worked out by Novozhilov, takes into account, in addition to the direct cost of production, the "costs of inverse relations", in other words the greater costs accruing to other productive sectors from renunciation of the use of a scarce commodity. In practice, Novozhilov's price is a "scarcity price", based on the marginal usefulness of goods. To me it does not seem very different from Fedorenko's price. Novozhilov explained to me: "I am completely in agreement [with Fedorenko] that the aim is to maximalise wellbeing; but unfortunately it is not yet possible to define the function of wellbeing; there is no unit of measurement. If this function could be expressed by consumers' demand [as, in effect, Fedorenko suggests], everything would be easy. But demand does not express optimal needs, but needs as they manifest themselves in relation to a certain distribution of labour and earnings. Our socialist market is therefore better than your capitalist market, but it is not the best market possible, it is not optimal. Today, therefore, optimal planning cannot be begun by setting out *only* from demand. Nevertheless, although Fedorenko poses the problem by setting out from demand whereas I pose it by setting out from the minimisation of the work needed for essential goods, the only difference between us is that of approach; in substance, there is no difference."

The thesis that there is no contradiction between the two orders of values, those deriving from demand and the market and those deriving from Marxian work-value (reinterpreted), also means that there is no conflict, according to Novozhilov, Aganbegian etc., between traditional Marxism and the modern theories of optimal planning. "According to us", Aganbegian said, "the optimal price as we define it corresponds completely to the methodology of Karl Marx." There has been much discussion about this, and some Westerners, such as the American Robert Campbell, have found themselves in agreement with the Soviet traditionalists, such as A. Y.

Boiarski, in maintaining that the contradiction exists and is unbridgeable. It is important for Novozhilov, Aganbegian, Fedorenko and their followers to demonstrate that this is not so, in order to be able to carry forward their innovating ideas without too many difficulties. In this demonstration they have employed all their ingenuity, with brilliant results which go far beyond a mere terminological argument or a debate on sources, and which in the end have produced a rethinking and deeper penetration of Marxism, and perhaps also an important contribution to the renewal of the structures of economic power in the USSR: in so far as theory can, by its own mysterious ways, contribute towards modifying reality.

Novozhilov and I discussed at some length how the Soviet economists' new theories came into being. I was curious to know whether they had been influenced by the decades-long dispute between the opponents and the supporters of planning, a dispute that extends from an essay of Enrico Barone in 1911, through von Mises and Hayek, down to the Lange-Lerner model of market socialism worked out in the 1930s. The subject of the dispute was whether or not it was possible to effect a rational distribution of resources in a planned economy ruled by arbitrary prices, not a market economy. This problem, which at that time was theoretical and discussed as such, has since the 1950s acquired an overwhelming practical importance. The Soviet "optimalists' " theories are to a great extent an attempt to solve precisely this problem, which faces the Soviet leaders and the Gosplan. I asked Novozhilov if he was familiar with this historic debate, and where his "model" came from. He answered, "From the link between economic science and our practical experience. I took part for years, as an adviser, in the work of several offices preparing projects. This experience compelled me to study the problems of the efficiency of investments and their optimal distribution. Practical needs (I began to publish my ideas in 1939) then brought me to the conclusions that I am still defending today."

In 1939, in Leningrad, a twenty-seven-year old mathematician, Leonid Kantorovich, who had been called on to solve certain transport problems, formulated the theory of "linear programming" which the American George Dantzig, a colleague of Wassily Leontief at Harvard, rediscovered on his own account some years later. Kantorovich realised that his mathematical methodology could also be applied to the general problem of the distribution of economic resources; but he needed a scale of "objectively determined values", and he invented a "scarcity price" very similar to Novozhilov's. "I met Kantorovich in 1939", Novozhilov told me, "and I became convinced that we were travelling along the same road. Then a great event in my life was my meeting with Nemchinov, in 1958—late in our lives, unfortunately. He was only a little younger than I, and we grasped at once how much we had in common. Our 'model' was born in this circle, which was then a very narrow one. There were very few of us. Today George Dantzig says—I don't know if it's true—that there are more mathematicians working in the economic field in Russia than in America." I asked him what he knew of Oskar Lange. "Not much, up to 1958. But he was a great scholar." (Subsequently Gregory Grossman, of the University of California at Berkeley, told me that it was he who sent Novozhilov a copy of Lange's works, towards the middle of 1960.)

We then talked about the future of the economy. Novozhilov is convinced that "the more the productive forces develop, the more complicated and difficult will the regulation of the economy, and especially planning, become" so as to avoid crises and cycles. Planning, he insists, is the *differentia specifica* of socialism; it will gain in strength in the future. He believes that both Western programming of the regulated market and planning according to market socialism as in Yugoslavia are inadequate ("Yugoslav society is socialist", he said, "but not at the level of socialism that Marx and Lenin regarded as socialist"). Though I realise that his planning would presuppose considerable autonomy for the "economic cells" and would respond to society's demands for prosperity, it seems to me that this conception of Novozhilov's is strongly influenced by that technocratic centralism that has always been present in Marxism, from Marx to Engels and Lenin. His idea of a planning that is constantly gaining in strength may also seem to be in contradiction to the rebirth in the Communist countries of certain market mechanisms which are trying to break the suffocating structure of Stalinist central planning. But I think he discounts that development and looks beyond it to a distant future: his picture of an economic society with vigorous autonomies, vigorously planned, embraces the whole of modern economy, both socialist and non-socialist.

With these ideas of his, not everyone would agree even here. Stanislav Menshikov said to me: "Stalin thought that in socialism market relationships would soon disappear, but that idea has been proved wrong, and most of our economists recognise the fact. Today, the fundamental difference between capitalism and Communism is not the market but ownership (though capitalist private ownership itself is changing today). As to the use of market relationships in our economy, economists' opinions differ: in any case, we ourselves make use of market relationships, in a market different from yours, and regulated (but that last is also true of the modern capitalist market)."

In these views, with their interesting shades of qualification, there is an implicit tendency towards the idea of "convergence" of the Communist and capitalist economies. This idea, propounded already by Jan Tinbergen in 1961, is not really in contrast with Novozhilov's great conception of modern economics. In my talk with Novozhilov we did not discuss the "convergence of systems" (an idea that fascinates and disturbs many people). But I did ask him, "Doesn't it seem to you that the unity of economic science has at last been reestablished, through the convergence of problems, theories and language? To me, after this journey, the thing seems obvious." Novozhilov, however, skated over my question and preferred to emphasise the differences.

We, he said, find our study of the Western economists very useful. But they "are interested chiefly in the present, and adopt a quantitative approach which according to us is insufficient to foresee the future of the economy. This depends mainly on qualitative changes, or on the evolution of the great economic relationships and the system of directing the economy: this is the decisive point. To me it seems essential that we should study the laws of development *(razvitie)* and not those of growth *(rost)*; the Westerners do not do this enough".

Novozhilov was perfectly right in this summing up of certain essential differences between Western—particularly American—and Soviet economic science. It is nevertheless open to argument whether theoretical discussion of the great economic principles and relationships is in fact as productive as the quantitative, analytical and practical approach. For the time being I am not sure that it is. In the Soviet Union itself, many practical economists regard the optimalists' theories as utopian and abstract, taking little account of the fact that economy is made up of millions of men, of individuals conditioned in their outlook and work by factors that are not only economic but social and political as well. I am told that the young Soviet economists, who can now be counted in thousands, are today divided between these two schools, the theoretical and the practical, the macroeconomic and the microeconomic (or "business" school). Meanwhile the great debate continues between Party and Academy, between reactionary and innovationary economists, and the first steps are being taken in a reform which, as Aganbegian told me, "is regarded not as a fact *una tantum* but as a long process". In such circumstances, the directions in which the theory and practice of economics in this country will develop in the next generation can hardly be imagined.

Leningrad

20. Reformers at a Congress

On the grassy banks of Lake Balaton in Hungary, the hordes of West German tourists who had come in their Mercedes cars mingled with the Hungarian bathers and even with the occasional group of Soviet officers who had exchanged their uniforms for swimming-suits. In the avenues of old poplars along the lakeside young girls were strolling in bikinis and old gentlemen in dressing-gowns, here to take the cure; and in the Kurhaus building, just opposite the fountain where glasses of the waters were being handed out, an economic congress was being held, promoted by a study centre in Milan, the Ceses (Centro Studi e Ricerche sui Problemi Economico-Sociali), and the Hungarian Economic Association.

It was the fifth congress of this kind to be organised by Ceses, but the first to be held not in Italy but in an East European country—quite a remarkable event. Among those who had come to take part in it were Gregory Grossman from Berkeley, California, Jean Marczewski from Paris, Michael Kaser from Oxford, the old and young Lipinskis from Warsaw, Habr and Urban from Prague, Horvat and Bajt from Yugoslavia, and many others—in all forty-eight economists from thirteen countries.

This congress had started badly: it was to have been held the year before, but the Russian armoured cars went into Prague and the whole thing had to be abandoned. Now it had come off, and this was a masterpiece of diplomacy on the part of Renato Mieli of Ceses and the Hungarian economists; but some of the journalists attending it had to leave before the end to rush to Prague, where the Central Committee meeting was being held which was virtually to liquidate Dubček. In the soft, gentle September climate of Balatonfüred, in a genuinely cordial and relaxed atmosphere, Czechoslovakia seemed at once far off and very near. Alarming telephone calls arrived for the exponents of the "new course" and the whole subject was discussed each evening at the Hotel Annabella. But at the congress itself no one talked of politics.

There was only one intervention from Czechoslovakia. A precise, detached review of the economic reasons for the new course, a detailed description of the plan of reforms that had been proposed, and then a brusque "Thank you, gentlemen" with which the Prague economist cut short his speech at the point where he would have had to raise too many questions about the future—and give too bitter answers. The suggestion of things left unsaid was striking.

In speaking of economic reforms in Eastern Europe and describing the new and various paths that the economists of these countries are following to build a more rational, human and productive economic society, it is impossible to disregard the present political conditions. Economic power is a form of political power, and the course of economic reforms is inextricably linked with the difficult transformation of the regimes. In the numerous episodes of violent rupture of the Stalinist model (Belgrade 1948, Warsaw 1956, Budapest 1956, Prague 1968, Danzig 1970) political and economic tensions were always present and intermingled: protest against the bitter injustices of the totalitarian party, but also the rejection of Stalin's command-economy because of its high social cost, the meagre benefits it produced, and its diminishing efficiency. The economic reforms, in their turn, with which the Communist Parties of these countries, enclosed by their past history within the circle of Soviet power, tried to confront the situation also had a political aim: by improving living conditions it was hoped to relax political tension. In some cases, as here in Hungary, the aim seemed for the moment to have been achieved. But in Prague it was just the opposite: it was the economic reform that opened the way to political revolution, which came to so tragic an end.

In these conditions, the subject of economic reform was a burning one. But the situation made it advisable to treat it in technical terms, and this is what happened at Balatonfüred. There was no repetition here of the lively debates that occurred at the previous congresses, when Czech, Hungarian, Yugoslav or Polish reformers took occasion to declare their "infatuation" for a return to a market economy as the panacea for the economic and political ills of their countries. I recall the bitter clash in Florence in 1966 between the old Soviet conservative Gatovski and the young and brilliant Czechoslovak Kyn. This time, discussion of the great alternative models and ideological choices was avoided. The Soviets were absent, the Czechoslovaks could not go beyond their single austere intervention, and there was only a faint attempt at lively discussion between the Poles and the Hungarians. The Poles took on the mantle of orthodox critics of the daring reform in progress in Hungary since the previous year. The congress proved extremely technical and not at all ideological.

Nevertheless this came about not only for reasons of prudence but also for another fundamental and more comforting reason. The fact is that today, throughout Eastern Europe, certain fundamental innovations are taken as a matter of course which only five or six years ago would have been regarded as deeply shocking. Only one of the Yugoslavs present (Soskič) thought fit to reaffirm categorically that socialism today can be a "market" socialism and that "modern planning must not prevent the functioning of the market and free initiative" (of socialist concerns). But his intervention passed off without causing any sensation: similar ideas can be found over and over again in the official texts of the Hungarian reform.

In fact an economist Rip van Winkle who had fallen asleep not more than ten or fifteen years ago and wakened up again in the congress hall at Balatonfüred would never have believed his ears, or would have thought that in the meantime some revolution must have taken place. Indeed, listening to speeches (in English, of course) like that of the Bulgarian Rumen Yanakiev on the adoption of systems analysis and computers in his country's economy (a speech so packed with quotations from texts of the American Management Association that an

American present remarked: "I've never liked quotations, either from Lenin or from the A.M.A."), the economist Rip van Winkle would have concluded that both the language and the theory of Eastern and Western economists had become unified, and that a common way had been evolved of looking at the problems—today very similar—of industrial organisation, planning and decentralisation, choice of investments, and so forth.

The technical character of the discussion, the absence of any trace of political polemics or ideological presupposition, and the complete lack of dogma or quotations from the classics in speeches constituted a political fact of considerable importance—even though we have so quickly become accustomed to this genuine *cultural revolution* which has happened in Eastern Europe that we almost take it as a matter of course. I don't want to err on the side of economic partiality and forget the seriousness of certain violent political manifestations in the Communist world: I merely confine myself to pointing out the important fact, not only in the sphere of economy but also of culture, which the achieved reunification of economic science represents.

The congress, moreover, had a concrete and passionately interesting central theme, the Hungarian reform. In the Communist world, at a pretty unpropitious moment for innovations, the conversion of the Hungarian economy from Soviet-type centralised planning to the new "planned socialist market system" was a very important fact, even though in the midst of so many more dramatic events few people were aware of it. After Yugoslavia, Hungary too has now broken up—irretrievably, as it would seem to many experts—the economic structure inherited from Stalinism. The experiment of "market socialism", in slightly differing forms, is spreading. The so-called "third economic model" of the contemporary world seems to be gaining ground, despite the political upheavals that prevented it from being carried out in Czechoslovakia.

It is, naturally, by no means clear as yet what will be the real significance of the "third model". Like the others, it probably has its good and bad points; the important thing, for the time being, is not so much to judge it as to understand it. The new system includes many unknown quantities, and certain lines of development could take it far. At Balatonfüred, Gregory Grossman and another American, George Garvy, of the Federal Reserve, developed the theme of the necessary creation of a real financial market in a socialist market economy. The Hungarians agree about this, but what will this market be like? The logic of the system, so the Americans maintained, would demand that money should regain its complete "power of choice": will this mean coming to socialist shareholding and a plurality of banks?

The Hungarians find such questions vital, and they are also highly topical in Yugoslavia, but they had no ready answers. On the other hand they reaffirmed another financial objective: to make their money convertible within a few years. Another unknown quantity about the new system is the risk of inflation; the Hungarians stated categorically that they would be able to avoid it because they will, by adequate measures of political economy, rigidly control the volume of wages—pursuing, in other words, that planned incomes policy to which, in the West, the whole strength of the trade unions, whether non-party, Communist, Labour or Catholic, and the arguments of free-trade economy are so strongly opposed.

Viewed as a whole, the "Hungarian model" emerged from this debate as an organism potentially capable of acquiring strength and vitality but still far from complete. Here economic science is advancing into new territory. The process of conversion from "Soviet planning" to "market socialism", which hitherto had been attempted only by the Yugoslavs and in very different conditions, is full of complicated political and sociological twists. The Hungarians, as Professor Csikos-Nagy told me, can so far boast of "an improvement in the political and psychological climate"; but this is possibly due to relief that the Hungarian reform has not been overthrown together with the somewhat similar reform in Czechoslovakia. Will this Hungarian reform, which is the most advanced among all those embarked on since 1965 in the Communist countries of Eastern Europe, remain an isolated instance, or will it become an attractive example for the other countries? We cannot tell, but the need for reforms will certainly continue to be felt.

An important study by the Yugoslav Alexander Bajt shows that the Communist economies in the last fifteen years have undergone even greater cyclical variations than the capitalist economies, and that their rates of development, which were originally higher (as was logically to be expected in more backward countries), are regularly falling, whereas those of the West are regularly rising. Even though two great revisionist schools of economics, the Polish and the Czechoslovak, are today practically destroyed (some of the greatest East European economists such as the Pole Wlodzimierz Brus or the Czechoslovak Ota Sik have been evicted from their institutes and chairs), every so often the Communist leaders will ask advice of the economists, and economic science will continue to suggest to them the course for radical reforms.

Even in the Polish economists' criticisms of the Hungarian "new economic mechanism" the signs could readily be seen of a pronounced interest in a reform so much more daring than the very cautious, Soviet-type, reform adopted in Poland. One of the Poles at the congress, when I asked him why his country had not adopted a radical reform like that of Hungary, gave me the candid reply: "Because the political leaders in Budapest have been more courageous; ours couldn't allow themselves to run risks, they were afraid of losing their posts."*

In history, the relationships between economic and political factors are complex. Politics often decisively condition economics, but sometimes, too, politics can be profoundly influenced and conditioned by economics.

Balatonfüred

---

* The lack of courage—or foresight—cost Gomulka his post, as a result of workers' protest against traditional "Soviet-type" planning, in December 1970.

21. Prudent Reform in Hungary

Building up a new economic mechanism opens up the way to the discovery of a new type of Communism. The East European economists are convinced of this fact and conscious of the seriousness of their undertaking, over and above the purely economic aspect. Jozsef Bognar, who today, in his early fifties, is the most authoritative Hungarian economist, said to me: "This will be not only an economic reform but a social and political one too."

For Bognar, "the series of reforms in progress in the East European countries opens up a new era in the history of socialist economy"; but in addition to the economy the political structure itself will be transformed.

"The reform", he has written, "takes account of the conflicting interests within socialist society; but it is not only in the economy that these group interests can express themselves. It is obvious that in future a system of counterpoises, such as the reform wants to create in the economy, will be necessary not only in the economic field. In order to bring about the social optimum and the confrontation between group interests we must develop political democracy and make public life more varied. The spirit of the economic reform will gradually pervade all spheres of public life." By the end of 1972 many of Bognar's predictions had come true, and the New Economic Mechanism had had important social and political consequences.

In the West too, of course, the economists are concerning themselves with social and political structures and not only with economic matters—but in a non-ideological way, and with less personal risk to themselves. Their lives are not complicated in the same way as those of their Eastern colleagues. Bognar today is an academician and president of the Institute of World Economics, and he has the typical ways of a don, but he also has behind him a remarkable political career. The son of an engine-driver, he was at school with Nicholas Kaldor, who subsequently emigrated to England. Bognar stayed in Budapest. At the age of 28, in 1945, he was elected deputy for the Smallholders' Party in the first post-war Parliament. He was Minister of Information in 1946, Mayor of Budapest in 1947, and then several times Minister of Trade. I am told that he supported Nagy in October 1956; but then, like many others, he become reconciled with Kadar, and though he has refused further ministerial posts he was one of the most influential initiators of the economic reform of 1968. He is a great expert on underdeveloped countries, but he takes a much wider view of economics than that of the specialist in any particular field. Above all, he is regarded as "a wise man", so Otto Gado told me.

"Political institutions", Bognar said to me, "political life, the parliamentary system, the methods of government, everything, and I mean everything, will be strongly influenced by the economic reform, in the direction of greater democracy. Since every problem has various possible solutions, a certain political and social freedom is necessary to find the best one, so that everyone can criticise other people's opinions and defend his own."

This evolution will naturally derive from the new type of economic organisation. "In the past", Bognar said, "when the Plan laid down from above particular tasks for the factories, a minimum of information sufficed to carry them out. But today they can take independent economic decisions, and so they need a great deal of information, close international contacts, and a knowledge of world problems; and an open society is generally also a more liberal society. The process of persuasion of the masses will also be much more complex." Another Hungarian economist, Csikos-Nagy, had said to me: "I know of no situation in the history of mankind, and I don't think a situation can ever arise, in which economics exists apart from politics."

The Hungarian economists are especially conscious of this fact. In 1967 two very similar economic reforms were coming near to implementation in Central Europe: those of Czecho-slovakia and of Hungary. They met with very different fates, and the Hungarians are slightly haunted by this comparison: they ask themselves with a certain anxiety whether they have been wiser, more prudent or merely more fortunate than the Czechoslovaks. They would not be human if they didn't believe they had been wiser.

In the Planning Office Otto Gado described to me with passionate enthusiasm the long debates and seminars that prepared for Hungary's economic reform of 1 January 1968, with the participation of all the political and intellectual forces, the Universities, the Institutes, and the Party: "If our reform has gone better than that of Czechoslovakia, that's the reason", he said. Bognar gave me a very detailed picture of the forces at work for this reform: it is a fascinating illustration of the way in which the economists, in their effort to make the economic set-up more rational, efficient and human, found they had not only to solve theoretical, organisational or psychological problems but also to arrive at a satisfactory relationship with the political powers.

This is not always possible. Bognar talked to me about Poland, the East European country that has had the most gifted economists, the real inventors of the socialist planned market (the "second model" of socialism, as Brus described it). "But their influence", said Bognar, "was very limited even in the days of Oskar Lange; and after the death of Lange, who was the only one who had real contact with the political leaders, it collapsed. We, on the other hand, were able to influence the Government. But to do that one has to sacrifice one's own individualism: if an economist lays too much stress on the importance of his task, he can create a situation in which the statesman refuses to accept his ideas."

The relationship between economist and politician in Communist Europe is certainly more difficult than that in the West, of which Heller and Kennedy provided the classic example. The process of economic reform which has been set in motion throughout Eastern Europe threatens, or pro-mises, to transform all the traditional mechanisms of party power. What were the forces, I asked Bognar, which started this process? What part, for instance, had the masses played? "An important part, but a secondary one", he answered. "The masses were dissatisfied with many things, and this was all to the good", because the idea of a reform was bound to please them in principle: but they had reservations too.

The masses wanted to live better (in recent years wages in Czechoslovakia and Hungary had gone up by around 1 to 1·5 per cent) and they realised that the central administrative planning ("command economy") inherited from Stalinism ended by provoking "sclerosis of the economic set-up". This pattern seemed no longer capable of directing a complex industrial economy in which ruthless exploitation of the masses had become politically unfeasible. Some Hungarian economists doubt today whether this system was the best even for an underdeveloped economy endowed with vast resources such as the Russia of Stalin was. But certainly, in a country like Hungary in the 'sixties, it caused a slowing-down or check in development; it restricted technological progress; it was incapable of satisfying consumers. In the advance towards wellbeing during the 'sixties the East European countries were left far behind those of the West. Czechoslovakia, which before the war was as prosperous as Germany, was now surpassed by Italy and Austria. The pattern of consumption was frozen at a level far below that of the West: this is true even of Hungary, although it enjoys a general and widespread prosperity as compared with the Soviet Union.

By comparison with Moscow, Budapest seems like a Western metropolis: the city is enchanting, the girls are charming in their elegant mini-skirts, there are a great many excellent restaurants, and the shops are well arranged. But though this is, all in all, still one of the great centres of European *savoir vivre,* when you look a little more closely at what the shops have to offer, at the quality and prices, you realise that there is a time-lag in the pattern of consumption of at least a decade as compared with an average Western country, especially in the field of durable consumer goods and in the variety and quality of the merchandise. Moreover, a national average of wages and salaries of 1950 forints, or about £27 a month (this was in 1969), permits only a modest standard of life, even if the cost of food and housing is lower than it is with us.

For all these reasons, there was a definite pressure for change from the masses. But it was not a revolutionary pressure, partly because the post-Stalinist "command economy" had also developed some internal compensations: security of employment, general equality, and toleration of slow rates of work in the factories burdened with supernumerary personnel. The coercion and fear of the Stalinist days had vanished, and there was less forced accumulation for saving. Moreover among the workers, so Bognar told me, "the egalitarian conception of socialism is very deeply rooted", and the announcement of even such negative stimuli as dismissals and of differentiated incentives aroused fears rather than hopes. The result of all this was that it was not the masses who took the initiative for the change-over to "market socialism"—and still less, of course, the government organisations which jealously administered the economy—but the economists, who had been preaching this reform ever since 1954, and also the Party.

This is the strangest aspect of the whole story. "Like kings in olden times", Bognar said, "the Party can be persuaded; but it is one thing to be able to persuade and quite another to have in one's hands the power to change things. Only the Party could do that; it alone could say yes or no, and at the same time had the means to convince the masses through its control of the press and television and its presence at all levels of social life."

Naturally, the Party did not decide for the reform without a political struggle: "The old Communists were faithful to their dogma and fearful of not being able to face up to a new and more complicated situation. The Party aroused a challenge to itself. But in a single-party system, the Party is forced to do this if it wants to change and survive: what else could it do? Only a strong government, of course, could carry through so fundamental a reform. It involved transferring power from one part of the population to another, changing certain conceptions or illusions that the Party itself had fostered in the past, and creating a new balance of forces. If the government is not strong, it cannot carry out such a process, which represents a great risk, because it might also lose power, whereas it merely wants to transfer or transform it. But the risk exists, because every political activity is a cumulative process, and one can't foresee everything."

The risks are still there. The process of economic, and potentially political, renewal will be long and difficult. Can it already be said to be irreversible? A Hungarian friend, when I asked him this, replied: "Where have you come from? Moscow? Well, why didn't you ask them there?" Bognar answered by saying that the running-in period of the new economic mechanism would last at least eight to ten years. But the process of renewal, he said, was "certainly irreversible as a whole". And he went on: "Internal resistances may develop; and, too, every movement is closely linked to the international situation and we cannot expect it to go ahead by itself. So we shall have some setbacks. But the process as a whole is irreversible."

A year after the events of Prague, I could only confine myself to registering this declaration of "historic" confidence, which was also repeated to me by other Hungarian economists, without expressing any opinion of my own.

For the time being, the experiment of the New Economic Mechanism, based on the productive autonomy of concerns in the market and on workers' participation in the profits, is going ahead; but it has had a slow start. The stern measures adopted to avoid an explosive inflation of wages and prices (prices are still largely controlled; and progressive taxes on the profits distributed by the concerns are so severe as to preclude, so Csikos-Nagy told me, wage increases of more than 2 to 2·5 per cent per annum) have proved too much of a curb on the stimulating effect of the new system. This severe wages policy has certainly managed to keep the economy in balance; but development has slowed down again. Industrial production in 1969, so Gado told me, was expected to rise by barely 1 per cent according to the new statistical methods, or by 4 per cent according to the old: in any case, a virtual standstill. The New

Mechanism, based on the stimulus of the firm's profits and the workers' share therein, on the firm's autonomy in decision-making, on market competition and partial liberation of prices, was still moving hesitantly; indeed, in many respects it was still merely on paper.*

But the Hungarian economists know what is not yet working properly; they are, in particular, aware that they "put the brake on too hard", in other words that in their first encounter with the market they imposed a too deflationary incomes policy, and they are preparing to slacken the brakes. Unforeseen circumstances apart, the internal situation seems sufficiently relaxed (Kadar is, together with Tito, the only popular leader in Communist Europe) to allow them the time needed to apply the necessary correctives and to give concrete realisation, step by step, in everyday practice as well as on paper, to their new economic system. It is not too farfetched to foresee that, if all goes well, this may take ten years to accomplish.

Then will begin the story, an uncertain story full of unknown factors, of this "neo-Communist" market economy, different from that of Yugoslavia because it does not include "self-management", but akin to it in the common, and ambitious, objective they share: to realise (in Bognar's words) "an efficient society, and a society in which there is equality: these are, from many points of view, contradictory goals".

Does this "contradiction" between equality and efficiency really exist? There is something profoundly realistic in Bognar's comment; but there would be some truth too in the opposite statement, namely that a society characterised by excessive

---

* By the end of 1972 industrial production had in fact risen much more rapidly than Gado anticipated; and Hungarian economists could in general see much more clearly how the New Economic Mechanism was working. Among problems encountered in the meantime were the overheating of the economy experienced in 1970–71, the result of extensive over-investment and consequent inflation; the emergence of a new middle class of enterprise managers, the beneficiaries of the de-levelling of incomes, and the resultant social tensions; and the response of the party in 1971–72 to keep matters within tolerable limits, attempting to reconcile economic demands (by means of greater flexibility) and ideological demands (by stronger central control).

inequalities cannot be efficient: the system of industrial production, as it exists today in the most advanced countries, demands a balanced social progress, and it would be unthinkable in a society in which a minority of rich exploiters stood in contrast to a majority of the exploited poor. It is the internal logic of modern productive progress that has prevented this historic Marxist hypothesis about the development of capitalism from being realised; the same logic may also urge the post-Stalinist economies towards decentralisation and perhaps to democratisation.

From the Hungarian point of view, in any case, the present problem is that of excessive equality, which reduces the stimulus to productive progress, with results, in the long run, harmful to all. This situation has been analysed in recent years with especial critical lucidity by the economists in Hungary, as also by those in Czechoslovakia. Today the latter are out of it; the former are still at work. Their argument is valid not only for Hungary but for all the post-Stalinist economies, beginning with the Soviet; in the attempt to reconcile workers' participation and productive efficiency other societies, if in very different conditions, are also involved. Various topics and problems recurrent in the Hungarian economy of today (control of inflation, incomes policy, reconciling planning with a market economy) are in fact present in all the industrialised economies in the West as well. The Hungarian experiment of a "planned and regulated market economy" (Csikos-Nagy's definition) has therefore an importance not confined to Hungary alone, or even to Eastern Europe. It is to be hoped that this experiment will be allowed to develop and flourish, and that in developing it may preserve its own individuality: to quote Bognar once again, "we want to improve efficiency without renouncing certain fundamental socialist ideas".

Budapest

22. *Belgrade: Halfway Reform*

Yugoslavia today is a country suspended between boom, crisis and Utopia. In this journey to the new frontiers of economics, my stay in Yugoslavia was one of the most stimulating, indeed entertaining, experiences. There is a touch of the paradoxical about everything here. Many people here speak of the (socialist) market with a missionary fervour, and with a complete faith in its beneficent powers, such as you find today only in that eccentric bastion of nineteenth-century liberalism, the Chicago of Milton Friedman. This similarity of attitude is not only curious and suggestive: it also gives one to think. On the other hand, the same people explain self-management and workers' participation in a passionate language which recalls that of some of the *avant-garde* strongholds of student protest in the West. Lastly, the Yugoslavs denounce the State and its over-weening power in a radical language which is unequalled today in any other country or society, which once again recalls Friedman, and which is, instead, the echo of a socialist tradition so old (running from Fourier to Owen and the anarchist-syndicalists) as to be almost forgotten.

Yugoslav "associationism" has caused the revival, in a developing Balkan country, of this tradition, which seemed to have been extinguished beneath the two-fold weight of Leninist-Stalinist centralism and neo-capitalistic organisational technicism. The most curious thing is that the same tradition appeals today to the youthful masses in the West who, however, programmatically scorn the Yugoslav experiments and all the revisionism of Eastern Europe, finding instead their mythical inspiration in the enigmatic experiments of the Chinese or Che Guevara. This, incidentally, is a cause of bitterness to the Yugoslavs, who feel like neglected and misunderstood prophets:

"happiness is not for export", said the "pure theoretician" Miladin Korac in a detached sort of way when talking to me at the economic faculty in Belgrade.

The sequence of paradoxes is not the only thing to give spice to a visit to Yugoslavia. There is also the fact that nowhere else is economic theory so closely intermingled with political and social reality: the economic adventure becomes, here more than anywhere else, a human and political adventure involving a nation of twenty million inhabitants in the crucial phase of its industrial take-off.

And then, too, the history of "neo-Communism" began here, away back in 1948. This was the scene of the first experiment in violent rupture of the "Stalinist model", and, paradoxically, it was Stalin who provoked it: the good Yugoslavs wanted nothing better than to remain faithful to it. The brutality of the excommunication and persecution that was to serve as a warning to all East European "nationalist" Communists caused them to lose their faith overnight, and it was a traumatic experience in every sense. Tito, they say, developed gall-bladder trouble, Kidrić got a stomach-ulcer and a skin disease, Djilas's hair fell out. All of them together invented revisionism, which can therefore be regarded as a psychosomatic reaction to loss of faith on the part of a remarkably tough and intelligent group of men selected in a hard school (that of partisan warfare). Without meaning to, they also initiated a revolution in the history of economics: they destroyed the dogma that equated "socialism" with State ownership and authoritarian planning, and they discovered that the market too can be socialist.

Their creation has survived, and twenty years ago few would have foretold this. Not only has it survived, but also during this period Yugoslavia "has had one of the highest growth rates in the world, has quintupled its industrial production in fifteen years, and from being a primitive country has become a European economic power, with a *per capita* income approaching that of pre-war France".

These successes, which Branko Horvat recalled to me at the Institute of Economic Research in Belgrade, are undeniable.

Yugoslavia's rates of development are higher than those of most other East European countries. Indeed one needs only to look around here in Belgrade or go to Zagreb during the industrial fair (the second in Europe after Milan) to realise in these violently expanding cities, afflicted with the first traffic jams of the East, how vital this country is. In short, the Yugoslav model (although it was for many years, and still is in several ways, a mixture of authoritarian planning and socialist market) has functioned better than a good many others, despite the crises it has been through. This experiment is therefore to be taken seriously, even if one plays it down like *The Economist* which called it the best system so far invented of human relations in industry. Even that says quite a lot, when one remembers all the winds of protest and revolt blowing in the rest of the world.

The Yugoslav experiment is also to be taken seriously because of the profound influence it has had throughout Eastern Europe as a constant stimulus towards renewal. This does not, of course, mean that everything has gone well. The difficulties became more acute after the reform of 1965, which aimed definitely to dismantle the apparatus of the centralised State. Industrial production remained stationary in 1967, it rose by 6 per cent in 1968, and it was not until 1969 that the boom exploded afresh, with an expected increase of 13 per cent. But unemployment went up: 400,000 unemployed in March 1969, as against four million employed in industry—a very high rate. And Horvat and others predicted a new cyclical decline for 1970, with an increase in industrial production of only 5–6 per cent.

Many Westerners—and also Russians, Hungarians etc.—think that the negative phenomena of these recent years are in fact the result of the reform, the fruit of a market economy based on social (non-State) ownership and on self-management of factories, which let loose violent inflationary pressures, due to the improvidence of the workers' councils in allocating to themselves a too high percentage of profits, or to the anarchy of a too free market. Opposition to the market also arises in the poor republics of Yugoslavia's "South", which see in centralism and authoritarian planning some guarantee of redistribution of income to their advantage (the dispute between the supporters of different economic systems thus runs the risk of becoming a quarrel between the rich and liberalising North and the poor and planning-minded South). So has the 1965 reform failed? And has the Yugoslav system failed with it, together with the tradition, revived here after long eclipse, of socialist "associationism", as well as the dream of the "socialist market"?

These were the central questions I put to some of the most brilliant Yugoslav economists: Branko Horvat and Miladin Korac in Belgrade, Jakov Sirotković and Rikard Lang in Zagreb. They are all of the same generation (41 to 45 years old), all passionate defenders of the Yugoslav model though they differ somewhat in temperament: some of them, for instance Korac, are particularly emphatic in their enthusiasm for the "socialist" market and their denunciation of State control.

Their answers coincided only in part; but their analyses of the causes of the 1967 crisis were very similar. "Our economy", Horvat said, "had become much more complex and difficult to direct, and it was changed in a great hurry; but the people responsible did not know how to guide a market economy, and they didn't realise that it can be planned with non-administrative instruments." They were, in fact, ignorant of the macroeconomic anti-cyclical post-Keynesian policy, or at any rate they applied it badly, by introducing a disastrous credit policy which in effect provoked the "artificial" crisis of 1967, beginning with inflation and followed by deflation and unemployment. "We economists", Sirotković said, "had made some useful diagnoses and forecasts in advance; but we were too late in convincing the authorities of the need for a change of policy." "The politicians", Horvat continued, "not understanding the economic causes of the crisis, talk about the hidden enemies of self-management who must be sought out and overcome: but the real cause of our misfortunes is insufficient knowledge. But we are learning our lesson; the quality of our economic leaders has greatly improved, and in two or three years the crisis of adaptation will be overcome. Then everything will be O.K."

I raised some objections. The technicians of OECD have criticised self-management, saying that in factories under this system the cost of labour is not something fixed, similar in all concerns, but changes according to the profits, being higher in the better factories: this would prevent profit from functioning as an element of natural selection among factories, and therefore an element of economic progress. This would compromise the functioning of the market as a mechanism for the rational distribution of resources. Horvat answered: "In the capitalist market too the better concerns pay wages above the average. But these are precisely the firms that offer better guarantees to the banks and can obtain funds for development. The rationality of the market is affirmed in any case."

The second objection, and one widely voiced, is that workers' councils tend to distribute excessive dividends and are therefore an innate factor of inflation. Horvat answered: "In capitalistic firms the owners tend to increase their profits and the workers their wages: the 'innate' factors of inflation are there too, but they are restrained by the market. The important thing is to know how to control the functioning of this complicated and delicate but extremely productive machine that the new system represents. It is true that we haven't got a wages policy, but not because it would be impossible to have it, merely because we don't know how to apply it."

I asked another question: how do cycles work out in a self-managed economy? Horvat answered: "They are easier to control than in a capitalist market, because the self-managed concerns spontaneously behave in an anticyclical way. If we had had a capitalist market economy in 1967, the crisis would have been much more serious." (This reasoning is based on the observation that it is more difficult to keep down wages, at a time of crisis, in a self-managed economy. More generally, the same argument has been advanced by many economists to explain why it is that cycles have levelled out in the present-day capitalist economy, as compared with that of fifty years ago.)

The last objection raised was: "Now that you have legalised private concerns (of up to five workers), and seeing how they flourish in tourism, trade, motor transport, and so on, is it possible that 'private capitalism' might revive?" "No. The private sector is, on the whole, static. There is no possibility that capitalism might revive. True, many people here still think that individual initiative is foreign to socialism; but in fact it is all part of socialism. We don't make a difference between private and non-private concerns, but between family concerns and, so to speak, 'incorporated' concerns—which, with us, are self-managed." (It is possible, in other words, to imagine in Yugoslavia the successful private businessman who carries his concern beyond family dimensions and towards self-management, just as in the West such a concern would move towards becoming a joint-stock company.)

In fact, none of the Yugoslav economists think that the crisis of 1967 was caused by self-management. Indeed many of them believe the exact opposite. "The main problem", Korac said, "is that the real, proper Yugoslav system doesn't yet exist." And Sirotković: "The fundamental cause of our misfortunes is the incomplete state of the self-managed economy. Centrally planned economy still occupies a much larger place here than one might think: ours is a mixed economy."

The 1965 reform wanted radically to reduce the "State sector", which in 1964 still absorbed 45 per cent of the net profit of factories. The system, in other words, was a sort of *métayage*—a product-sharing system—between the State and the factories, between central economy and market; and the result was a number of absurd political, anti-economic, investments on the part of the State. Under the reform, the State's share in net profits was to be reduced to 30 per cent in 1970, while the factories' share was to go up to 70 per cent.

In 1966 the factories' share did in fact rise to 60 per cent; but in 1967 it fell to 57·4 and in 1968 to 56·8 per cent, while in 1969 it went down still further, according to Sirotković, to whom I am indebted for these figures. In short, the State, whether from stubbornness or inertia, did not allow itself to be "expropriated", and deprived the factories of the financial means that were supposed to guarantee their autonomy. In addition, the factories are heavily indebted to the banks, and these are not independent, as they should be, but are

controlled by the State. In the data given above, the investment by the banks are in fact assimilated to those from the
State. From this point of view, as Sirotković said, "the reform
has not yet been carried out".

In March 1969 the Party's ninth congress decided to carry it
forward: this decision was being put into effect, and it was to
be a hard battle. I quote Sirotković again: "The two characteristics of our system, centralism and self-management, State
control and market, are still in sharp conflict. It will be
necessary to choose: if we cannot abolish the centralised
investments policy, we shall have to abolish self-management:
or vice versa."

Supposing self-management wins, what kind of economy
will there be then in Yugoslavia? The answers to this question
are extremely interesting but also very indefinite. The main
objective is to extend the mechanism and principle of self-
management from the factories, or from the "microeconomic"
level, to the "macroeconomic" and national level.

"We are aiming", Horvat said, "at an economy that will
be more decentralised, more of a market economy, than any
other in the world; and it can be so, because we shall have
eliminated any fundamental conflict between management
and workers, between the State and the factories. State intervention can be reduced because we shall carry out a process
of integration of factories, which will have to create organs of
coordination between themselves for productive ends." In this
atmosphere, it is claimed, planning too will be easier and more
decentralised ("more democratic", as Lang puts it) because it
will be based on coordination of the decentralised initiatives
and on agreement.

Even the most fervent supporters of self-management, such as
Sirotković, are convinced that Yugoslav society "will always
be centrally organised, and not based on a constellation of
independent producers" (in other words not a pure, completely
anarchical market). But this centralism will mean a series of
"associations of workers' organisms" (here again there is an
echo of long-forgotten pre-Marxist socialist traditions, from
Owen to Blanc and anarchist-syndicalism); it might even reach

the point of "creating a Parliament of productive units which would manage the country's economic policy".

They all say that there must be some sort of planning ("today it's State interference, not planning"), but it must not "do violence to the market". Here, however, they become more indefinite. They all admit that it is not yet clear what Yugoslav planning in the future will be like: "if they asked me to be the head of planning," Korac says, "I would answer, no, thank you, because I wouldn't know how to do it". In practice, the language of the Yugoslav economists on this subject is not very different from that of the French or Italian planners— even though they are convinced that their planning, like their economy, is something very different.

It is difficult to say how far these ambitions are likely to be realised, or even whether they are, in theory and in practice, possible of realisation. At bottom, the Yugoslavs too, like so many other people, are aiming at building the perfect market: but not by transforming it, as Fedorenko in Moscow dreams of doing, into an "electronic market"; nor by rationalising it by means of an enlightened technocratic planning, as the Hungarians would like to do, and also many Western economists in favour of a "mixed economy"; but rather by transforming it from within by means of self-management, which should suppress the conflicts that disturb the market at the microeconomic level (within factories, between management and workers) and at the macroeconomic level (between State power and the power of the factories).

The Yugoslav model is largely unfinished: it already exists, in part at least, at the "micro" but not at the "macro" level, and the leap from the one to the other seems difficult, ambitious, and full of unknown factors. The aim is to defeat State control, which is present even in the Hungarian-type socialist market, where the heads of firms are ministerial appointments ("that is market", Horvat says, "but it isn't socialism"); and to heal through self-management the functional disagreement between the worker and the industrial concern, whether private or State-controlled on Soviet lines.

The Yugoslavs believe that if they succeed in building their model of a "socialist self-managed market economy", a model which is certainly different from any other, it will be not less but more efficient than the others. Horvat told me: "All the studies on economies involving participation, including studies done outside Yugoslavia (and he mentioned some American ones), show that workers' participation increases productivity." Some of the research studies on the evolution of self-management in Yugoslavia would confirm the thesis that this model furthers technical and scientific progress. Certainly, so the Yugoslav economists whom I interviewed told me, if their model were to fail over this point, it would fail altogether; but they are convinced that it will not fail.

This brief sounding among the Yugoslav economists reaches no conclusion. The question of the validity of the Yugoslav formula is still wide open. It is even arguable whether the Yugoslavs will really succeed in building up the system they have in mind, and whether, once built, it will really prove to be as different from all the others as they think. Their problems are naturally the same as those of any other industrialised economy. Their solutions, as planned, are obstinately different on the two central problems of modern society: the relationship of power as between management and workers, and that same relationship as between the State and the industrial concerns.

At a time when the problem of the workers' situation is everywhere under discussion, when we are confronted with the troublous developments of trade unionism under participationist pressure, and when at the same time centralism is gaining ground throughout modern economy, the debate about the "Yugoslav model" is a highly stimulating one. Viewed against this background, it certainly appears to be much more than a mere curiosity of history—whatever its future development may be.

Belgrade-Zagreb

Footnote, December 1972. This was how Yugoslav economists were thinking in 1969—70. Developments since then—rapid inflation, two devaluations, the introduction of price controls, massive over-investment leading to serious overheating and other economic problems—have led to a recentralisation. In addition, political events, especially the Croat crisis of 1971 and its aftermath, have greatly changed the atmosphere of Yugoslav economic policy.

M

23. *Vranicki: Philosophers and Economists*

The most important Marxist periodical in Europe is called *Praxis,* and it is published not in London, Paris or Moscow but in Zagreb, that old city of Central Europe which is a provincial replica of Prague, Budapest or Vienna. At the foot of the upper town, mediaeval and baroque with its churches and fine houses, the lower town extends towards the Sava, with its avenues, tree-lined squares, rows of Hapsburgian buildings, theatres and museums. In his house in Marulicev Square I met Predrag Vranicki, philosopher and historian of Marxism and a member of the editorial board of *Praxis,* a periodical to which thinkers from East and West (but no Russians) contribute, among them Kosik and Kolakowski, Marcuse and Bloch. Scholars consider this periodical important in the history of Marxism and the post-Stalinist Left. At a more popular level, on the other hand, among the dilettanti of "contestation", *Praxis* is little known, as indeed is all Yugoslav thinking. The avant-garde editors, great translators of the more obscure prophets of guerrilla protest and revolt, have virtually ignored the difficult critical works of the sociologists of Zagreb and Belgrade, including Vranicki's great *History of Marxism.*

I did not ask Vranicki how old he was, but I should suppose he must be in the forties—like nine-tenths of the Yugoslavs who count today. This is a leading class that is homogeneous in age and background: first, the partisan experience, then the salutary shock of Stalin's excommunication, then feverish years of study, with the dogmatic barriers and ideological vetos falling one after the other, in an effort towards deeper understanding and discovery which ranged from the humanist "young Marx" to the Workers' Opposition destroyed by Lenin in 1921. Penetrating and merciless judgements on contemporary "socialism" emerged, Stalinist and even Leninist myths were destroyed, and a corpus of doctrines and political ideas was built up which has aroused echoes throughout the world. The most attractive and utopian of the Marxist ideas was rediscovered, that of the extinction of the State as a bureaucratic and dominating organisation; even the Party, it was declared, despoiled of its totalitarian power should suffer the same fate; the alienating character of State planned economy was denounced; the paleo-socialist idea of workers' self-management was re-invented; and the final discovery was the socialist value of the market, which would be able to confer concrete power on the self-managed concern.

From this fund of ideas the Western "new Left" has drawn some of its most powerful inspiration. But this cultural revolution, which has been going on for the past twenty years, is today at a critical stage. The Yugoslav intelligentsia is troubled by violent disputes. "People who for decades have known where they stood", Mihailo Marković wrote in *Praxis,* "now find themselves in a different situation, deeply divided in mind, torn and unable to put the pieces together again of their own unity of thought and practice." The Belgrade philosophers, Marković, Tadić, Stojanović, are deeply at odds with the Party and have in fact been expelled from it. They are accused of being Stalinist in economics, in other words against the market and for authoritarian centralism, and anarchist-liberal in politics, in other words favouring Western-style pluralism. In an acrimonious political fight the Belgrade philosophers have found themselves isolated. At the faculty of philosophy in Belgrade Ljubomir Tadić told me: "I and my colleagues are in a very precarious situation". However they still retain their chairs and their reviews, and they write, teach, and travel to America. *Praxis,* which is their most important review, has got over some difficult times and continues to receive financial support from the State.

But the visitor to Belgrade is non-plussed by the violence of the disputes and finds it hard to distinguish the rights and wrongs of the matter. You need to go to Zagreb to be able to discuss more calmly the ideas that are the subject of these political struggles. The Croat *Praxis* group, beginning with Vranicki, has remained in the Party and is trying to find a compromise. Vranicki explained the disagreements to me while reflecting on the differences of temperament of politicians and philosophers. He defended the philosophers' right to be critical, radical and utopian; but he recognised the motives of the politicians, who have "the problem of action; they are worried about the links in the chain, and all this is very difficult". Vranicki rejected as "quite absurd" the accusations of centralism and Stalinism made against the philosophers; he maintained that certain reserves felt by the philosophers with regard to the market had been twisted by the politicians. This seems to me a somewhat euphemistic version of the disputes. Ambition, as well as ingenuousness, caused the philosophers to become involved in a faction struggle. But anyway what interested me was to understand the motives behind it. So I asked, "What do the philosophers accept and reject in the Yugoslav model?" Let us first consider the economic side, then the political.

Tadić, when I talked to him in Belgrade, criticised the excessive freedom of the market, maintaining that under it the backward regions were exploited by the more advanced regions, and that Marxism proposed neither planned State control nor "the anarchical dissolution of the market" but "the association of producers"; the anarchical market, he explained, "leaves room for centralist, authoritarian and bureaucratic trends", just where the new central organs based on self-management should arise. I had seen similar ideas in an article by Mihailo Marković in the latest number of *Praxis*: according to him, the "economicism" prevalent today in Yugoslavia, with its insistence on the motives of profit and consumption as incentives for productive rationality, not only creates imbalances in development and unemployment but also "strengthens those social structures that socialism ought to weaken". This would mean a return to the alienation and "objectivisation" of the workers, while the spread of mercantile-monetary relationships in the name of economic rationalism would end in "sacrificing socialist humanism", causing mediocre petit-bourgeois consumer ideals to prevail.

I asked Vranicki whether he shared these criticisms of a Yugoslavia which was reverting from socialism to "paleo-capitalism". He did so, he said, only in part; he too thought that "the too-free market reproduces the fetish of things", and he remarked that it did not exist even in modern capitalism. But he recognised that the market served to weaken the powerful administrative structures, increased the real power of the workers, and effectively restricted the State-controlled sphere. He went on: "Self-government *(samoupravljanje)* exists today with us only at the lowest level, the microeconomic level of the factories. At the apex, the Plan and the Government still live on a detached plane, like organisms alienated from the base. The most difficult historic problem of our society, which it will need a whole era to solve, is to structurise the whole of society on the basis of self-government, creating centres of integration (I mean of collective action) which will be not political but social, so that the working class may create and do directly everything that belongs today to the political and State sphere."

Making a play on the translation of the word, I remarked, one might say that they want to go on from "self-management" to "self-government". Vranicki accepted this interpretation, although in Slav languages there is only the one word for it. Khrushchev too talked of *"samoupravlenie"*, or "self-government" of the social organisms, which, however, he thought of as subject to the iron direction of a Party constantly growing in strength. Here in Yugoslavia it is a very different matter. In the first place, economic self-management is supposed to go right up to the summit, through a pyramid of organisms independent of Party power; the Plan itself should be a synthesis of the individual economic wishes of the self-managed organisations. I must confess that at this point I found it rather difficult to understand the concrete significance of these ideas: would not a permanent organisational structure be created all the same, I asked? Vranicki answered cautiously: "This argument is inevitably somewhat abstract; in practice, problems will always arise. But when there is a political society, however democratic and representative it may be, it remains detached and alienated from the social and economic sphere. We, on the other hand, are imagining a quite new structure, in which there will be delegated powers (we aren't anarchists) but where they will represent the factories, the municipalities, the cultural organisations, all of them self-managed, and not a separate political organisation. The solution of our problem, in short, lies in the overcoming and withering-away of the political sphere, in the extinction of the State. We reject any type of traditional representative political organisation based on the Party or parties, and on Parliament. In a developed socialist society the problem of the party will be solved in this way." It too, in fact, should die away, together with the State, and with it the political class and function itself.

The fact is, it seems to me, that every explanation in solving one problem opens up many others; eliminating one doubt gives rise to other fresh ones. In Belgrade too, where Tadić had talked to me of his plan to set up "a Congress of workers' councils as the supreme political as well as economic authority" (much more powerful than the Leninist Soviets), the idea of this new structure remained somewhat vague and confused in my mind in spite of all the explanations. Tadić harked back to the ideals of the Workers' Opposition against Lenin's State-based policy and he quoted little-known nineteenth-century German Social Democratic thinkers, but my doubts still remained—including my doubt as to whether the Yugoslav utopians were right, and the realists of every kind wrong in being sceptical about the possibility of inventing a "polis" without politics or politicians.

Within this Yugoslav society, in any case, politics are still very much alive, and there is violent discussion about these things between the politicians jealous of their role and the intellectuals impatient of the "relics of authoritarianism". Explosive ideas emerge from the debate, such as the idea of multiple parties. Even Vranicki, who is against it because, so he says, "it would mean strengthening the political sphere and hindering its extinction", recognises that "if the attempt to extinguish the political sphere fails, some other structure will develop, possibly a multi-party one". It is natural that all these arguments should disturb the Party. No one likes to be told he'll be extinguished, even if the announcement is made in the name of Marx.*

Zagreb

---

* By 1973 the events of the previous two years had shown that Tito's party had no intention to permit its own extinction. The road to utopian Socialism is indeed a long and difficult one.

24. The "Socialist" Models

Before continuing my journey among the economists into Western Europe, I would like to try to explain rather more systematically the nature of the "socialist" economic models that exist or are emerging in the countries of Eastern Europe. I must begin by saying that in economy the system of centralised production under bureaucratic direction (what is known for short in the West as "command economy") is still dominant in almost all the Eastern European countries, and maintains a certain vitality; it continues to ensure fairly rapid rates of growth, though in some cases (the USSR, Rumania) these are falling, in another (Hungary) the rates are slow, and in yet another (Czechoslovakia) it has caused serious crises. But its efficiency is low: that is to say, the rates of return which it ensures on the capital employed are very low and consequently, while it secures growth rates comparable with those of many Western countries, it does so at a definitely higher rate of investment (and a much lower level of consumption). It provides definitely less good products in respect of quality and variety; bad services; and a decidedly lower standard of living.

Only in a few instances has the crisis of the economic system become the reason and occasion for a political crisis (as was the case, in part at least, in Czechoslovakia in 1967–68). Nevertheless the defects of the post-Stalinist economic system are by now so obvious that its reform is being undertaken in all the countries concerned.

The movement for reform is only in part socialist in inspiration, or a conscious protest against the economic expropriation of the worker at the hands of the Party, the State or the "new class"; for the rest, its origin derives from the spirit of efficiency of our times, which is offended by the crudenesses of this economic model. But criticism on more technocratic grounds also contains within itself some "socialist" motives: the absence of participation, of freedom of decision, of sense of ownership, of spirit of initiative, of the desire for research and innovation, all those negative characteristics which are deplored in the post-Stalinist system as results of the bureaucratic centralism of the economy, are equally defects of socialism.

The proposals for reform, which include greater autonomy for business concerns, greater participation of the masses in the profits of those concerns, a greater influence of the free choices of the citizen-consumer, through the reconstitution of market structures, on the lines of industrial development and on investments, are "technocratic" proposals with a socialist core. The objective is both more efficiency and more socialism.

This two-fold inspiration can be recognised in all the proposals for reform. But in economics, as in politics, the socialist "models" envisaged in the future or now in the first stages of construction both resemble and differ from each other; broadly speaking, they can be seen as "national" models.

Among the basic ideas of a new "socialist model" which have been worked out in the Soviet Union, two are of especial interest. The first is Fedorenko's principle that fundamental choices for development must arise out of free decisions taken at the bottom, and his conception of "optimality" which, as soon as it is put forward, evokes the need of a popular economic sovereignty (the "optimal plan" must be based on a system of particular choices decided on from below). The second is Novozhilov's thesis that productive autonomies must indeed develop, but contemporaneously, and in order dialectically to contain the more powerful divergent impulses that emerge from the market, the planning and organisational principle must be strengthened.

In practice, according to the rate of progress of the reform (and the inefficiency of the central bureaucratic planning system cannot be reduced sufficiently rapidly, by the adoption of more modern planning techniques, to render other structural transformations superfluous: therefore the reform will probably go ahead), the economic set-up will gradually approach a *mixed bureaucratic-market system* of the Hungarian kind.

I adopt this label provisionally to indicate that system of industrial production in which the heads of firms are bureaucratic appointments made by the ministerial apparatus, instead of being nominated, as in Yugoslavia, by a self-management committee elected by the workers and employees.

Another characteristic of the mixed bureaucratic-market economy is that the State will for long continue to reserve to itself very strong, indeed total, powers in the sphere of "incomes policy", controlling the sum paid out in wages so that it will not grow more rapidly than the increase in productivity.

A further point is that in this system the State will continue to reserve to itself (to the central plan) a disproportionate share of accumulation of profits and hence will retain very considerable powers in the choice of investments and of lines of productive development.

But the Yugoslav experiment demonstrates that in these sectors the transfers of decisional powers prove to be gradual, indeed almost imperceptible, more readily indicated by figures, statistics and percentages than by any broad description. The structures will apparently change very little, but certain channels of power expand while others dwindle. Means of production and socialist freedoms will flow more vigorously in certain directions, as in riverbeds that have been long dried up.

The Soviet Union is taking only the first steps along the road of bureaucractic-market socialism, but the fact that it is moving in this direction seems to me incontrovertible. It is reasonable to suppose that every step will lead sooner or later to the next one; not only because the courage of the reformers gradually increases, but also because every small reform weakens the pre-existing machinery and reduces its efficiency still further. The rate of progress will depend on the speed with which the efficiency of the existing system declines and opposition to the system increases. The thesis of the gradual "socialist" transformation of the post-Stalinist system rests substantially on the hypothesis that the vitality of that system is decreasing. So far the facts seem to confirm this view. But the consequent idea of a certain "economic inevitability" of socialism may nevertheless contain a certain amount of wishful thinking on the part of its progenitors.

Within the Soviet framework Fedorenko's work on the *optimal system of direction of the economy* proposes a mechanism which differs perceptibly from that of the *bureaucratic-socialist market* (or the Hungarian-Czech-Soviet model, in varying stages of elaboration), or from the "self-managed" market of Yugoslavia. Fedorenko's is one of the most original hypotheses of the "socialist model". The simulation of the market and of market bargainings with electronic "iterations", envisaged by Fedorenko as the premiss of a "plan" which will be, if I understand him rightly, the sum of the innumerable bargains of a normal market (a "sum" more perfect than the simple addition of its parts, since the electronic elaboration of the bargainings should allow the picture as a whole to be always present, and should at last make possible the realisation, for the first time in the history of the industrial world, of a perfectly fluid market), aims at being a real, proper model complete in all its parts. It presupposes, however, the "socialist-bureaucratic" economic reform, in as much as it demands that there should be a free market for consumer goods (a buyer's, not a seller's market, so well supplied that the consumer can have free choice to purchase or reject), upon the functioning of which the profit, success and development of the enterprise will depend. It is only in the bargainings between the productive enterprises that the "simulated market" *(rynok v kabinete)*, or the electronic simulation of the market, would be introduced.

Is it possible that there may be gradual and partial applications of the mechanism proposed by Fedorenko? What parallels can be found in the more advanced capitalist markets? It would be necessary to take into consideration the very big concerns with vertical and horizontal proliferations: within them, are not the elements perhaps partially present of a real electronic "simulated market"?

Fedorenko's work may find a place in that directive of economic research which aims at protecting, strengthening and developing the market and making it more efficient; even though, at first sight, it may seem that Fedorenko aims chiefly at the "optimal plan" and at improved planning. These researches therefore seem particularly interesting not only for the post-Stalinist economies but also for the post-capitalist market economies of the West.

We pass on now to Budapest. The *bureaucratic-socialist market* is the Hungarian economic model. How far is it, or will it be, socialist? When we recall that the headship of firms is by bureaucratic nomination; that wages policy, workers' participation in profit, and a large part of prices and taxes on profits are rigidly fixed from above; that the workers' syndicate has not the power to protest by strikes against these fundamental decisions of the techno-bureaucratic apparatus; and that the political channel of participation in power is still the Communist Party, Leninist, bureaucratised and authoritarian in its tradition and customs, then we are tempted to conclude that what the Hungarians are preparing (and possibly, later on, the Soviets too) is a market composed of a number of enterprises like IRI (the great State holding organisation in Italy) with above it a single-party Leninist government. This hypothesis has not much that is socialist about it, and it can perhaps be regarded as, at best, the last stage of evolution of the post-Stalinist Communist system from bureaucracy to technology.

It is however clear that this mechanism, in so far as it obliges the concerns to compete for a profit and allows workers' participation, if on a limited scale, in their profits, calls for a strong initiative, possibly for protest against the system, on the part of the workers. This bureaucractic market system is nevertheless more open to a socialist evolution than was the system of centralised authoritarian planning. A transformation of the Hungarian-type bureaucratic market in a democratic, and therefore socialist, direction would demand further radical changes in the trade union and political structures; but this system could also gradually acquire a more "socialist" character through a succession of reforms.

It is possible that, starting from the Hungarian model, a "more socialist" market economy might be achieved in which there would be State concerns with heads whose appointment would still be controlled by central organisations or regulations, but whose powers would be rigorously contested and "counterbalanced" by powerful autonomous trade unions. One can visualise an economy in which the central powers of the Plan in relation to policy on incomes, taxation on consumption and profits, and investment directives would still be very strong, and in which nevertheless these powers would be democratised by radical reforms, which would make possible an unrestricted political and economic debate and free political choices. One can imagine that in such an economy the workers' power in the factories might increase without necessarily reaching the point of "self-management".

The most characteristic note of the Hungarian model is the stern defence of the firms' individuality in relation to workers' participation: a purely "dialectical" (and potentially contestant) participation is envisaged, as in Western capitalist societies, not a direct participation, as in Yugoslavia. The Hungarians maintain that direct participation would deprive the concern of its character and its productive aims; the "consumer" mentality would be dominant, with disastrous effects on production, in self-managed concerns—and the Hungarians point to the example of their agricultural cooperatives. Thus a system of socialist market is sketched out which would nevertheless reject "participation" on Yugoslav lines.

Can a theoretical choice be made between these two hypotheses of "socialist" development? I would think not. The only possible and desirable thing is to try them out. One can also visualise "mixed economies" of a new kind, in which "self-managed" concerns would compete in the market with concerns "under bureaucratic direction" (I think the Yugoslav economy is to some extent an economy of this kind, by reason of the real imperfections of its self-management).

It cannot be denied, as a matter of principle, that a "dialectical", contestant kind of participation of the trade union, regulated in various ways by laws and customs, can also be real, in other words can serve to eliminate to some extent the workers' "alienation", no less than the Yugoslav variety of participation. The Yugoslavs, naturally, deny this possibility. In practice, the real forms of workers' participation in modern industrial economies are articulated in a thousand different ways, varying from country to country and from firm to firm. There can also be forms of indirect, political participation; participation can even be taken to be real when in fact it arises from skilful propaganda suggestions. It will be interesting to see how the economic mechanism of the Hungarian "bureaucratic market" will develop. To exclude *a priori* that it may acquire socialist characteristics unless it accepts the Yugoslav mechanism of "self-management" (as the Yugoslavs maintain), seems to me unjustifiable.

The "Yugoslav model", in its turn, goes far. The latest development of Yugoslav revisionism is the reacquisition by socialism of private entrepreneurial ownership. Confusion still exists as to the limits within which private ownership of the means of production by a private individual is not "exploitation" but a genuine and living fact of sociality, if not actually of socialism. At first it applied to a firm of not more than five dependent workers; but in practice it is expanding: various handicrafts concerns (carpenters, builders, glass workers, etc.) are coordinating their action and forming real private firms of quite considerable size.

At the other extreme of the Yugoslav economic evolution, the formation of a capital market in which the accumulated resources of the big self-managed concerns can be used creates new forms of participant economy, midway between the social and the private.

The reconquest for "socialism" of private initiative in the small-sized concerns is historically an important and stimulating event. It arises, indirectly, from the realisation of the "alienating" character of impersonal, State, bureaucratic or technocratic ownership in the big concerns. True socialist ownership must include participation; therefore direct, self-managed ownership by an individual or a small group of persons is socialist ownership, because it is not alienating.

In concrete terms, this means that a great many services (shops, tourism etc.) are much better run; the practical effect is extraordinary, and it can be seen even in Hungary. One cannot avoid the thought that a good deal of the drabness of Soviet daily life could be eliminated by readmitting private initiative and ownership in the small-sized concerns.

To what extent, I ask myself, can this make acceptable in a socialist society some of the largely positive phenomena of industrial life under the capitalist system, such as the transformation of small craftsmen or owners of small concerns or scientist-entrepreneurs into great "captains of industry"? (There have been numerous examples of this in recent years: in Italy, for instance, in the sphere of electrical household goods; in America in the more sophisticated spheres of industry with a high scientific and technological content.) In theory, there does not seem to me to be anything to preclude the evolution and growth of productive organisms of this kind, with the gradual passage, as the dimensions increase, from the personal concern to the "self-managed" or socialised concern or the concern in which workers' or State participation is realised in different ways. We are here, in any case, at one of the new frontiers of social evolution.

Experiences like that of Yugoslavia suggest the advisability of a far-reaching experimentation of various types of productive organisms, which may even coexist side by side. In short, the mixed economies should become much more mixed: for example, in Italy, why should not IRI try out in some of its concerns forms of participation, industrial democracy, or even self-management? Practice—and competition—could then show which type of concern would give proof of the greatest productive and social vitality.

III

WESTERN EUROPE

25. Balogh: The Incomes Policy

As our discussion of modern economics draws nearer home it becomes increasingly concrete and more closely related to our everyday difficulties. The Europe of today has both old and new economic problems. The old problems arise from shortages, underdevelopment and poverty (even the rich countries have their "depressed areas"); the new, from wealth itself, recently acquired and still uncertain, and from progress in production that has been too rapid and unequal to avoid arousing contrasts. Italy, with a dual economy, is perhaps the only country to be plagued equally by both these kinds of problems. In the rest of Europe, and increasingly in Italy too, the dominant problems are the new ones.

Although production in our countries doubles every 15 or 16 years (in Italy, every 12 or 13), at a rate hitherto undreamt-of, crises are nevertheless a constantly recurrent feature— monetary disorders, social unrest and strife which prosperity and full employment fail to attenuate. In the effort to explain these crises, the economists sometimes take on the guise of sociologists or psychologists. But as economists, they strive to meet them chiefly on their own ground, by diagnosing the reasons for the checks and setbacks that still often occur in productive progress.

That progress is, in fact, not continuous and stable as we should like it to be. Great difficulties are involved in regulating an economy of full employment, and the British scholars who, with Keynes, "invented" the economy in which we now live, and taught the politicians how to make it work, foresaw this from the beginning. In his report of 1944, *Full Employment in a Free Society,* which can be regarded as the birth certificate of neocapitalism and the welfare society, Beveridge himself wrote (p. 194): "There is a real danger that sectional wage bargaining, pursued without regard to its effects upon prices, may lead to a vicious spiral of inflation, with money wages chasing prices and without any gain in real wages for the working class as a whole." That prophecy has unfortunately come true; and no one, as Samuelson and Heller told me at the beginning of this journey of mine among the economists, has yet discovered how to have full employment without inflation in a Western society.

Many troubles derive from inflation, and to combat it governments are often induced to curb the economy. But the remedy is sometimes worse than the disease. Many post-war recessions, even if slight, have been decidedly artificial in character, in other words deliberately provoked by governments. Thus a new economico-political cycle has been installed: boom, full employment, inflation, balance of payments crises, deflationary measures, recession, measures to relaunch demand, boom—and the whole round begins again.

This cycle is much less destructive than the "natural" cycle of the old economy; but it slows up development and reduces the volume of goods available. In no country has this "stop-go" rhythm been so harmful as in Great Britain, the first country with full employment. It is in part the reason for its slow rate of growth; and the continental countries, as their economies mature, fear they may catch the infection of the "British sickness". The fact that British economists have not yet succeeded in breaking the vicious circle of stop-go is one of the great setbacks of modern economics.

Thomas Balogh opposes it with the idea of a "virtuous circle" with as its centre an agreed policy of prices and incomes. Balogh, now in his mid-sixties, is Hungarian by birth, Oxonian by adoption, and he was made a Life Peer by Wilson, of whom he is a great friend and adviser. He played a considerable role behind the scenes in Wilson's struggle with the trade unions to get them to accept a wages policy. For more than a decade he has maintained that "wage demands must be moderate, first of all, to allow of an increase in investments, and then so as to keep them within the limits of the increase in productivity".

That last is also the golden rule that the Communist planners impose by law in the countries of Eastern Europe. But England is not a Communist country, and many people think that Balogh is crying for the moon. Two Labour Prime Ministers, Attlee in the austerity years and Wilson in the late 'sixties, have tried to impose a calculated wages policy. But in both cases they had only partial and ephemeral success.

By the end of 1969, after months of bitter struggle with the trade unions, only some fragments of Wilson's policy of wages restraint remained intact. True, the Labour Party Congress had declared by a majority vote its belief in the vital importance of an effective prices and incomes policy; but it was doubtful whether these good intentions would be respected; and the attempt to regulate by law the rights and duties of the trade unions (including wild-cat strikes) had also failed.

Balogh is naturally conscious of the extreme difficulty of making his policy triumph—in other countries, too, it has registered few successes and many failures. But he refuses to abandon it, for he considers it vital: "If we fail", he told me when I saw him in his office at the Prices and Incomes Board* in one of the huge new glass-and-concrete buildings in Victoria Street in London, "inflation will end by provoking a revolt of the *lumpenbourgeoisie*—Fascism; this will happen, if the trade unions insist on demanding a free-for-all."

What precisely does Balogh mean by a prices and incomes policy? Something more, obviously, than a simple policy of wages control. "The present economic system", he said to me, "is by its very nature indeterminate. In a regime of oligopolies and monopolies, the banking system is no longer in a position to provide for stability, as in the theoretical models. That is now impossible *en principe*. The State must therefore intervene in wages negotiations, in which the consumer is never represented. How should the State's intervention come about? There are all sorts of ways: arbitration courts, as in Australia, or the policy that this Board has pursued (by applying a law

* This Board was subsequently abolished by the Conservative Government in November 1970.

which, temporarily, prevented wage increases beyond a certain limit), or wages guideposts. But the important thing is that effective figures should be fixed. Archimedes wanted a point of support to raise the world: this is lacking in the present economic system."

In defence of his proposals Balogh sharply attacks the trade unions. "Free" industrial bargaining, he said in a letter to *The Times* (8 September 1969), had not succeeded in increasing the wages slice of the national income cake: on the contrary, it had "achieved two things only: in the first place it undermined the country's competitive position . . . and in the second place (and through the defence action necessitated by the first) it caused unemployment, slowed down the growth of investment and productivity—and thus, paradoxically, the increase in real wages. Incidentally, it also increased inequality between the weaker and stronger among the working class".

In America these things are being said by a conservative such as Friedman. But Balogh is not a conservative, he is an ardent Labour man, and that is perhaps why he takes the trade unions so sternly to task. As he told me, "If the trade unions were to say 'Our price is that the taxation system should give us a redistribution of income in favour of the wage-earners', I should agree entirely. But I don't accept their saying that they won't have an incomes policy at any price. The trade unions came into being to help the poor, but today they have become centres of power with no responsibility to anyone. If we do not reach an agreement with the trade unions, we shall undoubtedly have a Fascist-type counterattack. The trade unions could use their enormous power to secure great advantages for their members; but for that reason they should recognise that they have certain fundamental duties to the community. The trade unions are certainly capable of damaging the currency; but they cannot, merely by trade union action, increase the share of wages in the national income. That they can only achieve through the State. Pure and simple trade union action only leads to chaos."

This wholesale attack on present-day trade unionism (Balogh is by nature an extremist in polemics) is the counterpart to some vast and rather vague ideas in his own and Wilson's thinking. What, I asked him, could persuade the trade unions to accept the incomes policy? In his answer Balogh traced the broad outlines of a real New Deal, a new pact with the trade unions which should consist of a number of agreed policies: "A taxes policy, a social security policy, a building policy, a regional policy, all coordinated, and, of course, very strong price controls." Balogh agrees that if the State wants to intervene with definite rules in trade union affairs, it is only fair that the trade unions should also want to intervene in the affairs of the State.

According to him, adequate machinery for this already exists in Britain: the trade unions have joint representation on all the planning committees. "If they were intelligent", he said, "they could use this power of theirs to secure new functions; but unfortunately they don't want that, they only want to force prices up; and that is madness, it's cutting off your nose to spite your face."

Balogh does not, of course, exclude the possibility that his grand design may prove impossible of realisation. Even if the trade union leaders were to be convinced, "such a situation of anarchy might arise in the factories that we would be unable to carry the lower reaches with us". In order to avoid that, "certain duties in the sphere of workers' social rights should be imposed on the bigger concerns." "In the factory", he added, "the shop stewards shoud be consulted much more. The truth is that many of our strikes are due to the fact that we have an antediluvian management. The industrialists have not yet grasped that, with full employment, people can no longer be ruled with a rod of iron."

Listening to Balogh's conversation one glimpses a vast design for economic and political renovation: we are no longer in the sphere of "modern capitalism" but in that of—to borrow the terminology of Eastern Europe—"capitalist revisionism" or, if you prefer it, of modern socialism. Wilson tried to develop this design—without much success. But what are the alternatives? Only, it would seem, that of deflation, already tried out (and precisely, and vigorously, by the Wilson Government), which creates productive stagnation and unemployment, with the aim of putting the foreign accounts to rights. For Wilson, this was intended as a temporary expedient. For others, it is quite simply the right policy.

What follows is the gist of a long talk I had with Lord Robbins, Lionel Robbins, one of the great English economists of this century, and a liberal-conservative. I saw him in his office at the *Financial Times,* of which he was chairman until 1971. "In my view", he said, "an incomes policy wouldn't work in inflationary conditions, not even if the angels of the Lord came down to Downing Street."

"Inflationary conditions" signifies full employment. "Keynes", said Lord Robbins, "foresaw before the war that if unemployment fell to 5 or 6 per cent serious problems would emerge; today an average level of unemployment of not much more than 2 per cent begins to have inflationary effects and upsets the balance of payments." The remedy, put briefly, would be a trifle more unemployment, a rigid policy of control of liquidity and public expenditure, and regional measures to relieve unemployment wherever it rose above the average: "There is no sense", he said, "in producing a boom and inflation in London simply because the rate of unemployment in parts of Scotland is abnormally high."

The alternative to the incomes policy and the vast political and economic revolution it would involve is not particularly attractive, but above all it is not new: we have seen it in operation in Britain, in the United States, in France, we saw it in Italy in 1963–64. We know its cost. The other way, as indicated by Balogh, that of a "new pact" between government and trade unions, may lead far, perhaps further than Balogh himself imagines; but no country has so far tried it seriously. Will there some day be a country that is able to do so?

*   *   *

In the history of the modern world, there is a true episode that seems like a fable: the fable of the spirit of Saltsjoebaden.

Saltsjoebaden is a seaside resort near Stockholm. In the most important of the dignified old-fashioned hotels facing the chilly shores of the Baltic Sea, the Grand Hotel, in the years between 1936 and 1938 a series of meetings took place between trade union leaders and industrialists, at which the foundations were laid of the industrial peace which still, after thirty-odd years, exists today.* There was born then what the Scandinavians call "the spirit of Saltsjoebaden".

Some years ago a big Swedish industrialist talked to me about it: "People believe that in Sweden workers and management get on well because they are Swedish, a placid cold-blooded people. But that isn't so. Before the Saltsjoebaden agreements we had as many strikes as any other country, and there were bitter industrial disputes. The Saltsjoebaden meetings were held precisely because the situation was so serious that the government threatened to intervene with severe controls over wages and profits. The only point on which the two sides agreed was that neither of them wanted State intervention. So they decided to meet, and once they met they discovered that, after all, they could talk together and even understand each other. The spirit of Saltsjoebaden is nothing else but that readiness to talk. But it is certainly not the result of the Swedish temperament, which has remained just the same."

Like all fables, the Saltsjoebaden fable has its moral. But what is it? The *Times,* writing about it some time ago, remarked that generally two quite opposite morals are drawn from it. According to some, there is more collaboration between the two sides of industry in Sweden than elsewhere "because the working-class is better educated". According to others, the real reason is because "the industrialists are much better educated and more competent than in other countries".

There are also other explanations. The State can be brought into it. In Sweden taxation is liberal towards a firm's income

---

* Though even Sweden experienced some industrial conflicts in 1970–71.

that goes into investment: it allows a firm, for example, to set aside a considerable part of its profits in special, controlled funds which it can draw on, tax-free, when the government thinks an economic recession is in the offing. On the other hand taxation of personal incomes is very severe. Sweden is not only the country where some decades of social democracy and social services have caused poverty to vanish. It is not only the country where the State assures for the masses, who are constantly being moved about by the industrial revolution, housing, work, social assistance, and vocational training. It is also the country where the scandal of excessive wealth has been for the most part eliminated.

The important thing is that social security and full employment have in no way reduced the incentives to economic progress: in this post-war period there has also been the Scandinavian miracle as well as those more famous miracles, the German and the Italian. Swedish trade union leaders maintain that it is the strong rights recognised to them by the State, and the real power enjoyed by the working class, that have enabled the workers and the trade unions to acquire a productive, creative and non-defensive mentality and to collaborate in discussion with the managers of firms instead of coming into headlong collision with them.

The technique of wages negotiation in Sweden goes from top to bottom. First of all the general lines of a global, top-level agreement are settled between the confederations of both sides; then they are broken down in successive negotiations at sector or local level in a series of operative agreements. This makes it possible to carry out a kind of incomes policy with no need of State intervention.

But if this is possible, it is also because there exists in the factories in Sweden a degree of industrial democracy unknown elsewhere. Through the factory committees the workers are given precise information about the firm's financial situation, its costs and its profits.

The fable of Saltsjoebaden, seen close to, is not a fable: it is the story of the laborious adaptation of a democratic society to the particular needs of the system of industrial production. This adaptation has involved many renunciations of traditional privileges and many concessions. The structures of industrial power have been profoundly modified.*

London

---

* By 1973 one was bound to modify these findings on the spread of worker participation or co-determination—so-called "industrial democracy"—as they had existed as recently as 1968–69. By the beginning of 1973, workers' rights to nominate a proportion of the members of company supervisory boards (though not, except for the personnel director, management boards) had become well established in West Germany. A similar procedure had become legally compulsory in the Netherlands and had been made the subject of a parliamentary Bill in Belgium. The co-determination principle had also been introduced as an option in France, though it was not yet much used. British employers and unions both for different reasons rejected the worker-director principle in its German or Dutch forms, but were nonetheless actively seeking some formula for worker-participation in the overall conduct of limited companies—as indeed they seemed likely to have to do by the mid-1970s in terms of EEC Draft Directive No 5 on the approximation of company structures in the enlarged community.

26. Robinson, Harrod, Kaldor: The Restless Keynesians

"If Keynes were alive," Roy Harrod said to me, "he would find the economic policy of today very little to his taste. He would be horrified at the increase in unemployment as a means of restoring the balance of payments to equilibrium." "I am convinced", Nicholas Kaldor explained, "that the implications of the Keynesian theory go far beyond Keynes, and lead to the complete rejection of the neo-classical theory in the framework of which Keynes was still functioning." And Joan Robinson: "After the war a popularised version of Keynes was adopted. Now, the point is this: Keynes was dealing with short-term problems, but following his criticisms the whole neo-classical theory was left in ruins. What I call the Cambridge Anglo-Italian school has applied itself to building it up again from the foundations."

In this journey among the economists, my meetings with the Keynesians have been among the most stimulating and at the same time the most difficult for the chronicler, because of the complexity of the subjects they raise. The people I have just mentioned, and others too, such as Piero Sraffa (accessible for fascinating conversations but not for interviews), have all inherited from Keynes a sophisticated and subtle taste for theory, and also a strong ethico-political motivation. But in Keynes the unity of theory and practice, under the influence of the great crisis of the 'thirties, was more obvious and essential. He was stimulated by the crisis and its disastrous effects to seek and propound a radical revision both of theory and of economic policy. But such encounters between a scholar and a vital problem of society rarely occur in history; with the Keynesians, the link between pure research and practical problems is less direct and drastic.

In London an important economic journalist, Norman McCrae of *The Economist,* had said to me, "Our economists, unlike the Americans, live in the clouds." Samuel Brittan, of the *Financial Times,* had remarked acidly, "The state of our economic science is as disappointing as the state of our economy." Andrew Shonfield had added: "In London, you have to listen out to catch the echo of the theoretical debates going on in the village of Cambridge." These judgements are exaggerated but not inexplicable. In Cambridge, one of the most brilliant exponents of that "Anglo-Italian" school I mentioned, Luigi Pasinetti, observed with a twinkle in his eye: "We concern ourselves with theory, and the practical consequences aren't immediately visible. Perhaps the good journalists in London won't find anything in it to interest them for another twenty years".

In the eyes of the journalists, however, the economic scholars seem like sorcerers' apprentices who have set in motion, with Keynes, the powerful machine of full employment but have failed to invent the means to guide and restrain it. In England too, the techniques, whether fiscal or monetary, for the regulation of that gigantic productive apparatus, post-Keynesian industrial society, have proved inadequate. Corrective interventions have often aggravated rather than attenuated the cyclical disturbances; and not infrequently the economists have given the governments bad advice, more from prejudice or factiousness than for scientific reasons. They have pursued theoretical diatribes rather than practical problems.

There may be some good foundation for all these criticisms. But I do not think it should be held against the principal British economists if they have directed their best energies towards the study of problems of theory: because this, in the intention of whoever pursues it, is the right road, if a long one, to arrive at a better understanding, and hence a better regulation of the economy. For years the post-Keynesians of Cambridge, England have been involved in a vast and profound debate with the "neo-classicists" of Cambridge, Massachusetts (who in America themselves count as neo-Keynesians).

The debate, which includes among its starting-points (so Kaldor told me) Piero Sraffa's new theory of value, touches on all the essential points of economic science: the theory of value, the theory of capital as a factor of production, the theory of the distribution of income between capital and labour, the theory of the profit rate, the theory of price formation, the theory of imperfect competition. In all these fields, the English Keynesians go further than Keynes (and than the Americans) in criticism of the traditional theses on the natural equilibrium of the market. They go further than Keynes, too, in the search for a "dynamic" theory of economics.

For Keynes, the problem was to utilise existing resources to the full; today, on the other hand, everyone talks about the development or growth of resources. But the theoretical bases of this research are weak: "There is no theory of growth", said Roy Harrod, the friend and biographer of Keynes, when I saw him in the lovely Georgian house in Norfolk to which he has retired from Oxford. "The politicians try to carry out a growth policy while the fundamental theorems for it don't exist: it's like trying to build a bridge without the laws of dynamics."

This general re-thinking of economic theory has so far produced only partial results. But that was to be expected. "Our theoretical work", Kaldor said, "may still seem very abstract. But I regard it as very important. What is economics? It is the attempt to understand how a market mechanism functions. And it is not only the immediate practical conclusions that matter but the whole way of thinking. In 99 per cent of cases, Einstein's and Newton's theories give the same answers; but they are quite different theories, and in critical cases they offer divergent answers."

The inspiration of these researches is not merely theoretical but also ethical and political. Joan Robinson criticises Paul Samuelson and his "neo-classical synthesis" not only because she considers him inconsistent ("He has played a foremost part in relaunching some silly old ideas, although he is a Keynesian about problems of employment and money; his famous 'synthesis' isn't a real synthesis but two different boxes put together") but also because she puts the worst construction on his practical aims: "Behind the old anti-scientific theology, which the Keynesian revolution was supposed to do away with", she said, "there is the whole weight of the desire to justify capitalism. It is no longer the ideology of *laissez-faire,* because the State has a great part in the economic game, nor yet the ideology of perfect competition, because there are oligopolies and monopolies. But what is proposed is still a market ideology which tries to justify the old economy in the eyes of the new generation. And now we have to carry on a tremendous struggle to clarify the simplest points."

In the post-Keynesian English economists traces crop up of the old radicalism, that precious flower for which the aristocratic atmosphere of the great colleges acts as a hothouse. (In America, the economist who best represents these ideas, with greater talent as a writer and with less wealth of theory, is Kenneth Galbraith.) Joan Robinson's polemical energy is typical of this frame of mind. I saw her at the Institute of Economics, in one of the university's most modern buildings. She was wearing old trousers and a flowered tunic, and she had a great crown of white hair, luminous blue eyes, and a penetrating voice; her enthusiasms for China and North Korea disconcert many of her admirers, who describe them as "juvenile".

She looks at the society of today with the eyes of the perpetual radical socialist, and says that full employment "is now a conservative slogan", whereas what matters today is to decide what it is to be used for: "whether to manufacture arms, or to produce greater profits, or to ensure better social services". She is unhappy about the post-war boom, because she fears it may be due more to rearmament than to the new economics: "Perhaps the cure is worse than the disease".

About the relationship between full employment and inflation she said: "Twenty years ago I wrote that full employment, far from being a position of stable equilibrium, might become a peak from which the value of money would be precipitated into an abyss. But the moral I wanted to draw was that we should practice some socialism, in other words give the worker a greater share in the national income so as to free him from having to carry on a continuous struggle. If profits are allowed to increase, why should the workers have to impose limitations on their own wages?"

Nicholas Kaldor too, when I saw him in London at the Treasury, in one of those picturesque nineteenth-century buildings between Westminster and Scotland Yard that misguided planners want to destroy, gave a radical criticism of "neo-capitalism". "I believe", he said, "that our world will change a great deal; but it won't be economic conditions that will cause capitalism to fall, but dissatisfaction because of its inequalities. Even though there is less injustice than there used to be, people are more aware of it, because today people feel more equal."

Kaldor regards the Communist and the capitalist systems as equally unstable. In the Communist system there is an intolerable political centralisation of power; in the capitalist system it is the big international industrial groups that are becoming uncontrollable centres of decisions. "The remedy", he said, "may perhaps be the assumption of ever greater powers of control by the State. But I don't really know how this society will change: human society has always developed of itself through the action of impersonal forces, not because it was guided by the philosophers."

Animated by this critical view of post-Keynesian society, Keynes's friends have carried forward the attack on the theories of the perfect market, analysing the present-day society of the imperfect market, vitiated by oligopolies (whether entrepreneurial or trade unionist), in which the rate of profit and prices do not naturally find their "right" level but may be determined arbitrarily. "This", Joan Robinson said, "is the economy of the new mercantilism, without natural equilibrium, and with continual struggles and contradictions."

The Keynesians propound afresh such problems as the relation between capital and labour, exploitation, the structure of economic power, and the mechanisms of development. "Keynes", Pasinetti said to me, "had sensed the theoretical evolution that we are now going through, although he saw things from the practical standpoint. Keynes did not go very deeply into theory, but he brought out something important that wasn't right in the traditional theory of the market, something that put a spanner in the works, and by so doing, as Galbraith said, he saved Western economy."

The post-Keynesians have indicated other spanners in the works of society today. But they do not promise salvation; their work is still a long way from producing a system, a model of what post-Keynesian economy is, or should become. They reject any other model, whether Soviet or Yugoslav, with a certain fastidiousness of the pure intellectual, but they offer no global alternatives. This is somewhat unsatisfying; but it is no good taking the British head-in-the-clouds economists to task about it. All the political and economic forces at work in our society, from the most integrated to the most revolutionary, are acting today without reference to models, be they real or ideal, historical or utopian.

This fluidity and imprecision in the ideological field is a typical characteristic of our times. It is not surprising that in going back to the most direct and richest source of European economic thought, the Keynesian school, a similar practical restlessness and theoretical incompleteness should be found. Here too there is no global answer to the present problems. This answer, Kaldor says, will come not from philosophers' ideas but from "impersonal forces": thus action comes first and thought after. It is the typical mark of an era of great upheavals. The restlessness of the Keynesians arises, it seems to me, not only from their radical conscience but from the dissatisfaction of this unfinished search.

Cambridge—London

27. Marjolin and Shonfield: The Structure

Where is European society going? Where is modern capitalism going? To what extent do the social agitations of recent years, the student revolts of May 1968 in France, the "hot autumn" of the 1969 strikes in Italy, foreshadow a general crisis of the whole system? And what kind of crisis, what kind of change or transformation or renovation? These are questions that everyone is asking today in the West: the revolutionaries are no longer the only ones to talk of revolution. In his speech of September 1969, reminiscent in tone of Mendès-France, M. Chaban-Delmas, then Pompidou's Prime Minister, said: "There are few moments in the life of a people in which it can ask itself, other than in a dream: what sort of society do I want to live in?—and at the same time effectively build that society. I have the feeling that we are approaching one of these moments." Well, what "dream" is Europe pursuing?

I put these questions in London to Andrew Shonfield, who, after his splendid book on *Modern Capitalism*, has now definitely abandoned an illustrious career as an economic journalist. When I saw him he was dividing his time between the Royal Institute of International Affairs (he became its Director in 1972) and the National Council for Social Research, one of those organisations of a scientific-cum-technocratic nature with which Labour under Wilson hoped to speed up the modernisation of Britain. It was there that I saw him, in one of London's new skyscraper buildings: seen from above, you realise how greatly the city has changed, punctuated as it now is by these glittering towers.

I put the same questions in Paris to one of the great personalities of France and Europe today: Robert Marjolin, former vice-President of the Common Market Commission, before that

Secretary-General of OEEC, and collaborator of Jean Monnet as Commissaire Général Adjoint of the Monnet Plan. Marjolin has the severe, aristocratic look of a French *commis d'état*, but he is not an aristocrat: he is a carpenter's son, and at fourteen he left school to work in a factory, later resuming his studies to carry them on intensively. He is one of the great Europeans, and one of the few authentic American-style self-made men in the Europe of today. Since leaving the Common Market he has divided his time between business, studies, and university lecturing ("I am also thinking about a book", he told me, "but I don't yet know exactly what about—there are so many problems that are still unclear").

I saw him in his apartment overlooking a boulevard packed with traffic: a pleasant bourgeois flat with lots of books and some good pictures, and Marjolin in a pullover smoking a thin cigar and talking in his quiet, convincing way. After all those years of the Common Market and of battles with jealous governments, one thing at least is certain—Marjolin is, as *Le Monde* says, *un homme persuasif.*

"It is obvious", he said, "that economic progress and a higher standard of living do not produce that calm and contentment that might have been hoped for. Expectations grow more rapidly than their satisfaction. Large categories of the population think they haven't got what they ought to have. The modern age, appearances notwithstanding, has witnessed a certain increase in inequalities. There is a very wide span between those who have more and those who have less: and we have not yet reached the point (as they have, in some ways, in America) where those with less have at least the essentials of what they desire."

To explain what he had in mind, Marjolin recalled the time when as a youth he was working in a factory in Northern France. "In those days", he said, "people never came to Paris, or only for the big exhibitions. A peasant never thought of comparing his situation with that of a factory-worker. Today, with the rural exodus, the comparison is inevitable. What counts today even more than inequality is the amount of change—vast and profound changes, with migrations of population, as for instance from the South to the North of Italy. In America that is normal: but to become Americans people had first to make an immense long journey, so the change was taken as a matter of course. In the European tradition, on the other hand, there was the centuries-long immobility of village life. Change leads to comparison, and comparison to reaction against inequality: this sociological chain-phenomenon is at the root of the agitation and unrest."

Marjolin continued in his calm voice: "And the situation will get gradually worse as we witness the formation of ever vaster urban agglomerations where people live very much alone, while television enables every modest family to contemplate daily the life of those who have everything: how can you expect people to remain quiet?"

I asked him what remedy economics could offer for these tensions. "Economics presupposes great fluidity of the means of production, and that doesn't exist, or if it exists it raises its own problems. To make it possible for each individual to give his maximum marginal production, incessant changes would be needed; but men are made of flesh and blood, and every move is an uprooting and a drama. Thus the vicious circle of modern society is born. To satisfy the demands created by the changes, there needs to be a rapid and constant increase of the national product: the economy is fundamental. But to secure that increase, a certain amount of change has to be admitted, and those changes in themselves create very serious social and human problems."

If economics has no global answer to these problems, where is the answer to be found? For instance, I asked Marjolin, did he believe in "participation"?

"Yes, I believe in participation. I think it is a mistake to suppose that we can go on living under a system in which the management of a firm has virtually no other relationship with its work people beyond hiring their services and paying their wages. I consider it indispensable that that relationship should be humanised—first and foremost through information, which is the beginning of participation. People must know what is going on. And then gradually the factories must be turned into a place where the man who works there feels that he is in some sense at home, as it used to be in small firms. The way must be found, I don't know how, to recreate that sort of relationship in big firms; perhaps through a reform of the factory committees."

I asked Marjolin what he thought about workers' shareholding.

"I don't think it gives the feeling of participation", he answered. "I wouldn't exclude it; but there must be a much more concrete, more direct participation."

These were Marjolin's views. Also in Paris, in the course of a long interview about which I shall say more later on, Pierre Uri, another former colleague of Monnet's, touched on the same themes. "In my view", he said, "participation, envisaged rather on American lines, is useful for economic progress. Our European firms are much more monarchical than the American concerns: the best we have are enlightened despots. We must change things gradually, learning as we go. But I am not in favour of participation in the Gaullist sense of distribution of shares to the workers: the wage-earners must participate as wage-earners, not as pseudo-capitalists. The road to participation lies in decentralisation in the factories: that is also the road towards increase of productivity. What needs to be discussed today", he concluded, "is methods of management rather than distribution of profits. Changes in the methods of management also seem to me useful as a means of combating workers' 'alienation' and developing productivity."

Shonfield too was concerned about defence of the productive process, which is obviously the necessary premise for any social progress. He did not think that the Italian strikes of autumn 1969, and the trade union and student agitations of recent years in general, were the forerunners of a widespread crisis. "In general", he said, "it doesn't seem to me that there is a crisis in the traditional relationships between trade union and entrepreneur, between worker and management; it's rather a particular crisis in the Italian and French trade unions, which need to become more modern, and therefore stronger: strength will bring them greater patience." "The trade union", he went on, "was an organisation of *pauvres diables* who were defending themselves. How? By violent struggles, which called for total discipline, but which didn't last long. Now, while the *pauvre diable* is no longer so *pauvre*, the 'Latin' trade union has not yet got that financial strength that comes from a large number of registered members and their contributions, such as the Scandinavian and German trade unions have." Its methods are still the same old ones, and it continues to choose, whether from necessity or tradition, "the violent and brief collision". It is, in fact, going through a "difficult period of transformation"; but the basic trend, as seen with the detachment of the historian of modern capitalism, will lead the "Latin" trade union towards the methods and conduct of its Scandinavian counterpart.

But Shonfield's diagnosis does not stop there. He sees a "new pact" developing between the trade unions and the other productive forces. In his analysis such a pact would set out from the need for an incomes policy, "to prevent wages-bargaining from merely leading to an increase in prices".

He went on: "If they want a more rational 'division of the cake', the firms' activities must come out into the open much more. It is unreasonable to expect the trade unions to believe what they are told with their eyes shut. The German experiment in participation is important not so much because it gives the workers powers in the organisation, but because it lets them know something about what is going on."

So much for relations between firms and trade unions. What about relations between the trade unions and the State? "In this new framework", Shonfield answered, "there will have to be participation by the organised workers in political procedures too. For example: if an incomes policy is to be introduced, the Budget ought also to be discussed with the people who will be asked, for economic reasons, to moderate their wage claims. That is to say, a new institutional pact will be needed (a difficult thing to do, as a matter of fact, when part of the workers' leadership is 'anti-establishment'); and the organised workers will need to be represented in some specific political council. To give an Italian example again: it is a striking fact that a successful economy like yours runs into difficulties because some people send large sums of money out of the country. But this is an important fact in relation to a wages policy: if people want such a policy, they must also be prepared to have strict controls against the flight of capital."

"The trade unions", Shonfield concluded, "cannot stay outside the political system and come into it only occasionally. In England too we are in a phase of revolt of the trade unions against the Government, which has made use of them for a policy that they aren't keen on. But our trade unions are gradually becoming converted to the point of view that they cannot remain outside the legal system. Political and institutional arrangements are still inadequate for a solution of the problem of calculated distribution of incomes. But if people want to have, at the same time, stable prices, full employment and rapid growth, they must face up to this question in all its aspects."

London—Paris

28. *Uri: Market and Plan*

Two economic ideologies have dominated Europe in the post-war period: that of the European market, as a means of strengthening capitalism; and that of national planning, as a means of disciplining capitalism. These two ideologies were only apparently opposed to each other: in reality, such opposition was so far from the truth that both were born from the same "brains trust". Jean Monnet and his friends, the initiators of the French Plan immediately after the war, were, a few years later, the real inventors of the Common Market. Though imposing controls with the Plan and liberalising with the Common Market, Monnet and his followers were not schizophrenics but perfectly rational people in their search for a synthesis between two inspirations which they considered equally necessary to the economic and social wellbeing of Europe.

Today, more than a dozen years after the establishment of the Common Market, more than twenty-odd years after the French Plan, the two ideologies still retain their vitality, if in a state of crisis. Some people regard as certain, after de Gaulle, a historical relaunching of Europeanism; but some maintain that the Europe of the Six is on the verge of collapse and protectionism will return. Some say that today in Europe everyone goes in for planning; others aver that the French Plan itself, first-born of all the Western plannings, has now lost strength in face of the market. To get an idea of the state of the two ideologies, I talked in Paris to Robert Marjolin, Pierre Uri, Pierre Bauchet (one of the main experts on the French Plan), and lastly with the Plan's Commissioner-General, René Montjoie.

Marjolin, with the realism born of many years on the EEC Commission, did not believe either in a general crisis of Europe or in an imminent leap forward towards unification. "I do not believe", he told me, "in the possibility of making real advances towards monetary unification without advances on the political plane: a common currency is inconceivable without a European government. On the other hand, the customs union for industrial products does not require monetary unity, it is compatible with separate national currencies—on condition that the Governments don't govern too badly. If we stay within the framework of moderate inequalities, with monetary adjustments every so often, the inconveniences are very slight."

He did not attach much credence to the hypothesis, put forward by the *Nouvel Observateur*, that France might revert to protectionism in 1970 and that monetary difficulties were likely to lead to a general crisis in the European Community. Even the Common Market in agriculture, he thought, would survive. But "a common economic policy is, for the moment, to a large extent an illusion" because the differences between the various countries are too deep. Marjolin's programme for Europe is cautious and by slow stages: it consists of a series of initiatives to strengthen the customs union, to create the statute of a "European society", or to build up gradually a less heterogeneous fiscal system. But that too "will need a long time, a social evolution that may take twenty years".

Marjolin's timing for Europe is, in fact, the long-term timing of structural, social and economic evolution, not the short-term timing of revolutionary political initiatives. Pierre Uri's view is not very different, if more aggressive. I met him at the Atlantic Institute, where he is principal adviser. Uri came to economics from philosophy. It was he who "did the accounts" for the Monnet Plan, the first post-war plan for France's economy. He was among the creators of the European Coal and Steel Community and author of the Spaak report of 1955 which served as the basis for the Common Market treaty. When I met him he was giving the last touches to a full-scale study on the competitive position of Europe, as rapporteur of a committee set up by EEC.

Like Marjolin, Uri did not fear a return to protectionism. "I think", he said, "that exchange adjustments will be made in time to allow us to avoid the worst. It is difficult to imagine what Europe would be like today if there had been no Common Market. One can't see what the countries that returned to protectionism would manage to do on their own." Uri is however conscious of the seriousness of "monetary disintegration" in Europe, which is a manifestation of the divergent or unbalanced evolution of the economies of the individual countries. How, I asked him, were such phenomena to be avoided? How could Europe become more competitive and accelerate its rates of development?

Uri's answer to these problems lay in propounding "a new policy of structure". He said: "New policies must be progressively built up—a new incomes policy, a new technology policy, and a new employment policy. By degrees the internal political problems in the individual countries will change, and will change in the same way. Thus internal resistance to unification will diminish, and we shall even arrive at a common foreign policy instead of the play-acting that it is today." For Pierre Uri, Europe is growing in a hurry, but not fast enough. "Why", he says, "can't it develop at the Japanese sort of rate, perhaps 8 per cent a year? The businessmen's usual answer is to put the blame on the heavy burden of the State. My answer—and I hope to show its truth in the study I am writing—is that we are too indulgent in dragging along behind us too many unproductive sectors and concerns—in agriculture, in trade, in subsidised branches of industry (textiles, railways, etc.). We in Europe have too little competitive drive; and we have too rigid an employment policy."

Uri criticised the lack of an incomes policy: "The present situation", he said, "is leading to a social explosion. It is no use getting wage increases that are absorbed by price increases. The explosive and discontinuous evolution of wages must be eliminated and replaced by gradual and fair increases, such that the sum of monetary incomes corresponds to the development of real resources, or of productivity." This is not incompatible with certain redistributions of income. But the essential of a new employment policy is to further development, by increasing the mobility of manpower and moving it from the backward to the more productive sectors. This is done, by very different methods, in America, Japan and Sweden. The Swedish method—strong guarantees against unemployment and for social security, adoption of adequate programmes for the re-training and settlement of workers in their new jobs and places of residence—is obviously the best suited to European conditions. "We shall make specific recommendations to EEC," Uri concluded, "on the subject of policies for employment, technology, money, and incomes. We shall propose an economic and social strategy favourable to a more rapid growth of Europe, a policy conceived by Europe for Europe." It is in fact obvious, in his view, that all these things can only be done on a continental, not a national scale.

Uri would like, in short, more "plan" in the European market. His idea is to develop the "medium-term planning" which Marjolin and the Italian Franco Bobba set in motion. He wants to plan in Europe a policy of structures—not an economic policy in the narrow sense of the word—which will make the European market more vigorous. He wants more "plan" so as to have more market: is not this perhaps the philosophy of the "European miracle" of the last twenty years?

But what is meant today by "plan"? Marjolin, who was also with Monnet on the French Plan, remarks prudently: "The effect of the plan is still uncertain. It plays a part, but what part we don't know exactly. The plan is affected by economic circumstances rather than creating them, it is more of a coordinating than a programming agent; and it does not fundamentally change the functioning of the market."

In point of fact, the ideology of the French Plan has undergone subtle changes over the past twenty-odd years. The Plan, so Pierre Bauchet told me, has moved away from the direct, and often physical, planning of certain key productions to become mainly "the planning of State activities". He explained it like this: "The market, chased out of the door by the Plan, has returned through the window of the Common Market. As the Plan gradually showed itself to be increasingly powerless to direct the life of business concerns, it gave greater importance to collective and State initiatives. French planning therefore still exercises a considerable influence on the country's economy: directly in the basic sectors (energy, transport, space, electronics), indirectly by rationalising public expenditure. Today there are no longer any big public investment expenditures which are not illuminated by a sort of rational long-term perspective."

The famous sectorial committees, typical of French planning, still exist as the meeting point of the three partners, the State, the firms, and the trade unions. Thus planning as concerted action is still alive: indeed it is from this concept that "contrattazione programmatica" (planning of private investment through bargaining between the State and the big corporations) in Italy derives. But the influence of the Plan has gradually moved away "from the factories to the environment in which the factories are situated". So René Montjoie told me when I saw him in the attractive house in rue Martignac where the Plan's offices have their headquarters (the staff then consisted of only some 170 people, not more than 50 of whom were officials engaged on the actual work of planning).

The next Plan (the sixth, for 1971–75) was to be drawn up taking into account the fact that the French concerns, like those in all the other EEC countries, "are operating within an increasingly competitive and international system", Montjoie said; and this observation is important because it belies, on the basis of an unequalled practical experience, the theories of many economists about international big business killing the market. The governments' aim, Montjoie went on, must therefore be to create "the infrastructures best suited to the development of productive organisms".

The sixth French Plan will concentrate on such problems as the development of telecommunications, organisation of the financial markets, education and vocational training, and research: "everything that constitutes the sphere of operation of the business concerns and contributes to their efficiency and vitality", as Montjoie said. And he added: "There is no withdrawal on the part of the State. The Plan applies to the whole of the economy."

This conception of the plan that creates the conditions in which the market can function better, the plan that "rationalises" State expenditure and interventions (on the basis of methodologies similar to those of American planning), is now accepted everywhere in Europe. The best planning of public finance, so Marjolin told me, is done by the Germans, who were ardent free-traders. When the representatives of all the Western planning offices met together for the first time in 1968 in Paris, Marjolin said, "we discovered, somewhat to our surprise, great similarities in the philosophy and basic ideas of the plans, even though the methods were different".

The premises for a structural European plan within the framework of the European market already exist to a considerable extent. From the synthesis of the two European economic ideologies, will a real model of the modern economy perhaps come to birth?

Paris

29. *Aron and Garaudy: Reform or Revolution*

In France the debate on "Reform or Revolution", a fundamental theme in many Western countries of recent years, is not left merely to the students and the politicians; it involves also many people in the world of culture, and in France culture still has a depth and amplitude that is impressive. I fancy, though, that Anglo-Saxons must find something disconcerting about the frequent use by French writers of an abstract philosophical rather than social or economic language. I quote, to give an example, from a key-book of the 1960s, *Lire le Capital*, by Louis Althusser: "We have read *Das Kapital* as philosophers. To go straight to the point, let us confess: we posed to it the problem of its relationship with its object, and therefore, at the same time, the question of the specific nature of its object; and the problem of the specific nature of its relationship with the object."

Nevertheless the French debate on liberal-democratic neo-capitalist society and its present tensions and protests, both because of its successes and its failures, is more satisfying than similar debates now in progress in other European countries. This is partly because it is more concrete, in the sense that it has as its point of reference a definite experience, the abortive, or betrayed, or illusory revolt of May 1968. I had some interesting conversations about these problems with Raymond Aron and Roger Garaudy, the gist of which I report here. Both of them approached their theme from an angle at once economic, sociological, and political.

Aron, who has been involved for the past twenty years in an iconoclastic debate against the current myths of "left-wing culture" (his *Opium des Intellectuels*, of 1955, is still valid in part), observed that "the New Left has endeavoured to formulate a new ideology, but it has not succeeded in finding the equivalent of the obsolete Soviet orthodoxy". In its negative part, on the subject of capitalism, the new ideology still uses "the old Marxist analysis, corrected by some elements of Maoism, but basically still the same thing". In its constructive part, the New Left, "rather than having a positive utopia, nourishes itself on activism; it oscillates between a Marxist criticism of capitalism and a romantic vision of the rational society". About the disillusioned philo-Soviet intellectuals like Jean-Paul Sartre, Aron said: "It's all as if they found some extraordinary merit in detaching themselves from their earlier delirium, but without asking themselves why they ever indulged in that delirium, or whether they haven't embarked on some new form of delirium."

Aron does not underestimate "contestation" and the May revolt, though he regards it as "a psycho-drama". "In countries like France and Italy", he said, "modern productive organisation is enclosed in a pre-modern shell, and production lacks the widespread, egalitarian character that it has, for example, in the United States. In our two countries, prestige hierarchies obstruct the modern professional hierarchies." He also admitted that the organisational constrictions of industrial society weigh heavily: "During the May revolts people were happy, because they were freed from the obligations of daily life; students addressed their professors as 'tu', people talked to each other as they'd never done before, and they still remember that May as the great moment of their lives." It is a fact that "a great many of the young generation do not accept without protest the typical values of bourgeois industrial society, of a society that questions its own aims and does not know how to give itself an adequate representation of the 'good life': to produce is not an end in itself".

Aron therefore regards cultural criticism as a more valid element of the ideology of the New Left. "Modern industrial society", he said, "undoubtedly brings with it psychological tensions and human frustrations which the New Left, like many others before it, has the merit of recognising and denouncing." Though the economic advances of the past 25 years have surpassed the most optimistic hopes, this is nevertheless "an incomplete society"; it is not yet really "a society of abundance", and the distribution of wealth is unsatisfying.

"The individual", Aron said, "does not have the feeling that he can determine the course of this society of monstrous dimensions. True, Western society has absorbed some of the socialist criticisms, in managing to raise the level of working-class life and reduce crises and depressions; and in the same way it will absorb some of the criticisms of the New Left, by modifying the over-hierarchical and authoritarian organisation of business concerns, making the bureaucracy less rigid, and respecting the law of the equal dignity of men. But I believe we shall continue to go through a period of mounting dissatisfactions derived both from the imperfections of industrial society and from those of pre-industrial society. In any case, the New Left has no miraculous panacea for these ills of industrial society. Nobody has.

Aron is convinced that we are faced, not indeed with a crisis of civilisation, but certainly with "a profound change in culture and habits". But he does not think that the myths of self-management are a valid answer to the problems of the method of industrial production, nor does he find a valid alternative in the revolutionary ideology of the New Left. "None of the left-wing intellectuals", he said, "has offered us a model of democratic Communist society. Sartre, instead of outlining great theories, would do better to explain to us how he envisages reconciling centralisation with intellectual freedom, or the single party with his own right to evolve a new theory every ten years."

Aron himself does not claim to have an exhaustive answer to present-day problems; he suggests profound innovations in the style of human relationships in factories and, whimsically, he thinks it might not be at all a bad idea to have "periodical saturnalia, during which all restrictions and hierarchies would be suspended, as they were in May 1968". But he does not think other people have found solutions either, and he deplores the fact that "it will take at least ten years for the terrible

fright of May to be forgotten": indeed the road to reform seems
to him more difficult than before.

*   *   *

Garaudy, the revisionist philosopher who was expelled from
the French Communist Party for his criticisms of the Soviet
Union, still believes in revolution and, adapting an old concept
of Gramsci's, visualises a new "historic bloc" of workers, intellectuals and technicians. His new revolutionary class which will
be able to prevent the degeneration of the victorious revolution is
at bottom the same as Galbraith's "techno-structure". He is
convinced that the new industry of the cybernetic era is by
nature democratic. "There is an increasing contradiction",
he said, "in demanding the maximum initiative and responsibility from a worker, and at the same time expecting him to
give unconditional obedience to the owner, whether individual
or collective, of the means of production. The workers are
aware of this growing new contradiction, and so too are the
technicians, who are conscious of the contrast between the
logic of profit, which makes them mere executants, and their
own technical, if not yet socialist, rationality." On such ground,
he imagines, the future revolution will plant its roots. But the
traditional working-class Communists do not believe this; they
call him a "computer mystic".

His vision of contemporary society is also contradicted by
the ranks of economists and sociologists who regard "techno-
structure" as already in power, and consider it sensitive to
organisational and productivist ideals but virtually indifferent
to profit motives. Is it thinkable that such a class should really
want to initiate a revolution and adhere to the ideals of self-
management under the guidance of the Communist Party, even
if it were (as Garaudy would wish) a new party completely
different from that of Lenin? Is not the technicians' philosophy
more nearly represented by the slogan recently, and surprisingly, propounded by Mao for the Chinese: "Revolution
must not take the place of production"?

Garaudy himself, moreover, told me that the technicians,
engineers and officials, though they took part in the May revolt,

P

"did not want a revolution; nor, indeed, did the workers and students, as a whole". How could a revolution happen in such circumstances? And even if it did, how could it fail to degenerate?

On this point, which Garaudy solves by maintaining that the technicians would already have conceived a taste for anti-bureaucratic "self-management" before the revolution, even Sartre expressed himself pessimistically. In an interview in the *New Left Review* he said: "If revolution were to triumph in any Western country, there would be a great and constant danger of bureaucratic degeneration. The idea of a total and instantaneous liberation is utopian. We can already foresee some of the limitations and constrictions which would be imposed on a future revolution. But anyone who finds in that a reason for not fighting for revolution and propagating it is simply a counter-revolutionary."

In the end, the prospect of a revolution carried out by the technician masses, under the guidance of repentant ex-Stalinist politicians and intellectuals already convinced that it will degenerate, dissolves in uncertainty; it ends by being entrusted to the improvisations of history, to Sartre's "groups in fusion". The prospects for the post-revolutionary period are equally obscure. Garaudy proposed in effect the Yugoslav economic model (which is more revolutionary than he, and a good deal less concrete). But the Yugoslav model, interesting though it is, may suggest tentative experiments, not revolutionary leaps in the dark.

But the main uncertainty concerns politics, not economics, and it affects all the Western Communist Parties. Garaudy is undoubtedly a sincere intellectual, seriously convinced of the need for a new, less Leninist and less totalitarian party; it was for this reason that he was expelled from the French Communist Party. But for him too "multiplicity of parties" has a curious meaning. I asked him whether he did not think that the Communists' promise of multiplicity would, to make it credible, require a specific rejection of Leninism. He answered: "Not at all. Lenin himself had envisaged collaboration with other parties. But in the situation as it was in Russia, the other parties moved over to counter-revolution, there was a national betrayal. The Russian situation was born of that move by the other parties to counter-revolution." It is a paralysing answer for anyone who recalls the pitiless elimination of the other socialist and revolutionary parties at the hands of the party of Lenin.

Paris

30. Galbraith: The Absurdities of the Society we live in

John Kenneth Galbraith has left literature and returned to economics, at any rate for the time being. He gave me this news himself, and I am delighted, much as I admire his first satyrico-political novel, *The Triumph*. He had started on a second novel: "But I realised", he said, "that I didn't like or dislike the people in it enough to make me write a good book. So I've set it aside." I met Galbraith, whom I had not managed to see in America, in Rome, where he had come for a few days from Switzerland. That is where, for the past fifteen years, he has gone to write his books. Thus he loses touch with politics: "But I have discovered", he said, putting on the poker-face he uses when making a joke, "that I can leave the United States for five or six months without anyone noticing."

This time he was working, he said, on "two little books": the first a systematic and theoretical exposition of "the central nucleus of ideas of modern economics" and the second "a programme of social action", in which he would try to clarify what needs to be done "to escape the tensions of the high production economy" in which we live.

In an hour-and-a-half's conversation in the morning, over a cup of coffee in the breakfast-room of his hotel, Galbraith, sitting in an armchair (he is immensely tall, and even sitting, if he hadn't been stretched out, I should have had to twist my head up to hear him), gave me a sort of preview of his two next books. It was a fascinating experience which I had already had once: in 1966, in his fine Edwardian house beside the university at Harvard, he had talked to me about what later became *The New Industrial State*.

What follows is a report of what he said. His starting-point is the recognition that we had cherished illusions about the power of economic progress. "We imagined", he said, "that by rapidly increasing production all the social problems would be solved. The Communists and the Keynesians thought so", and thus the ideology developed of production as the dominant aim of society. But it happened, and we have realised in the last ten years, Galbraith went on, "that the problems of this model, dominated by the aim of production in itself and for itself, have proved intractable, like the problems of unemployment".

What are the new problems? First of all, inflation: "There is no way of reconciling a high level of employment and price stability except by adopting controls of prices and wages". But these controls have been adopted only for short periods and in an incomplete way, and Galbraith blames the economists for this, for their failure to grasp the importance of the prices and incomes policy.

The second problem is inequality. Here Galbraith referred to the United States and said that to get the Keynesian economic policy accepted "a moral compromise with the Right was necessary on two points: an amnesty for the rich, and the renunciation of nationalisation". The result was that the distribution of income became more unequal. Third problem: "The levels of efficiency are very different. Efficiency is very high in the industries producing automobiles, electrical domestic machines, everything that is sold in the shops; it is low in house-building or mass-transport."

Fourth problem: gigantic size and bureaucracy. "If production is the fundamental objective", Galbraith said, "you get very big productive organisations. The Keynesian revolution, in bringing into operation a full-employment economy, has changed the structure of the system, creating an environment suited to the greatest technological virtuosity and to great productive organisations. Thus power has passed from the consumer to the producer, in alliance with a State which ensures him the conditions favourable for development (armaments industry). Thus we have a highly bureaucratic industry which works together with a highly bureaucratic State."

*   *   *

At this point Galbraith indicated what seem to him to be the fundamental contradictions of the society in which we live, of the "new industrial State" dominated by "techno-structure". "The greatest conflict of our times", he said, "arises from the fact that this system creates a highly educated intellectual proletariat whose individuality is cultivated, but who has then to accustom himself to accepting the discipline of the State and of General Motors" (this discipline, in Galbraith's view, includes such things as the Vietnam war).

"The system", he went on, "thus comes into collision with the people it itself has created. A conflict is created in the factory between discipline and the expression of personality." This is the first big contradiction. The second is that "the system is self-defeating. The unrestricted increase of consumption cannot go on indefinitely. Within five years or less, all the big cities, Rome included, will have to recognise, for example, that free consumption of cars is impossible in urban environments." Third contradiction: "This system involves an enormous use of raw materials and thus creates collateral effects such as the pollution of air or water which can seriously threaten human life. This too arises from the ideological primacy of production."

This is Galbraith's critical analysis of the situation. What remedies does he propose? First, "It would be a grave mistake to regard this situation as revolutionary. A distinction must be made between the discontent that leads to a social action and the discontent that leads to a revolution." Galbraith therefore does not agree with Garaudy, whom he describes as "the most unpredictable of my disciples", about the latter's dream of a revolution carried out by the technicians. Galbraith is thinking instead of a "social action", and his first target is the State: "The State must be regarded as the captive of the system; for Marx, it was the administrative council of the bourgeoisie, today it is the administrative council of the techno-structure. The first problem is to free the State from the control of the techno-structure."

Revolution cannot do this, and is in any case impossible because the trade union movement, inured as it is to industrial discipline, does not want it. "These problems", Galbraith went on, "will be solved within the system itself. The problem is to develop techniques and methods which will allow the individual will to express itself against bureaucratic power. In the United States, the legislative power, Congress, must first be freed from subordination to bureaucratic power; and this can be done, because bureaucratic arrogance has now become unpopular with the electorate." Galbraith was chairman of an organisation called "Referendum '70", and he proposed "to disqualify in the eyes of the electorate, in view of the coming elections, those Congressmen who are subservient to the Pentagon".

Once legislative power has been restored to "the democratic forum", Galbraith said, various other things must be done. The main thing is to cut down, indeed destroy, the myth of production as the supreme aim. Then the "unrestrained drive for consumption" must be brought to an end, and here again his first target is the automobile as a means of urban transport. "When I was a boy in Canada", he said, "nothing thrilled me more than the longing for a car. Today I have two sons of 18 and 19, and they haven't even learnt to drive. They say it would complicate their lives, and they certainly aren't particularly radical." Another thing is nationalisation (Galbraith was speaking here of the United States): the railways, the armaments industry, and the firms that increase social inequality must be nationalised. Lastly, national economics must be freed from the excessive tutelage of the "Zurich bankers" and from the excessive obligations of an open economy.

Galbraith does not include in his plans for reform projects related to the idea of participation. He doesn't believe in it: "The French preoccupation with participation", he says, "is romantic rather than realistic. If scientists or technicians or workers' representatives were added to the administrative councils, a new bureaucracy would be created: unimportant people would merely be added to a body of other unimportant people." Nor does Galbraith believe in nationalisation of factories as a determining factor: "There is no essential difference", he says, "between the big private or State concerns, between General Motors or Fiat or Volkswagen or Renault. It is the type of organisation that deprives the individual members of the techno-structure of power."

What he would like to change is, rather, the dominant ideology of production. "The big concern", he says, "is a marvellously efficient thing for productive ends. It suits perfectly if the main aim is production. It is therefore destined to dominate the society that has this fixed idea of 'production above all'. If we want a society in which the individual can express himself in a different way, if we want there to be external forces which will limit the concern's field of action, then we must emancipate ourselves from this dominant idea of production; and in that way bureaucratic power will also be reduced."

*   *   *

I have reported as faithfully as I could Galbraith's present ideas. But even in a long and intensive talk there are inevitably omissions or gaps in reasoning. To form a real opinion about the new Galbraith we must await his two coming books.* What seems clear to me so far is that Galbraith is seeking a way out of the contradictions of the "new industrial State" in a reform which is political and moral rather than economic and structural.

This seems to me typically American. It would never enter the head of a European to start a reform of the system by going to work on parliamentarians. Faith in elective democracy is obviously still strong in America, a country in which a candidate's personality counts for much more than his membership of a party.

I also observe that Galbraith, in proposing a political and moral reform, recognises that the "new industrial State" is not so monolithic as it seems. Unlike Garaudy, who wants a revolution, unlike the young, who dream of the myths of China and Cuba ("countries sufficiently far off to be romanticised", Galbraith says, "also because they are still pre-bureaucratic States"), unlike Marcuse, who talks of "single-dimensional man", Galbraith considers that reconstruction

---

* His *Guide to Economics, Peace and Laughter* came out in 1971.

can be brought about from within. His social message is therefore not too pessimistic. Now in his middle sixties, John K. Galbraith, economist and writer, "member of the establishment on its least respected fringe" (as he says), is as combative and confident as ever. "Ten years ago", he says, "I used to wonder when my ideas would be listened to. Today everyone is talking about these things. In the history of economic ideas, the next ten years will be the most interesting since the early 'thirties."

Rome

31. Dow, the Reluctant Optimist

Ragnar Frisch, who was one of the two 1969 Nobel Prize winners for Economics, has a favourite story that he tells. The Finance Ministers of all the countries are meeting in Oslo. Each of them explains how his country intends to produce a favourable balance of trade in the coming year. Last of all the Norwegian gets up. Gentlemen, he says, I'm sorry, but we are too small a country to be able to bear so enormous a deficit in the balance of trade. "The international monetary system", said Joan Robinson, who told me this story, "is simply crazy."

This "craziness", as shown in the sequence of crises (gold, sterling, franc, Mark), is one of the reasons which cause some economists to foresee a new great economic collapse like that of 1929. Recently the cries of alarm had multiplied. Kenneth Galbraith prophesied a collapse of the Stock Exchange (even though the economic consequences might not be disastrous as they were in 1929). *Le Monde* expressed the considered opinion that "the desirable and necessary slowing-down of economic activity in Germany, the United States, France and Britain may lead to a world recession". *The Economist* explained how Nixon ran the risk of provoking a recession in America but without checking inflation, with the result of precipitating the country, for the next three to seven years, into a disastrous stop-go cycle like the British. All the experts fear new speculative *coups* from that huge mass of mobile or stateless currency which can move about with great speed from one market to another (25–30 billion Eurodollars alone), and which threatens, so *Le Monde* said, "all the balances of payments and all the currencies".

Two things are making world economy unstable: the increasing difficulty of curbing inflationary processes, as if the economies had become inured to "anti-inflationary drugs"; and the consequent development of economic and monetary inequalities which are at once accentuated by the speculative factor. For these reasons, neither the readjustment of exchanges in 1968–70 (devaluation of sterling and the franc, revaluation of the Mark, devaluation of the dollar), nor the creation of Special Drawing Rights (which increase international liquidity), or the subsequent adoption of measures aimed at making monetary parities more flexible, would make it possible to avoid imminent and serious crises: the "miracle of the 'sixties" is unlikely to be repeated in the 'seventies.

I came to Paris to discuss the reasons and plausibility of these pessimistic forecasts with the OECD, the Organisation for Economic Cooperation and Development, formerly known as the OEEC, to which all the industrialised countries of the West belong; it is a unique observatory for anyone who wants to get an overall picture.

I talked with John Christopher Dow, author of a well-known book on British economy and now Assistant Secretary-General of OECD after an illustrious career as economist and adviser to the British Government. Dow is a quiet man who looks like a don and expresses his opinions with great circumspection. He is a reluctant optimist: he enumerates all the disasters, risks and dangers that are threatening, but in the end he arrives at mainly positive conclusions.

Our talk began with the past. In the 'sixties, the OECD countries had undertaken to make their economy grow by 50 per cent, and this undertaking had been considered by many specialists to be absurd and propagandistic. Now it looked as if it would be "comfortably exceeded": the increase over the decade might well be around 55 rather than 50 per cent.

I asked Dow whether this was exceptional, or whether it could continue in the 'seventies.

He answered: "We are made to grow, and there isn't much that the governments can do to stop growth. It has been going on year after year for about thirty years. It began with the war and continued after the war. There are no clear signs of acceleration, but the impression of the economists is reassuring for the public: the phenomenon will continue at least until the year 2000, and by then the population will be immensely rich. The problem is not whether growth will go on, but how to make use of it. In the last thirty years the production of the industrialised world has at least tripled; if it continues to grow at the rate of 50 per cent in each decade, it will be tripled again before 2000.''

It is easy to calculate that at the present rates of development by 1980 there will be four or five countries (among them Canada and Sweden) which will have overtaken the per capita income of the Americans in 1967—$4,000. Japan will be near to it. The French and Germans will have an average per capita annual income of around $4,000, the Italians around $3,000, the British (unless there is a speeding-up) around $2,500. Meanwhile the Americans will have risen to $5,500. On the supposition of an annual rate of increase of 5·5 per cent, before 2000 A.D. the average Italian will have reached an annual income of around $8,000, or double that of an American in 1967.

This will happen within a bare generation: the machinery of compound interest has revolutionary effects. Within the space of thirty years, when our children are as old as we are today, all-pervading problems such as the permanent semi-poverty of large strata of the population will have been over-come: every manual worker will live as a white-collar worker lives today, so to speak. In the course of those thirty years, each one of the OECD countries will reach or surpass the point at which, so Dow said, "every addition to income will be over and above the margin of essential needs. This will make possible a much greater choice" between the various kinds of public or private consumption.

These are the forecasts of prudent economists. What, then, about the fears of serious crises? Dow, reluctantly, didn't believe in them. He did think there would be a slowing-down in the American economy and an increase in unemployment in the U.S.A.: "If you want to call that a recession", he said, "it will probably happen. But if it goes too far they can easily correct it. I believe it's a mistake to think we are living on a razor's edge."

Dow knows perfectly well that the efforts of governments to regulate the economy are largely imperfect, and that "certain deviations of the ship from the right course are caused more by untimely jerks of the steering-wheel than by gusts of wind". "But", he added, "it is foolish to paint a picture of vast unpredictable forces. I don't mean to say that there are no more dangers ahead; there are always events that can't be foreseen. But I think that unless we go very wrong indeed—and I don't believe that will happen—we shall be in time to take the necessary corrective steps before it is too late. We may make mistakes, but they won't be disastrous mistakes."

And what about the international monetary situation? "The abscess we have had ought with a bit of luck to be on the way to recovery", Dow said. No one at OECD thinks that the difficult phase of the past years is completely overcome. But it is thought that the "demonetisation" of gold and the various adjustments of monetary parities should guarantee greater stability in the coming years. Other currencies might run into difficulties, and the dollar might go through phases of weakness; but the increase in liquidity as a result of the Special Drawing Rights, and the greater flexibility in the rates of exchange, should make acute crises less likely.

"In any case", Dow said, "one of the lessons of the last twenty years is that, in spite of all the Finance Ministers' fears, in spite of all the talk about monetary crises and all the panic, economic growth has continued very regularly. The financial disturbances haven't strangled development."

Many other economists I have met in Europe on the whole share this calculated optimism. Uri simply says: "I don't believe in the great crisis. We have learnt too much about how to avoid it." Harrod: "I am optimistic, thanks to the American negroes. Thanks to them, the American leaders can't do what they would have done twelve years ago under Eisenhower: they can't allow themselves a recession, which would give rise to disastrous unemployment among the negroes. The negroes are the safeguard of world economy. Thanks to them, the world is in a much better state." And Kaldor: "There is no reason why what happened in the 'sixties shouldn't be repeated in the 'seventies" (provided, he adds, that there are successive "competitive" monetary devaluations).

Joan Robinson, who regards this monetary system as "crazy and very bad" because it facilitates the useless game of speculation (though, on the other hand, "a system of fluctuating exchanges would create impossible problems"), thinks that "we shall end by reaching a compromise between the various needs, and the situation will be better. We shall continue to muddle through".

I have set out the anxieties of the pessimists and the reasons of the optimists. These very different views nevertheless all show clearly how close the relationship is between the internal evolution of the individual economies and the international set-up as a whole. Internal problems (and first of all inflation) continually give rise to disturbances in the relations between the various economies. On the other hand, in a world like ours in which national economies are increasingly open, the prosperity of many countries depends on a high volume of trade exchanges, and consequently international disturbances can have tremendous internal repercussions. This means that the problems of each one of the great industrial countries— Italy among them—are the problems of all: in the long run, the progress of each one will depend on the success of efforts to coordinate the individual economic policies. The increasing unification of world economy, by now a fact, calls for a corresponding unification of law: otherwise, serious disasters may lie ahead.

It is to be hoped that they will be avoided and that economic development will continue; but all the problems that development carries with it will also continue to manifest themselves and perhaps to grow worse. "Modern society is terribly complicated", said Dow, "and it calls for great discipline and order in the productive process. But it is asking too much of people to expect them always to be disciplined, orderly, and ready to collaborate. It is human that this system should have its crises; but to me it seems more important that there is now much less absolute poverty. However horrid and complicated our society may seem, it is all the same better than it was."

The problems of prosperity are very real: but who would want to go back to the problems that arose from lack of resources: unemployment, poverty, hunger, ignorance? We can console ourselves with these considerations as we confront the new technical and social problems of adaptation. "Rapid economic progress", Dow concluded, "creates great difficulties: urban overcrowding, pollution of air and water, destruction of natural surroundings. These will be the dominating problems of the century's last thirty years."

Paris

32. Carli: Money and Society

I have before me Guido Carli, Governor of the Bank of Italy: and I have in mind a sentence in Walter Heller's latest *Newsletter* which reached me a few days ago from Minneapolis, in which Heller, the economist friend of Kennedy and father of the long boom, praises the "sophisticated and flexible directors" of Italy's Central Bank who have "facilitated an expansion of unprecedented length and vigour". It is nine o'clock in the morning. Carli has been in his big dark study for over an hour. The desk is littered with books and papers. On a little table the black screen of a close-circuit television lights up every so often to show some lines of green writing: these are the financial data transmitted from the Bank's central electronic brain. By pressing the knobs on a keyboard the Governor has at his disposal all the immense mass of data of every description stored up by the computer.

Carli put down the book he was reading as I came in, a first work by one of the brilliant young and less well-known Italian economists. Our conversation started from that point—from the very high degree of proficiency of the new generation of economists, who are possibly better known and appreciated abroad than in Italy. The universities have been undergoing upheavals, but all the same there are some very good economic brains there. Carli told me that all the universities were being presented with the latest econometric model of the Italian economy, prepared by the Bank of Italy; it was an important model, "because it will serve to concentrate the economists' interest on the problems posed by the correlation between real economic phenomena and monetary phenomena".

It is upon this correlation that the "sophisticated and flexible" mind of Guido Carli is concentrating today; and this was the central theme of our conversation. It was not so much the complex and difficult architecture of the international monetary system but the economic reality behind it that Carli wanted to explain to me.

What connection is there, then, between the two? "Let us consider the monetary crises of these recent years", said Carli. "They have been due essentially to two causes. The first is the very high degree of interconnection between the national economies, at all levels, mercantile, monetary, or financial. The crisis of the monetary system, from this point of view, is the product of the system's own success: interdependence and interconnections have far surpassed the most optimistic expectations and even though some relics of exchange control remain here and there, the unity of the system can be said to have been realised." But this makes it all the more difficult to make this machinery with its different and interrelated parts function when within the individual economies constant imbalances arise between demand and productive capacity.

Here we come to the second cause of the monetary crises. "It is becoming increasingly difficult", Carli said, "to adapt institutions to the evolution of our societies. The social groups within those societies are seeking to satisfy aspirations which we do not manage to coordinate in a convincing way. The social groups do not find in the existing system ways in which these aspirations can be met. The demand (and I am thinking not only of wage claims but also of the immense social needs) always tends, in the short term, to outstrip the system's productive possibilities. The result of these imbalances is that our economies are constantly subject to inflationary pressures."

"We do not succeed", he went on, "through the conscious actions of the various groups, the firms, trade unions, and State organisations, in carrying out a policy of regulation of demand by fiscal means or an incomes policy. Thus the balance is impaired, and this is shown in the rise of prices. How is the balance to be restored? In all the countries, recourse is had to a monetary policy. But a policy of this kind produces deep lacerations, because there are rigid areas in the system, such as the volume of public expenditure. A monetary policy from its very nature bites harder into other sectors—to begin with, into private investments."

Societies in a rapid state of advance, such as Italy, are especially prone to stronger pressures from the various social groups. "It is in these societies", Carli said, "that one is increasingly aware of the inadequacy of any recognised authority capable of reconciling the different demands: this is partly because our economies have shown themselves unable to provide adequate answers to the new social needs. The shepherd who drove his flocks along the wellworn tracks from the Abruzzi to Lucania had far fewer worries than he would have if later on he became a factory worker in Milan. Because of our inability to coordinate and take conscious decisions to adapt demand to the productive potential, we are suffering from sharp price increases, and these in turn let loose forces that prejudice the capacities for ordered development. So recourse to the monetary system becomes necessary. Unable rationally to regulate the volume of incomes, we end up by regulating it by reducing employment. Thus the balance is restored—but in what I can only call an uncivilised way."

Thus Carli explained to me in condensed form the main essentials of his economic thinking. Its nucleus is a lucid understanding of the limitations of a monetary policy which, so far as Italy is concerned, has nevertheless won praises throughout the world because it "has made possible an unprecedented expansion"—"for the time being", Carli commented drily when I reminded him of these successes. (Italy's economy was in fact to experience a serious crisis in 1970–72.)

Let us now follow the thread of his reasoning in two different directions. The first concerns the international monetary system. Carli prefaced his remarks by saying, "What is in crisis is modern society, not the international monetary system. That is only a gigantic amortisator of the shocks produced from end to end of the system. How is it to be made to function?"

To begin with, Carli rejects Rueff's thesis of a return to the gold standard. "It is doubtful", he says, "whether it ever functioned, but anyway it no longer functions today. Marx, in his day, had grave doubts about the advisability of entrusting the economy to this exogenous factor. It might work all right when the adjustments it caused to the level of employment were accepted without question. Today it is unthinkable that the mere fact of transferring some bars of gold from the vaults of one bank to another can compel the leaders of any country to adopt troublesome constrictions." So what is to be done? The system can finance imbalances by means of bilateral credits (e.g. "swap" agreements) or multilateral credits (e.g. Special Drawing Rights); or it can accept adjustments in the rates of exchange.

In recent years both these things have been done, and Carli is not dissatisfied with the results. "The international monetary system", he said, "has shown that it can put these adjustments into effect without ever breaking the thread of international exchange. Moving from 'crisis' to 'crisis', we have, in fact, put into operation a regime in which the volume of inter-national exchange has increased to a remarkable degree. We have coped with situations which in the 'thirties would have broken up the system, throwing it back on to segmentation of the markets. Modern society is no longer prepared to accept the prison of national frontiers. And this immense international exchange has been an essential factor in growth and in tech-nological innovation, carrying the impetus of innovation even into the smallest-sized economies. The results have been almost incredible when we consider that all the economies are on the move, and that the movements do not coincide."

These, then, are the conspicuous virtues of the monetary system. But Carli is also conscious of its limitations. "It must guarantee continuity of communication between markets that are subject to continuous tensions, to intense vibrations. Supposing all the economies get into a chaotic state, how can you hope to have an ordered monetary system? These pheno-mena have to be looked at from the angle of the economic structure, not from that of the superstructure that the international monetary system represents."

So we return to the structure. "At the basis of everything, what is there?", asked Carli, "There is the fact that modern society has not yet evolved the formula for producing an authority capable of coordinating the social groups. I am talking, of course, about an accepted authority, not authoritarianism."

I asked how this authority could develop. Carli answered: "First of all there must be much wider information about facts, decisions, and their motivations. Administrative decisions that affect the lives of the community are open to attack when no good reasons are given for them, even though they may be legally unexceptionable. The reasons must be known and accepted. That means that we must establish—but we haven't yet done so—a system of real participation in these decisions that today explode suddenly over people's heads." I asked him whether a more involved participation in economic decisions by the social groups, the firms and the trade unions, might perhaps require institutional changes. "I can't say", Carli answered, "but I'm not sure that they may not be needed."

I do not know whether Carli is very hopeful that these "adaptations" can be carried out with the necessary speed. He is not pessimistic; he explains insistently that the economic imbalances he is talking about occur in the short term: "I set out from the premise that in the long term, or in the course of two or three decades, mankind will find solutions for all these difficulties: and the problem will no longer be the economy, but the peace of the spirit." But in the short term, if I understood him rightly, he considers it best to prepare for a succession of crises (in the limited sense in which he defined them, of something that "does not break the thread" of international exchange and growth). He expects the alternation to continue of inflationary periods and monetary corrections which provoke deflationary phenomena: "This discontinuity is hard to avoid", he says.

Clearly, in his view, it could only be avoided if action were taken about the economic, political and social structures rather than the "monetary superstructures"; if a new "accepted authority" were to be created, fruit of that much-talked-of participation, which would be capable of regulating the economic and social forces. I asked him whether there were signs of a greater awareness of this problem. "I couldn't answer that," he replied. "There are too many signs pointing both ways, not only in our own country but everywhere. The causes of crises are always to be sought, at bottom, in the conscience of individuals. If we are coming into a period in which unrest becomes a permanent element in the individual countries, and if the economic vibrations arising therefrom were to penetrate to the whole international system. . . . " He left the argument in suspense. But he resumed: "I am convinced that a process of adjustment is going on in Italy which will contribute towards improving this country. What is needed is to get people to discuss things in a more reasonable way. But these adjustments will continue to be difficult."

Carli concluded his reflections by reverting to his theme of modern society, where he clearly had in mind, in particular, the uncertainties arising from the trade union agitations in Italy. "In the society we all hope for", he said, "everyone will have to do his duty, like Nelson's sailors at Trafalgar. But he must begin to do his duty now. This means that we must not seek the easy agreement, we must not show favour to anyone. A Governor of the Central Bank must do his duty too, which is to defend monetary stability. This is his job, and it is well that that should be known: there must be some elements of certainty in the system. It is for others to draw conclusions from this knowledge, and, if they wish, to offer alternatives and substitutes for a monetary policy."

Rome

33. Tinbergen: The Nobel Test

About two months before my journey among the economists came to an end, I had decided to conclude it by interviewing the Dutchman Jan Tinbergen, a great figure in the contemporary economic scene. But I never managed to reach him because he was constantly travelling about the world on behalf of the United Nations. By the time I did see him he had got the Nobel prize, which was awarded in 1969 for the first time to economic science; Tinbergen was chosen as the first Nobel prizewinner in economics, together with the Norwegian Ragnar Frisch, for the work they did on econometry more than thirty years ago.

Since then Tinbergen, who is now in his late sixties, has been concerned with many other things: he was the creator of planning in Holland, and is one of the chief experts on developing countries. He came to talk on that subject to an economic congress in Turin, where at last I met him. I began by asking him a question that was not included in my original plan for the interview: "Has the time really come for economics to win a Nobel prize? Have economists the qualifications to pass the Nobel test?" He answered, "Yes, I think so. This prize seems to me to be a recognition of the fact that economics has become quite a bit of a science."

Tinbergen, despite his Nobel prize and his recognised international authority (he had been for many years chairman of the UN Committee on Planning and Development, and is the father of the world plan for economic development that the UN is launching in the 1970s), is a modest, cautious man, not given to snap judgements. He doesn't say economics is a science, merely that it is "quite a bit of a science". All his opinions during the interview were qualified and objective. Like Frisch,

Tinbergen is a professed socialist; but he is one of the most anti-ideological men I know. The American Paul Samuelson (who was himself also to win a Nobel prize in 1970) said of the two new prizewinners: "These two socialists, by helping us to acquire the necessary knowledge to make a mixed economy function, have done more to save the freedom of the world than all the *laissez-faire* ideologists."

Jan Tinbergen can be said to be the main theoretician of the "mixed economy" in which we live. He is increasingly convinced of the truth of the theory, which he was among the first to expound more than ten years ago in a celebrated article in *Soviet Studies*,* that the Western and the Communist countries are converging towards forms of "mixed economy", and he thinks the convergence of these opposing systems will come near to the "optimal model of the economy". As he explained to me: "The optimal order is a complex of institutions, such as the markets, the State, the local authorities, the trade unions, and education, which together should maximise wellbeing." The optimal system does not yet exist. But Tinbergen, this shy, quiet, reserved man, is sincerely convinced that we are on the right road towards achieving it, step by step.

I asked him, "What are the typical, essential features of a mixed economy?" He answered: "Two things. First of all, we have discovered, in theory and practice, that a certain number of tasks are performed better by the community than by private, or anyway independent, concerns. But it is no less essential that other activities should be left to autonomous units. Welfare economy also needs competition."

Tinbergen explained in theoretical terms what are the conditions which make it advisable to entrust certain activities to public bodies: in particular, those activities which have strong "external effects", in other words which can improve or worsen the condition of persons or concerns extraneous to the activities in question. The theoretical principles have practical applications which vary from country to country; but they provide the rational justification for the phenomenon, common

* April 1961, Vol. 12, No. 4.

to all Western countries, of the enlargement of the State's functions. Tinbergen does not think this harmful, on the contrary, he regards it as favourable to the better functioning of a market economy.

"The State", he said, "must intervene in those markets which are by their nature unstable, such as agriculture. But it seems to me that the great majority of industrial markets are not unstable, and do not call for State intervention. These markets are useful, because they ensure the uniformity of prices which is necessary for the welfare economy to achieve the optimal position." There may be other ways of achieving this end (Tinbergen mentioned, with a mixture of interest and scepticism, the "electronic market" of the Russian Fedorenko); but the essential thing is that the mixed system functions.

"Experience shows", Tinbergen said, "that the mixed economy works better. Since the war the mixed economies have done very well, growing at a rate of about 5 per cent per annum, or much more than when they were freer economies before the war. In spite of heavy taxes and the increasing influence of the trade unions, they have grown more rapidly; and in addition the economic cycles have been kept in control. These are the two great results that have been achieved."

Tinbergen is enough of a socialist to put himself the problem of private ownership; but he does so in an unprejudiced way. "When someone says that income from private capital is unjustifiable", he said, "my answer is, if private activity can be shown to be more efficient, then a compromise must be worked out." And he went on:

"Today the debate about ownership is not the most important thing. What is ownership? As Gunnar Adler-Karlsson has shown in his book on *Functional Socialism*, ownership is only a combination of powers of decision: the freedom to decide what to produce, what prices to ask, how many people to employ and for how long, how much to pay them, how to use the profits, and so on. A hundred years ago the owner-entrepreneur decided all these things. Then, bit by bit, this combination of powers was reduced by law and the evolution of society.

"Today, the mixed economy is mixed from this point of view

too. It is no longer true that ours is a private economy, as the Communists say. Our business concerns are only superficially private. In reality, our private ownership has been so whittled down and restricted that certain essential functions in it have become socialised. For example, today the State takes on an average half the profits, and trade union agreements or the law restrict other powers of the owner. It is no longer true, therefore, that there is a fundamental difference between ownership in our mixed system and ownership in the Communist system: our ownership is no longer so private." (And Communist ownership, so Yugoslav revisionism maintains, has never really been social ownership.)

Tinbergen therefore says he sees "no particular urgency" about changes in this field. The mixed economy requires that modifications of the system should not go beyond certain limits. Not only must it continue to be a market which will guarantee the efficiency of the independent concerns (and these concerns must be prevented from eliminating competition by forming trusts); but also the machinery of "industrial democracy", or of "participation" as it is called today, must not be pushed to extremes.

The Dutch economist is convinced that "beneath the surface" some progress is being made towards industrial democracy, and he thinks that further advances must be made in that direction. He believes, for example, that firms should discuss with the workers' councils such questions as the dismissal of workers or mergers with other companies. But he cites works by American and French writers to show that participation must have some limits set to it: "It has been found", he says, "that in cases where there is very little participation, productivity is low. When participation is increased to a certain extent, productivity increases. But if it is increased still further, productivity begins to fall again. I don't think one can aspire to 100 per cent participation. A middle course must be found, a synthesis" (the Yugoslav economists, as we have seen, hold a different view).

Although Tinbergen thinks that "the structures of our mixed economy are sound and function satisfactorily", he believes they will continue to evolve. He would like to see a more egalitarian distribution of incomes, and he deplores the fact that in recent times "there has not been more progress towards a greater equality", as is shown by research done in Sweden. He would like to increase taxes on inheritance and lower those on income but he would tax accumulated wealth more severely. He considers that only by means of such reforms will it be possible to achieve an incomes policy, persuading the trade unions to renounce excessive wage increases which produce inflation.

If I interpret Tinbergen rightly, these reforms should not, however, destroy the essential feature of the mixed economy: the delicate balance between autonomous initiative of competing firms and communitary action. Experience and science, theory and practice, justify, to his mind, this complex and difficult model which is being carried out in the West.

Talking with Tinbergen one realises, however, that the most urgent problems, in his view, are not those concerned with the greater perfecting of the mixed economy, but other problems relating to the creation of an "international order", both in the military and in the social and economic spheres. "There is absolute need", he says, "for a minimum of supranational organisation to which a part of sovereignty is yielded." He argues vigorously that it is in the interest of the rich countries to make concrete sacrifices to help the poor countries to grow more rapidly, thus preventing the increasing difference between peoples from reaching explosive dimensions.

But Tinbergen is not a utopian, and he does not ignore the reluctance of the rich to give. He confines himself to explaining insistently that, from the technical point of view, and if the developed countries assume in the 1970s the definite obligations he suggests, an increase of 6–7 per cent per annum in the income of the backward countries should be perfectly possible to achieve. But will his voice be listened to? Tinbergen answers: "I am no prophet, and I don't make prophecies. But I believe I can say what ought to be done. I repeat the maxim of William the Silent, founder of the Low Countries: you don't have to believe you will succeed to go on trying. And I say to the sceptics: this scepticism of yours is highly unproductive."

Looking at the immense problems of the impoverished part of the world, and dreaming of his "world plan of development", Tinbergen is sure that economics is still a key-science of our times. He recognises that "material prosperity is not everything, for human happiness depends not only on actual income but on the system of relations with your neighbours". But he has, instinctively, no great sympathy for those Western intellectuals who, from the secure pedestal of their high incomes, regard the economic problem as a thing of the past and condemn or deride the production-and-consumer mentality.

"We must not forget," he observes, "that a large part of the world is still so poor that economic questions retain a tremendous importance. Even in our own countries there are many social groups that would be happier if they had a higher income: the incomes of intellectuals are not typical. With the population explosion that is going on in the developing countries, economic problems will remain with us for many decades to come. Economics still retains its full usefulness."

Turin

34. *The Debate Goes On*

Looking back on my long journey among the economists, and before giving the green light to the English and American editions of this book, I decided to address once more a few of the economists whom I had met: some important economic events of the more recent past seemed to demand further comment.

An international monetary crisis, more serious than all the preceding ones, had seemed to threaten, during the second half of 1971, that huge flow of goods among countries on which so much of today's economic expansion is based. At the same time, not only the United States but also quite a few countries of the Old World had experienced a new kind of economic disease, or at least a new variation of an old one, for which the term "stagflation" had been coined. New economic policies of wages and prices control had once more been adopted or attempted, on a scale not known before. How were we to assess all these events? What lessons must the "science" of economics and economic policy draw from such developments? I submitted these questions to some of the economists I had interviewed including the first and second winners of the Nobel Prize for Economics, whom I had originally chosen, with some foresight, as my last and first interviewees. Here are some of the answers.

Let us begin with "stagflation", and let us hear first, once more, Professor Paul Samuelson of the MIT. How did Professor Samuelson view the economic future as seen in the summer of 1972? "Recent experience in the United States", this is what he writes to me, "does not make one more optimistic on the problem of 'stagflation'. Since 1969 the Nixon Administration has engineered a considerable degree of slack in our system; but never has so little in the way of inflation abatement been realised in return for so much. The fact that President Nixon, on 15 August 1971, had to throw away his old-game plan of 'gradualism' in favour of the rather extreme measure of direct wage-price controls is testimony to how disappointing the American Phillips-curve dilemma has been."

What about the economic experience in the rest of the world? "As I look abroad", says Professor Samuelson, "I seem to see the same unhappy story. It is a duty of modern economic science to admit that no jury of experts can today agree on a proper 'incomes policy'. We can agree on proper fiscal and proper monetary policies."

To sum up: "I conclude from this that in the coming decade of the 1970s, America will go through bouts of creeping inflation, contrived slow-downs of the stop-go variety, and intermittent flirtations with direct wage-price controls. We can live and grow in such an environment, but one must admit that it reflects a blemish in the post-Keynes economy".

So far, Professor Samuelson: not a pessimist by nature, quite the reverse; but a realist, who seems to admit that there are limits today beyond which the science of economics cannot claim to be moving on safe ground; there are difficulties through which economists and governments can only hope to "muddle through", with a pinch of common sense and a pinch of luck; certainly not as conquerors of a new world of safety and plenty for all.

From Hawaii, via Chicago, I received a remarkably similar opinion from Professor Samuelson's chief American "opponent", the head of the great monetarist school of America, Milton Friedman. We had last met, for a couple of days in September 1971, on the shores of Lake Maggiore, at Stresa. In the hall of one of the great "fin de siècle" hotels we had discussed the then rampant monetary crisis as well as the Italian economic difficulties and the latest developments in the economy of Eastern Europe (this last being the theme of the conference in which we were both taking part). Not even such a powerful array of subjects had been sufficient to repress the inexhaustible zest of Professor Friedman, while we sipped some Italian "aperitivo", more often than not forgetting our glasses in the heat of the discussion. He was then no optimist about the possibility of reconstructing the international monetary system around some structure of fixed parities. How did the new situation look to him, eight months later, seen from the other end of the world?

If one were to sum it up in three words, I would say: "Still not good". First, the international monetary crisis: "This", Professor Friedman wrote to me, "has been an inevitable outcome of the defects of the Bretton Woods system", which, "despite the intent of its founders, produced rigidity and instability in exchange rates, rather than moderate flexibility and stability." The crisis itself "served a very desirable purpose by formally certifying the death of Bretton Woods". But the Smithsonian agreement of December 1971, while restoring the form of the Bretton Woods arrangements, "lacks its substance, because of the end of even the formal convertibility of the dollar into gold: it cannot, in my opinion, last". What then can we expect? "The outcome", says Professor Friedman, "is likely to be much more frequent changes in official exchange rates by smaller amounts, with occasional intervals of floating exchange rates" (which is exactly what happened to the pound a few weeks after this opinion had been written). Looking to a medium-term future, Friedman says: "No new internationally agreed arrangement, in my opinion, will be reached; but rather the present effective dollar standard will continue more or less indefinitely—with all the participants, including the U.S.A., refusing to admit that that is what it is."

Let us now turn to the second part of Professor Friedman's views sent to me from distant Hawaii—stagflation. This is where the chief monetarist's views and expectations coincide to an unexpectedly large extent with those of Professor Samuelson: not in the analysis of the causes of it (on the contrary, one can recognize a distinct "I told you so" flavour in Professor Friedman's opinion), but in the forecast for the American economy in the 'seventies. Professor Friedman says: "With respect to 'stagflation' in many countries, that is the delayed effect of inflationary policies. These policies appeared to stimulate economies so long as the public was fooled into believing that inflation was temporary. Once the public catches on, the game is up. Further stimulus can only come from more rapid inflation and even then only so long as the public does not catch on. Price and wage controls are an evasion of the issue. They will for a time distort the economies, and will then collapse. Yet, given the political situation, I shall not be surprised if the next decade sees continued attempts to inflate through monetary and fiscal means, on the one hand, and to repress the inflation through direct controls, on the other."

A more precise and short-term forecast follows: "For the United States, a sharp confrontation is likely to come in 1973, when resources are again fully utilised and yet inflationary pressure is still strong. Political pressures explain President Nixon's reversal of policy in August 1971. On economic grounds, I believe that reversal was a great mistake, that it slowed down economic expansion without contributing to halting inflation, and that we shall have to suffer from its heritage for many years".

Bearing in mind what Professor Friedman hoped (or even expected) to get from President Nixon—a real fundamental change in economic policy, similar to that originated by President Roosevelt—Nixon's conversion to the policies of direct controls was obviously a great disappointment to the head of the Chicago school: it was not surprising that he should seem even less confident than the head of Boston's neo-classic school, Professor Samuelson, on its possible effects in the 'seventies.

*   *   *

Economists move around the world all the time: having heard from the "Chicago wizard" from Hawaii, I received an answer—brief, dry, and effective, as is his style—by one of the "grand old men" of English economics from Claremont, California. Sir Roy Harrod, Keynes's friend and biographer (whom I had first met in his lovely country house in Norfolk, on a fresh damp early summer day, and then listened to him again during a passionate monetary debate at the Johns

Hopkins Bologna Center), views the world of economics, from sunny California, with a distinctly benevolent look. How does he assess the present state of the Western economy? "I would say", he writes to me, "that the present state is fairly good. The need for a prices and incomes policy has now been recognised, both in the U.S.A. and the U.K.". What lessons must the science of economics draw from recent political events? "There is no 'science' of economics", says Sir Roy. "Economic policy will continue to limp along, but I guess that its mistakes will not be large enough to interfere with natural forces of expansion." Comforted by these words of wisdom, let us continue, our "mini-journey" among the economists. As we shall see, moving now to Europe, the talk is still all the time of wages and prices policy, of the pros and cons of direct controls, of the social and political implications of such a policy: but Samuelson's disbelief in it and Friedman's active dislike of it give way, as we move over to the other side of the Atlantic (as of course Sir Roy's words from California had anticipated), to a much more positive attitude.

Let us begin with one of the creators of the European Economic Community, Pierre Uri. He writes to me from Paris: "Monetary restraint, as was tried by the Republican Administration (in the U.S.A.) and by other conservative Governments, had produced what the Keynesians could expect: a slow-down in activity and employment rather than in the price rises. It would be a pity", says Uri, "if the U.S.A. were again to revert to it."

Was then President Nixon's later attempt to impose direct controls a correct choice? "The prices and incomes policy which the President has tried", says the French economist, "lacked any general principle and created too much uncertainty." Uri goes on to explain in a few lines the "general theory" of an incomes policy, at which he has been working for quite some time. He says: "In the U.S.A., and even more so in Europe, a completely new concept of incomes policy and an original set of instruments to implement it are urgent. Money incomes cannot be kept within the limit of real resources unless inequalities are progressively reduced. But this cannot be done by decree. Inequalities in incomes stem from disparities in structures. The differences in wages in the same countries according to areas, to industries, to firms, are enormous. Regional policies which develop the necessary infrastructures and give temporary forms of aid to overcome the external diseconomies are necessary to help backward or declining regions to catch up their arrears. An adjustment policy, as was promised in the European Community as well as in the American Trade Expansion Act, must dispose of large sources of funds. And credit policies must more and more be geared to the birth and growth of new firms, which will compete with the long-established ones and reduce their monopoly margins."

This is how Pierre Uri ends his "oeconomia in nuce": "This narrowing of the various gaps which plague our economies would go hand in hand with a new type of town and country planning, aiming at the development of medium-sized cities instead of the tentacular megalopoles. This new over-all policy for balanced growth would thus at the same time represent a genuine and effective social policy and a tool for the conservation of the environment."

It is a long road from an attempt to control inflation or "stagflation" through incomes and prices controls to the "over-all policy for balanced growth" recommended by Pierre Uri: but do not let us make the mistake of thinking that this is a utopian way of looking at things. The picture which Uri draws with bold strokes hides a whole series of "ironlinks" in logical thinking. One could, I believe, rephrase it more or less like this: you cannot avoid stagflation with purely monetary and fiscal policies; you must have a prices-and-incomes policy to do that. But in a democratic society you cannot have a prices-and-incomes policy unless you progressively reduce inequalities in incomes. And in order to do that you must radically modify, through an "over-all policy for balanced growth", the uneven social and economic structures which are behind it all, and you can do that only through regional policies, regional planning, development policies, all within the framework of a general plan for balanced growth: this is where the failures of the economic policies of the 'sixties lead you.

257

R

The message from France may seem very difficult to implement: but one cannot deny the Gallic clarity of the reasoning behind it. One can also easily sense the much stronger social and political tensions of Europe and of France (one of the only two "provinces" of the Western realm, together with Italy, where the workers' movement is still in large part Communist-orientated), which ineluctably lead economists from a purely "economic" view of economic affairs to a much finer sensitivity for the wider socio-political implications of economic policy.

A very similar view comes (still remaining on "the Continent") from Professor Tinbergen, writing to me from The Hague. This is the voice of a Social Democrat: and once again, the point of departure of this brief but profound analysis is wages policy. Once again, the problem of all problems—how to apply a wages restraint—is seen in all its social implications. In order to apply a certain economic policy which is considered necessary for purely economic and theoretical reasons, a certain social policy *must* be applied: at least, in European political conditions.

Answering my "simple question" on "the present state of Western economy and stagflation", Tinbergen writes to me: "The subject is too vast to deal with in all detail. Let me therefore stress one aspect of it that may not always receive sufficient attention. One of the roots of wage demands is a degree of dissatisfaction with income distribution as a whole. Wage policy in isolation is not a very efficient means of attaining less inequality in income distribution. In a general way, less inequality among incomes can be lastingly attained only if demand for and supply of the various types of labour, from highly qualified to unskilled, are in balance. My impression is that there is still too small a supply of highly qualified and too high a supply of unskilled labour. We may have to see to it that more people find their way towards schools and training appropriate for them."

Educational policy seems to be, says Tinbergen, a necessary element of political economy today. And not only that. The Dutch Nobel Prize winner continues: "Apart from this educational effort, higher taxes on estates have a place: they will bring us closer to the 'equal opportunities' which we so often discuss but which are still far from being attained. For a better understanding of the effect of education on income distribution expanded research on this effect is required. Recently increased attention has been given to this subject by a group of American economists with whom I am in correspondence now."

European economists, as we have seen, are very keenly aware of what is behind the wages pressure of our times: the widespread desire for equality in the masses (or, should we say, the whole trend towards equality of Western society, ever since the French Revolution?). This reminds me of what Raymond Aron was telling me in a recent conversation in Paris: "Modern societies are, by their very nature, unstable societies, because they are changing societies, and also because they never wholly achieve their democratic and egalitarian ideals: they are torn apart by the very liberties which they enjoy. But one must not allow oneself to be too deeply impressed by political tumults. As Montesquieu said, echoing Machiavelli, 'it is when I see no tumults in the streets that I worry'."

So what Machiavelli called a "Repubblica tumultuaria" (he claimed that Rome had been a really free State just because it was a "Repubblica tumultuaria") still stays with us: the economic contemporary manifestation of a "tumultuary Republic" being an excess of wages pressure and the impossibility of achieving wages control without deep structural reforms: so say Uri, Tinbergen, and a large majority of Western Europe's economists of democratic feelings. The same phenomenon, seen from America, can be described in a detached and coldly matter-of-fact way which in Europe would be inconceivable. From the Brookings Institution in Washington, Gary Fromm, one of the creators of the great Brookings econometric model of the American economy, in a letter to me describes the problem of stagflation thus: "It has been due to erosion of competition in product and labour markets, the use of emulation and comparability for setting wages and prices, and the expectation that Government will act to prevent or offset any sizeable reductions in output, employment and income. Unemployment insurance, welfare payments, and other transfers all tend to reduce the cyclical sensitivity of wages and prices. Thus, when product and labour demand slackens, workers are not prone to lower their wages demands, whether they are employed or not. The reduction or elimination of stagflation will require a reversal of labour and business concentration of power, better government forecasting and fiscal and monetary policy management, and more efficient and effective labour and product markets. Until we get these in abundant measure, we will be saddled with intervention, incomes policies and direct or quasi controls or limits on wages, prices and other factor costs". Of course, if this return to the dry logic of the pure market were impossible in present-day society (can one seriously think about doing away with the unions, with social security, with business concentration and all that?), it is quite possible that we must learn to live with "stagflation": unless we move on, as Uri and Tinbergen suggest, towards much greater "structural" changes.

Let us end this rapid excursion through today's main economic problems of the West by moving over to England. There we can hear two more voices of great authority: Lord Balogh from Oxford, Joan Robinson from Cambridge. Let us first listen to their opinions on the monetary crisis. Milton Friedman, as we recall, was forecasting the continuation of a "dollar standard", with more flexibility in official exchange rates and "floating bouts" in various countries. Joan Robinson undoubtedly shares the view that the dollar will maintain its central position in the international monetary system, but likes it less than Friedman. Mrs Robinson writes: "Stability of the international monetary system, with fixed exchange rates, requires every national economy to follow the rule of maintaining an outflow on capital account equal to, but not greater than, its surplus on income account, except for the country whose currency provides the international medium of exchange; it can maintain an outflow greater than its surplus to the extent that international monetary balances are growing."

Having thus reminded us of the general theory behind the

"fixed rates dollar standard", Mrs Robinson goes on to say: "In recent years, the U.S.A. (with wars, 'aid', and overseas investment) has been maintaining outflows in excess of what the international monetary system can comfortably accept. President Nixon's policy seems to be to attempt to build up a surplus on commercial transactions to match the outflow, instead of curbing the outflow to match the surplus. This is very unlikely to be successful, but the process of trying to do it, by depreciating the dollar against other currencies, using political pressure to increase exports and protection to curtail imports, puts the rest of the trading world into grave difficulties."

Which leads Mrs Robinson to conclude (though this curtly philosophical summing up refers also to the general state of economics today): "These developments show how little the world has learned from past experience and how far short-sighted political expediency dominates over economic enlightenment."

Should President Nixon read these judgements and feel hurt by them, he could, I think, find some consolation in the opinion that follows. It also comes from England, and it very neatly puts the weight on the other foot—the European one. Lord Balogh writes to me: "The so-called monetary crisis is the result of the continental countries' schizophrenia between wishing to do down the dollar and force deflation on the U.S.A. They want to maintain employment in the world, none of them apart from America is willing to enforce an incomes policy, yet a sharp devaluation of the dollar, if successful, would of course mean a ruinous change in the balance of payments of the rest of the world. If on the other hand (as is likely until the election), the President pursues an expansionary policy, the effects of devaluation on competitiveness will be destroyed and further decomposition of the monetary system will threaten. Fortunately Nixon has refused to re-introduce convertibility and so long as he sticks to this viewpoint his bargaining position is splendid."

These judgements lead Lord Balogh too to a final philo-sophical assessment of the state of economics. But I will keep

that in reserve for the end of the chapter; in the meantime,
I will confine myself to pointing out that the divergences
between economists on "the so-called monetary crisis" can be a
little confusing for the layman. But of course, so long as "the
system" continues working—which means, so long as "the
system" allows the great flow of goods and resources and
technology between all countries of the world to continue
unabated—the layman will not allow himself to be unduly
worried by the constantly recurring monetary crises. This is
what has happened so far: let us hope that it will not induce
an excessive state of complacency in us all.

Let me now go back to the problem of managing the economy, maintaining full employment, and stopping stagflation.
In two words: the problem. The fact that there is no solution
in sight, Samuelson says, "reflects a blemish in the post-
Keynes economy". Of course, Samuelson does not like or
much believe in the efficacy of direct wage-price controls; for
once, he is in some agreement, on this point, with Chicago's
Friedman. From England, the voices of Joan Robinson and
Lord Balogh have a very different sound: their view practically
coincides with what we have already heard from Uri and
Tinbergen, even though their approach is more theoretical,
more "purely economic". And if Robinson and Balogh disagree on the monetary crisis, they express coinciding views on
stagflation, its causes and remedies. Let us once more hear first
Joan Robinson's view. This is the "Keynesian Left" speaking;
it is also another small chapter of the great "Cambridge versus
Cambridge" debate (with a spare and especially sharp arrow
aimed at Chicago).

"It was an obvious corollary of the Keynesian revolution
(Mrs Robinson writes) that, if an industrial nation succeeded
in maintaining near-full employment for a run of years,
without changing the institutions and habits of wage bargaining,
it would be subject to continuous inflation. The notion that
'just a little' unemployment would keep money-wages and
prices in check was never plausible, and is now proved false."
(I would remark in passing that, so far, Mrs Robinson's
analysis does not differ substantially from Gary Fromm's,

though the conclusions drawn from the same experience are quite opposite.)

"For a time," Mrs Robinson goes on, "economists, especially in the U.S.A., were inclined to seek refuge from this awkward question in a revival of the Quantity Theory of Money. This theory was always completely hollow and policies based on what it was believed to mean have led to disillusionment."

So, Mrs Robinson concludes: "Nowadays it is widely recognised that it is impossible to combine continuous prosperity with stable prices unless the whole system of industrial relations is radically changed. Such a change involves very deep political issues, which no capitalist country is yet willing to face."

"A radical change in the whole system of industrial relations": no small assignment; perhaps a revolution. The very fact that Mrs Robinson does not spell out in detail what this would imply (though those acquainted with her radical-reformist thought are aware that the implications are indeed revolutionary) leaves the field quite open to everyone's imagination; near the end of this journey among the economists, this sentence is one of those that will stay with us as a stimulus to further enquiries.

Lord Balogh can perhaps help us a little more along our road. A very similar thought to Mrs Robinson's is laid wide open by him in this passage of his letter to me. Writing from Oxford in April 1972, Lord Balogh says: "The events of the past year have completely vindicated my attack on both Keynesians and Friedmanites, that is to say the neo-pseudo-liberals who wish to achieve stability (both of prices and of balance of payments) *and* full employment by *global* measures: the first by fiscal and the second by monetary policy. They have now all beaten their breasts and together with econometricians and mathematical economists have confessed their failure. This is no little satisfaction to me", says Lord Balogh, "as I was, with Galbraith, one of the very few who steadfastly adhered to the view that if the Western economy wanted to survive, and with it democracy, *more direct means would have to be found* to achieve stability. An incomes policy without a price policy and without a new social compact is not possible except if we break Trade Unions and are prepared to use violence against labour. This would transform what are relatively pleasant countries into fields of savage class war: a solution which no man of good will can advocate."

I suppose we can now abandon the great debate on how to manage the economy, how to insure growth, full employment, stability of prices and wages in today's world. We have heard some of the more authoritative advocates of the principal theories, we know their reasons and their expectations. We can only be slightly puzzled by the fact that the policy of "direct controls" which European (and especially British) economists advocate more strongly has been more directly tried out nowadays in America by, of all people, a Republican President who was widely expected to dismantle rather than to augment economic controls! The astuteness of History always surprises even the cleverest men. Let me however point to the fact that when Europeans talk about "a social compact" or a wages policy—as spelt out more clearly in Uri's and Tinbergen's letters—they go a long way beyond President Nixon's policy of controls.

I shall leave to Lord Balogh the final word of this chapter. Referring to both problems (control of the economy, and control of the international monetary system), Lord Balogh says: "These events prove that economics 'as a science' needs radical rethinking. The number of variables is so great and their variation through time is so considerable that each great historical situation has to be analysed afresh." After a more technical consideration (Balogh criticises such economists as Samuelson for "trying to force the Keynesian system into the old Marshallian or Walrasian static straitjacket with schedules giving determinate answers through their crossing"), the Oxford economist concludes his analysis of today's economics thus: "It will no doubt take a few more crises before professional economists will accept a more modest role in the universe and will talk to political scientists and sociologists before they pontificate on economic policies which are in fact applied moral and political judgements."

35. Conclusion

1. Economics, Tinbergen says, still retains its full usefulness, in as much as economic problems, or the problems of scarcity and need, will remain with us for a long time to come. Even a sober scientific person like Tinbergen already glimpses on the furthest horizon of the foreseeable future the day when, in the words of the Italian economist Sergio Ricossa, "prosperity, which has brought the economists fame, will end by taking it away from them, and will take away their trade at the same time". But this prospect is still very remote: there is no need for alarm among the tens of thousands of economics students in the universities of the world; they are not likely to have to look for a new field of activity.

Thus the problem is not whether economics is becoming obsolete because of the disappearance of economic problems. It is rather a different question, namely, whether economics as a science justifies its existence, whether it provides the effective and important contribution it should to the solution of economic problems and towards improving the conditions of human existence. How far are economists useful to society? How should we regard contemporary economic science?

In the course of this journey of mine among the economists this theme has been touched on repeatedly. I have reported some widely differing opinions, but I think I can sum up the predominant view by saying that to the majority of economists and men of culture economics seems like a scientific research, incomplete and imperfect, exposed to making even serious mistakes, but able to correct them and gradually to accumulate a body of doctrines and knowledge which can be applied with increasing certainty to ensure rapid economic growth, thus procuring undoubted benefits for human society.

I believe that the economists and intellectuals of both West and East would be fundamentally in agreement with this view; and although my economic "grand tour" did not include the developing countries, everyone knows to what extent they entrust themselves, in their efforts to emerge from that unhappy position of inferiority, to productive processes and to the analyses and plans of the economists.

Do economists, then, enjoy the same unquestioned prestige as scientists? That is perhaps too much to say: the economists are still today not so certain as, shall we say, the physicists that they are pursuing a positive science. But while we may be conscious of the fact that the very material of economic science, namely human society in certain particular aspects of its activity, is constantly changing and so causes the systematic conclusions of economics to change; and while we may be convinced that economic research will never be exhaustive or arrive at a final point except on the utopian hypothesis that economic problems will vanish altogether; we can nevertheless be equally confident that this endless research is necessary and beneficent in its effects. By comparison with a hundred and fifty years ago, this confidence in political economy as a science has immensely increased both among economists and among the ordinary public.

2. By comparison with ten years ago however, one is tempted to suggest, the generally favourable view of economic science has become tempered with reserves and limitations which have, as a whole, enriched the economists' powers of self-criticism but have also developed their sense of their responsibilities and hence their ambitions. To a great extent, the objections which have been raised with regard to economics impugn this science as the instrument and part of a "productivist ideology", a "consumer philosophy", and these are the real objects of attack. It did not fall within the plan of my journey to examine those ideologies that repudiate economics wholesale because they repudiate the "productive ideal", but it must be mentioned that economists today are well aware of these objections. They are, above all, aware of the fact that economic science, precisely because it furthers productive progress,

contributes towards creating new problems as it solves the old ones: for it creates new social tensions, provokes the destruction and pollution of natural resources, and does not always increase social stability but even, paradoxically, sometimes reduces it. Economic progress cannot of itself suffice to solve the problems of human happiness and justice; indeed it may give rise to protest and agitation, because it makes attainable desirable things that formerly seemed beyond the bounds of imagination: but between the desire and its attainment a long lapse of time intervenes, which to the impatience of people today often seems intolerable.

The constant multiplication of desires, which is nourished by the rapid progress of production, prevents such progress from being the complete panacea for humanity's ills that some had supposed. In this sense, economics could be called "the god that failed". Neither the vastly increased rates of production nor the profound changes in social structures have so far enabled mankind to achieve that "leap from the rule of necessity to the rule of freedom" of which Engels spoke, and which was the foundation of the optimistic ideologies (both Marxist and anti-Marxist) of the nineteenth century.

More or less consistently, Maoists, Marcusians, hippies, and neo-Gandhians reject, at least in theory, the ideology of economic progress as affirmed in the "North of the world", both capitalist and Communist. For some neo-Gandhians, the multiplication of desires, which is the mainspring of social evolution both in Western and in Soviet-type countries, will inevitably lead mankind to a terrible crash. Happiness should be sought in the limitation of desires, not in the vain incessant effort to satisfy them, with the sole result of creating new ones. For Maoism (or rather, for a certain phase and version of Maoism), the real aim to be pursued is the creation of a "new man", not the realisation of that economic progress which alone, according to traditional Communist ideology, can serve as the "material basis" for the subsequent flowering of a new humanity that will be purer and more just and free from those egoistic ambitions which are still the instrument and vehicle of progress today.

Even in the West (but much less so in the Soviet Communist
hemisphere) these "anti-economic ideologies", if they can be so
described, have penetrated sufficiently deeply into the common
consciousness to cause economists themselves to take a much
more sober and less triumphalistic view of their profession than
was the case some years ago. Ingenuous optimism is no longer
fashionable among them. Nevertheless their belief that they are
doing something useful for ordinary people—in as much as
productive progress contributes to cure or reduce concrete and
widespread evils such as poverty and backwardness—remains
unshaken; just as it has not yet really come to pass that mankind, either in developed or in underdeveloped countries or
even in China, seeks happiness in the flight from terrestrial
wellbeing. It may come to pass one day. For the present, that
revolutionary change has not happened. So the economists still
think their work is justified. Only, they are much more conscious
of the difficulties of their work; they distinguish much more
clearly the collateral social effects, both positive and negative,
of productive development; they take more fully into account
the complex nature of the relationship between increased
production of goods and improvement of social conditions.
All this tends to transform the economists from technicians of
the productive process into social scientists. In short, the
"ideological" objections and global confrontations encountered
by economic science have served to enlarge the economists'
cultural horizon and field of action and to develop their
ambitions rather than to shake their faith in their own profession
and science.

3. Leaving aside, then, discussions of a philosophical or
ideological nature, we come to another kind of reservations
and criticisms with regard to the science and profession of
economics, criticisms which come from within, rather than from
outside, the "economic" ideology dominant in the world today.
An article by Michael N. Postan, appearing in the January
1968 issue of *Encounter* under the title "A Plague of Economists?", started up a lively debate about the merits and defects
of economics and economists in the world in general and Britain
in particular. It is not unreasonable that British economists

should come under attack, for modern economic science is to a large extent the offspring of British scholarship and culture; while at the same time the British economy, the prototype and original model of all the contemporary industrial economies, has in the last quarter of a century shown little capacity for growth.

The British are annoyed to find themselves constantly last in those rates-of-development tables which are the economic equivalent of the Olympics or the World Cup. In these circumstances it is quite understandable that they should want to take it out of their famous and authoritative economists— even though, as a matter of fact, the accusers themselves are more often than not economists.

In the debate sparked off by the *Encounter* article, however, the most extreme anti-economist line was taken by a historian, Max Beloff. According to Beloff, the best that can be said of present-day economists is the equivalent of the dictum about a famous Harley Street doctor: his medical knowledge was fabulous and it was only a pity that all his patients died. "Historically", says Beloff, "the record of economists since the discipline became a recognised one has been almost uniformly dismal." Even Keynes, despite some merit, "was probably never so harmlessly occupied as when pursuing his homosexual amours". Happy are the countries that do not contribute to economic science, such as "Scandinavia, Germany, France, Italy and Holland": they are the ones that grow fastest. Beloff's conclusion is: "It is possible for an economist to be intelligent, in the same way as it is possible for a 'starlet' to be chaste. It is just very difficult."

Beloff's thesis is Anglo-centric as well as eccentric. *Pace* his comments, the first Nobel prize for economics went to a Norwegian and a Dutchman. To reproach economists for their mistakes is just like reproaching doctors for theirs. It is certainly more probable than otherwise that a doctor may kill somebody or an economist drive his country to disaster. That will not, however, I imagine, stop Professor Beloff if he is ill from going to a doctor, despite the attendant risks, rather than to an economist. In the same way governments will continue to seek advice

269

on economic matters from economists rather than from doctors or historians.

4. I heard an almost equally radical criticism of economics in London from Lord Balogh, who read me extracts from a book he was then writing called *The Limits of Expansion*. I wrote down one or two of his concepts: that it was not economics that made full employment, but full employment that "made" economics; that economics is not, as people think, a science but a scientology, or pseudo-science, or better still an art, "a historic art in which each new situation gives rise to new problems, and this proves absolutely intolerable to many economists". But there are no absolute truths, no equations that give absolute answers: "equations can always anticipate the past, not the future".

In defining economics as an art rather than a science, Lord Balogh, who is one of its most eminent representatives, was not meaning, I think, to condemn it as something harmful to humanity, but rather to indicate its limitations, in contradistinction to the view of his more enthusiastic or ingenuous or presumptuous followers. I heard a similar, if at first sight opposite, criticism in Cambridge, Mass., from Jay Forrester, who dreams of a global science of man and society, and criticises economics for having "artificially restricted its point of view and interests", creating the abstract idea of "homo oeconomicus", something inadequate and unreal seeing that the motivations of human actions are not solely economic.

These objections and criticisms express a disquiet common to the followers of all the "social sciences", of all those disciplines, that is to say, which concern themselves with human events and to which, because of the complexity and mutability of the subject, the epithet of "science" can be only imperfectly attributed. Michael Postan, too, is motivated by this disquiet when he accuses post-Keynesian economics of being too abstract because it is too much devoted to "macroeconomic" problems. Economic research has always moved awkwardly between Scylla and Charybdis, between the charge of being over-abstract and that of being merely a collection of facts from which some general truths can be extracted which are, however, valid only for the past but not for the future. Economics has seemed sometimes too mathematical, aprioristic and deductive, sometimes too empirical and inductive. These are also the traditional reservations of Benedetto Croce in relation to economics—that it does not keep enough to the concrete, the particular, the individual historical fact, but navigates uncertainly between abstractions and pseudo-concepts. These reservations were also taken into account by W. W. Rostow in the introduction to his well-known book on *The Stages of Economic Growth*; but that did not cause him to abandon his analyses and syntheses, even though they might not represent an ultimate and absolute truth but merely an instrument for the understanding of economic reality.

We can say, therefore, that economists today are conscious of the provisional and hypothetical nature of many of the "truths" they have discovered. They are also very conscious of the fact that history never tires of creating new and surprising facts in the light of which their ideas and theories must be continually adapted and renewed. They do not, I think, for that reason consider their research less useful and positive. Is not the ideology of doubt a typical and particular characteristic of all contemporary science, including science in the strict sense (physics, chemistry, biology)? Are not all modern scientific theories hypothetical, provisional—until a better one has been found—and subject to incessant revisions? The economists of today may well say, "I doubt, therefore I am a scientist".

5. It would perhaps be fairer to say that certain economists are abstract, aprioristic, deductive, absolute, and useless, rather than accusing economics in general of these faults. In some celebrated instances, it has been precisely the abstractions and theoretical elaborations of the economists that have illuminated certain obscure historical facts, certain economic mechanisms that would otherwise have been impossible to control and harmful: we need only to recall Keynes' theoretical work and the problem of depression and unemployment.

The fact is that debates of this kind form part of the internal dialectic of economic science, they represent stages in its own evolution and progress, and are the expression of a research carried on by many hands in which both critics and criticised take part.

Is modern economics really too much devoted to "macro-economic" researches, is it concerned with too general economic categories and too "aggregated" values? Possibly yes, at certain times and in certain countries; certainly no, at other times and in other countries. Indeed, sometimes the very opposite charge is made: in New York Murray Rossant deplored the fact that present-day economics was exhausting itself in too many detailed analyses and was lacking in synthetical and systematic capacity, unable to see the wood for the trees.

The French economic review *Entreprise* had this sort of thing in mind when it deplored the lack of geniuses in economics. "Since Keynes", it said, "the world has known no great thinkers in economics. Today economic thinking awaits a new genius, a new general synthesis. Who will make the synthesis? Who will be the point of convergence? Who will be for economics what Einstein was for physics?" These questions are both stimulating and pertinent; I too would regard Keynes as the Newton, not the Einstein, of economics. But despite the desire of the human mind to rest in the shadow of great definitive syntheses and revealed truths, the most fruitful periods of research for human thought have probably been the periods that were dominated by uncertainty, by the multiplicity of theses, theories and schools, by the dialogue and debate between the "greatest systems". And an Einstein or a Newton can, indeed, be invoked but not, alas, evoked. Meanwhile I think there is a lot to be said for Gardner Ackley's argument that, until the perfect economic methodology has been discovered (to my mind a utopian hypothesis), the multiplicity of centres for research and the branches it covers is fully justified and useful. The absence of what Samuelson called "a Copernican revolution in economics" does not make economic research useless.

6. Moreover, it is by no means true that there is an absence of general theories and great syntheses. Looking at a single, particular economic system it might seem so. But if one

makes an even partial economic "grand tour" of the developed countries, one finds that in these countries not just one or two but at least three or four general and systematic theories of economics are being put forward.

I leave on one side theoretical debates, important in themselves but not global, such as that between the "monetarists" and the "fiscalists" in America: both theories move within the orbit of the same general hypotheses, the same economic system—the system of a mixed economy. The same can be said, I think, for the present at least, of the debate between Cambridge, Mass. and Cambridge, England. But the theory of mixed economy is not the only great theoretical hypothesis or organisational system of industrial society in these last decades of the second century of its existence. There has been, and still is, a global alternative which has been at least partially realised for some decades—the Stalinist "command economy", involving the centralised planning and distribution of resources adumbrated more or less completely in the "wartime economies" of the West: Germany's control of economy in the First World War had, as is well known, a direct and determining influence on the theory and practice of Soviet planning. But today the Eastern, Communist, half of industrialised society advances other hypotheses and achievements which are, as we have seen, of considerable interest. Among the hypotheses, one of the most novel and forward-looking is certainly the "simulated market" of Fedorenko in Moscow; among the achievements, the mixed, planned-cum-market, economy in a regime of self-management of factories, in Tito's Yugoslavia, and the incipient mixed State-cum-market economy of Hungary (it is beginning to be difficult to find the right labels for each of these economic systems).

One sometimes has the feeling that the boundaries between the various models are partly confused and uncertain (for instance, in the big Western State concerns such as IRI in Italy, which operate in an international market regime). But there is no doubt that behind these economic realities in evolution there are a corresponding number of "general theories" of economics.

273

S

Seen, as it should be, against the background of these concrete economic realities and of the great social and political facts which influence and are influenced by them, present-day economic science appears as a typical manifestation of industrial culture and civilisation, or as one of the attempts of industrial society to acquire consciousness of itself, and also an instrument and manifestation of the wish of that society to organise and adapt itself better. Economics carries out this task by producing and experiencing powerful social and political pressures, transfering on to the plane of theoretical elaboration, but also of action and economic policy, extensive demands which arise from men's aspiration to improve the conditions of their existence.

7. Within this framework, economics and economists represent, it seems to me, a well defined and recognisable force. At the end of my journey among the economists in the industrialised world, both capitalist and Communist, I am even tempted to speak of the existence of an "economists' party", which is in some way mingled or allied with the wider "technocrats' party", or the party of those social strata that are in the forefront of the work of transformation and improvement of industrial society. The economists' party has an ideology of its own, the particular characteristic of which is to be anti-ideological, or anti-mythmaking, since it is inspired by a problematic and experimental conception of social evolution. Economists, like scientific men in general, are fundamentally radical reformers, men of the Enlightenment. They too participate in the movement of "contestation" or protest against existing industrial societies, whether capitalist or Communist, but they differentiate themselves sharply from what might be called romantic or anarchical "contestation". The economists think that we shall have to live with this industrial society for a long time, and that it is no use just condemning or rejecting it *en bloc*: instead, we must try to correct and improve it, bringing the imperfect reality in which we live before the tribunal of reason. Economists are in general against traumatic and revolutionary transformations of society, because they know by experience that they are often

illusory. Consequently they inevitably clash with those arbitrary political forces which believe they can transform society and man at a single blow and which often end by taking refuge in the magic of rhetoric or flinging themselves into the abyss of constriction and violence. A whole generation of economists, including some of the most brilliant in this century, ended up in this way, condemned and trampled down by Stalinism.

Since the economists have, whether consciously or not, an ideology of their own, a difficult but stimulating dialectical relationship is inevitably created between them and the professionals of ideology, in other words the politicians. The distinction is naturally empirical: economists are in reality politicians, and vice versa. In practice, the relationship between politicians and economists, whether in the form of dialogue, collaboration, or dispute, is one of the essential and typical links of modern industrial society. For the economist, in whatever society he operates, the politicians represent a big practical problem. In relation to them he sometimes assumes the office of pedagogue and teacher, or of collaborator; at other times he seems to be their opponent and critic.

In the *Encounter* debate, Michael Stewart opposed Postan's theory about the "plague of economists" by the theory that the world is suffering, rather, from a "plague of politicians". According to Stewart, "the economy has not got into a mess because there has been too little microeconomic intervention by economists. It has got into a mess because the economists' advice on macroeconomics has not been listened to". Stewart's comments on the political misfortunes of the British economy have their counterpart in Heller's comments on the misfortunes of the American economy in recent years owing to the failure of the politicians to accept the advice given them by the economists. In the Soviet world, the battle of the economists for reform of the "command economy" has always manifested itself in a difficult relationship with the holders of political power, in other words with the leaders of the Communist Party. Here the "economists' party" has really taken on the characteristics of a political grouping or of a pressure group which often represented well defined social strata. As a result, the

Communist economists, from Liberman in Russia to Ota Sik in Czechoslovakia, have not had easy lives. They have had fame and often much power, but they have run grave risks; to avoid them, they have had to act, as Jozef Bognar told me in Budapest, with great diplomacy. In inserting themselves among the ranks of the innovating "intelligentsia" and echoing the demands of vast social masses (both consumers and producers) eager for prosperity and greater autonomy, the economists of the East have had and continue to have a function of primary importance in the troubled process of renovation of those regimes.

More generally, the economists, as Kenneth Galbraith says, form part in the world today of that vast intellectual community, that "educational and scientific estate", whose task it is to humanise the reign of technology, or the industrial society. The new economic theories have been fundamental factors in transforming contemporary societies, promoting the passage from "paleo-capitalism" to "neo-capitalism", from "paleo-communism" to "neo-communism". The economists are among the protagonists of what has been called the "revolution of the North of the world". "The effective revolutionaries seem, in the North of the world, to be the men of knowledge rather than the men of passion or representation; the multitudes of studious apprentices, taciturn, impassive, dedicated to 'thinking the unthinkable', rather than the ideologues."* Perhaps they, rather than the professionals of romantic revolution, are the real transformers of the world, together with the biologists, geneticists, chemists, physicists, and mathematicians.

8. In Western societies, political economy seems today to have reached a turning point, expressed in the ever increasing involvement of economists, as political scientists, in a reform of society, over and above the pure and simple administration or transformation of economic structures. Doubts as to the ability of productive progress to act as a panacea for social ills have contributed towards this new awareness. Economic progress in the industrialised societies of the West has been tremendously

* Alberto Ronchey, *Prospettive del pensiero economico contemporaneo*, Turin, ed. Utet, 1970.

rapid over the last two hundred years, but now that is not enough. What are the conditions for growth to continue but not to be wasted or actually to harm the social and psychological stability of these societies? The economists, it seems to me, answer this question by an analysis conducted on three planes: the planes of economic theory, economic policy, and pure and simple politics. There is surprisingly wide agreement among the experts today on the theory of regulated development and also on the economic policy that governments should follow. For some time, however, the economists have been taking their analyses a step further: they discuss what political and social conditions are needed in order to put into effect the measures they advise the governments to adopt.

Thus their theme moves from pure economics to embrace politics and sociology as well. This was not so thirty years ago. Faced with the then very serious problem of mass unemployment and the collapse of production, the economists who counselled new solutions concentrated chiefly on theoretical battles. Keynes began by reinventing economics and writing a ponderous treatise, his *General Theory*.

Subsequently, when the new theories had triumphed in the academic world, the economists became involved in the next stage, that of economic policy. The mantle of Keynes passed to the shoulders of the political economists such as Walter Heller. After convincing themselves they convinced the leading statesmen. The great post-war progress was born, at least in part, of their twofold success.

In recent times the economic debate has become more complicated. It no longer suffices to persuade a president or a minister. It no longer suffices to have the stage-manager on one's side; one needs to be able to count on all the actors. By dint of invoking participation, we have failed to perceive that it had already arrived, like the Kingdom of Heaven, silently as a thief in the night. So far it has shown itself chiefly in negative ways; but even "contestation" is a form of participation. The economic problems of today are much less dramatic than those of thirty years ago, but their solution calls for a much greater degree of understanding and agreement.

The "new millennium" of abundance is relatively near. But in order to reach it, it will be necessary to act prudently: to defer and plan ahead for certain urgent claims, to renounce certain immediate benefits, not to kill by excessive demands the goose of the golden egg that is the mixed economy in which we live.

However, to use a phrase of Balogh's, with full employment you can't rule people with a rod of iron. You have to persuade them, and to let themselves be persuaded people want to be sure that there is justice in the distribution of resources; and they want their new responsibilities to carry with them new powers.

It is at this point that the economists' theme ceases to be purely economic and becomes political. With monotonous regularity the experts in West and East alike counsel, for example, an "incomes policy", or a relationship of regulated balance between the increase in income consumed or invested and the increase in income produced. No less monotonously the economists propound today that the achievement of this more rational economic policy should be sought by means of a new agreement involving all the interested parties, government, business concerns, and trade unions. There are some residual obscurities in the new slogans we hear: those about the "new social contract", "participation", or "recognised authority". But some hints are already pretty clear. One is the need for a new economic education which will embrace both the governing class and the masses. "We must get people to discuss things in a more reasonable way," said Carli. And Marjolin: "Information is the beginning of participation."

Decisions need to become consensual and to stop—to quote Carli again—"exploding suddenly over people's heads". But here a whole series of new debates opens up: on the trade union and its responsibilities and powers; on the factory ("It is a mistake", Marjolin says, "to suppose that we can go on living under a system in which the management of a firm has virtually no other relationship with the work people beyond hiring their services and paying their wages"); on the obligations which the government must assume in relation to the great social needs. Two hundred and fifty years after the birth of

Adam Smith, "capitalist" or market economy has become much more difficult to manage—perhaps as a result of its own successes.

The conditions of economic progress and social serenity are revealed as much more complex than when the economists' debate was carried on only on the plane of theory or of government policy. Society today, says Dow, is "terribly complicated, it calls for great discipline and order in the productive process". The task is difficult. But the stake is very high. A widespread and sure prosperity can be seen ahead which will be able to offer tranquillity, confidence, and responsibility. The importance of the end to be achieved is such as to call for deep reflection and mature judgement on the part of everyone—but also for much courage to face the necessary innovations.

Within this framework of an industrial society in rapid evolution, restless and anxious to change itself even more rapidly and radically than the social and productive forces in it are already doing spontaneously, and anarchically, the function of the economists, as scientific experimentalists, as intellectual protagonists of the "permanent bourgeois revolution", seems to be twofold. They serve as instigators of new ideas and proposals for renovation and reform, but also as destroyers of the illusions inevitably let loose by the vital tension of the society in which we live: and here even the myth of productive progress as the ultimate answer to the eternal search for human happiness cannot go unquestioned. And in any case, the myths and fables that mankind tells itself are often a necessary inspiration, sometimes even a guide along its way.

Turin, 5 June 1973

BIBLIOGRAPHICAL NOTE

The subject of this inquiry—modern economics—is so vast that I cannot hope to provide an exhaustive, let alone a complete, bibliography for it. I shall therefore confine myself to mentioning some of the works which I have consulted and found especially interesting in the course of the inquiry. The list of publications is divided into two parts, Western economics and Communist economics. The second part is based on a much fuller and more systematic bibliography prepared for a course on Contemporary Eastern Europe which I gave at the Bologna Center of Johns Hopkins University in the academic year 1967–68.

WESTERN ECONOMICS

Baran, P. A. and Sweezy, P. M., *Monopoly Capital: an Essay on the American economic and social order*, New York, Monthly Review Press, 1966.

Bauchet, P., *La planification française*, Paris, Ed. du Seuil, 1966.

Becker, G. S., *Human Capital*, New York, National Bureau of Economic Research, 1964.

Denison, F., *The Sources of Economic Growth in the United States*, New York, Brookings Institution, 1962.

Denison, F., *Why Growth Rates Differ: Postwar Experience in Nine Western Countries*, Washington, Brookings Institution, 1967.

Drucker, P. F., *The Age of Discontinuity*, New York, Harper & Row, 1968.

Forrester, J. W., *Urban Dynamics*, Cambridge, Mass., M.I.T. Press, 1969.

Forte, F., *Introduzione alla politica economica*, Turin, Einaudi, 1964.

Friedman, M., *Capitalism and Freedom*, University of Chicago Press, 1962.

Friedman, M. and Heller, W. W., *Monetary vs. Fiscal Policy*, New York, Norton, 1969.

Fromm, G. and Taubman, P., *Policy Simulations with an Econometric Model*, Washington, Brookings Institution, 1968.

Fuchs, V. R., *The Service Economy*, New York, National Bureau of Economic Research, 1968.

Galbraith, J. K., *American Capitalism*, London, Hamish Hamilton, 1956.

Galbraith, J. K., *The Affluent Society*, London, Hamish Hamilton, 1961.

Galbraith, J. K., *The New Industrial State*, London, Hamish Hamilton, 1967.

Gordon, K. (ed.), *Agenda for the Nation*, Washington, Brookings Institution, 1968.

Harrod, R. F., *The Life of J. M. Keynes*, London, Macmillan, 1951.

Heilbroner, R. L., *Worldly Philosophers*, New York, Watts, 1967.

Heilbroner, R. L., *The Economic Problem*, Englewood Cliffs, N. J., Prentice-Hall, 1968.

Heller, W. W., *New Dimensions of Political Economy*, Harvard University Press, 1966.

Heller, W. W., et al., *Politique Budgétaire et équilibre économique*, Paris, OECD, 1968.

Kahn, H., and Wiener, A. J., *The Year 2000*, London, Macmillan, 1967.

Kaldor, N., *Strategic Factors in Economic Development*, New York, New York State School of Industrial and Labor Relations, 1967.

Kaldor, N., *Essays on Economic Stability and Growth*, London, Duckworth, 1960.

Kaldor, N., *Essays on Value and Distribution*, New York, The Free Press of Glencoe, 1960.

Klein, L. R., *Introduction to Econometrics*, Englewood Cliffs, N.J., Prentice-Hall, 1962.

Klein, L. R., and Evans, M. K., *The Wharton Econometric Forecasting Model*, Philadelphia, University of Pennsylvania Press, 1968.

Leontief, W., *Input-Output Economics*, New York, Oxford University Press, 1966.

Leon, P., *Structural Change and Growth in Capitalism*, Baltimore, Johns Hopkins Press, 1967.

Levy, M. E., *Fiscal Policy, Cycles and Growth*, New York, The Conference Board, 1963.

Lutz, V., *Central Planning for the Market Economy*, London, Longmans, 1969.

Mansfield, E., *The Economics of Technological Change*, New York, Norton, 1968.

Napoleoni, C., *Il pensiero economico del 900*, Turin, Einaudi, 1963.

Oulès, F., *Economic Planning and Democracy*, London, Penguin Books, 1966.

Pen, J., *Modern Economics*, London, Penguin Books, 1965.

Perroux, F., *L'Economie du XXème siècle*, Paris, Presses Universitaires de France, 1964.

Phelps, E. S. (ed.) *Private Wants and Public Needs*, New York, W. W. Norton, 1965.

Philip, A. *Histoire des faits économiques et sociaux*, Paris, Aubier-Montaigne, 1963.

Robinson, J., *Economic Philosophy*, London, Watts & Co., 1962.

Robinson, J., *Essays in the Theory of Employment*, London, Macmillan, 1937.

Rostow, W. W., *The Stages of Economic Growth*, Cambridge University Press, 1960.

Ruffolo, G., *La grande impresa nella società moderna*, Turin, Einaudi, 1967.

Samuelson, P., *Economics*, New York, McGraw Hill, 1964.

Saraceno, P., *Lo stato e l'economia*, Rome, Cinque Lune, 1965.

Shanks, M., *The Innovators (The Economics of Technology)*, London, Pelican Books, 1967.

Shonfield, A., *Modern Capitalism*, London, Oxford University Press, 1965.
Sraffa, P., *Production of Commodities by Means of Commodities*, Cambridge University Press, 1963.
Stewart, M., *Keynes and After*, London, Penguin Books, 1967.
Sylos Labini, P., *Oligopolio e progresso tecnico*, Turin, Einaudi, 1964.
Tinbergen, J., *Lessons from the Past*, Amsterdam, Elsevier, 1963.

COMMUNIST ECONOMICS

Antonov, O. K., *La pianificazione sovietica*, Florence, Vallecchi, 1968.
Bernard, P. J., *Destin de la planification soviétique*, Paris, Les éditions ouvrières, 1963.
Bettleheim, Ch., *Planification et croissance accélérée*, Paris, Maspero, 1964.
Bettleheim, Ch., *Problèmes théoriques et pratiques de la planification*, Paris, Maspero, 1966.
Bettiza, E., *L'altra Europa*, Florence, Vallecchi, 1966.
Boffito, C., *Socialismo e mercato in Jugoslavia*, Turin, Einaudi, 1968.
Bognar, J., *Economic Policy and Planning in Developing Countries*, Budapest, Akadèmiai Kiadò, 1968.
Brus, W., *Ogólne problemy funkcionowania gospodaski socjalistycznej*, Warsaw, 1961; Italian translation, *Il funzionamento dell'economia socialista*, Milan, Feltrinelli, 1965.
Cech, J., *Praga, 1968—Le idee del nuovo corso*, Bari, Laterza, 1968.
Ceses, *Problemi attuali della pianificazione sovietica*, Milan, Comunità, 1965.
Ceses, *Le riforme economiche nei Paesi dell'Est*, Florence, Vallecchi, 1966.
Ceses, *Il sistema dei prezzi nell'Est Europeo*, Milan, Angeli, 1967.
Ceses, Texts (some awaiting publication) of Congresses at Rapallo (1967) and Balatonfüred (1969), and seminars at Tremezzo (1967) and Venice (1969).
Diskussia ob optimal'nom planirovannii (Discussion on optimal planning), Moscow, Izdatelstvo Ekonomika, 1968.
Djilas, M., *The New Class*, London, Thames and Hudson, 1957.
Dobb, M., *Soviet Economic Development since 1917*, London, Routledge and Kegan Paul, 1948 (6th edition 1966).
Fedorenko, N. P., *Ekonomika i matematika (Economics and mathematics)*, Moscow, Izdatelstvo Nauka, 1967.
Fedorenko, N. P., *O razrabotke sistemy optimal'nogo funktsionirovaniia ekonimiki (On elaboration of a system of optimal functioning of the economy)*, Moscow, Izdatelstvo Nauka, 1967.
Hayek, F. A. (ed.), *Collectivist Economic Planning*, London, Routledge and Kegan Paul, 1963.
Horvat, B., *Towards a Theory of Planned Economy*, Belgrade, 1964.
Hutchinson, T. W., *Economics and Economic Policy in Britain, 1946-1966*, London, Allen & Unwin, 1968.
Jelenski, K. A., *La realtà dell'ottobre polacco: gli articoli di "Po Prostu"*, Milan, Silva, 1961.
Lange, O., *Political Economy*, Oxford, Pergamon Press, 1963.

Bibliographical Note

Liberman, Nemchinov, Trapeznikov et al., *Piano e profitto nell'economia sovietica*, Rome, Editori Riuniti, 1965.

Lippincott, B., Lange, O., Taylor, F., *On the Economic Theory of Socialism*, Minneapolis, University of Minnesota Press, 1938.

Lisichkin, G. S., *Plan i rynok (Plan and Market)*, Moscow, Izdatelstvo Ekonomika, 1966.

Marczewski, J., *Planification et croissance économique des démocraties populaires*, Paris, Presses Universitaires de France, 1956.

Meister, A., *Socialisme et autogestion: l'expérience yougoslave*, Paris, Ed. du Seuil, 1964.

New Directions in the Soviet Economy, Washington, U.S. Printing Office, 1966.

Nove, A., *Was Stalin Really Necessary?*, London, Allen & Unwin, 1964.

Nove, A., *The Soviet Economy*, London, Allen & Unwin, 1961.

Reform of the Economic Mechanism in Hungary (edited by Istvan Friss), Budapest, Akadèmiai Kiadò, 1969.

Richta, R., *"Civilizace na rozcesti,"* *Marianskyeh Laznieh*, 1–6, Dubna, 1968; Italian translation, *La via cecoslovacca*, Milan, Angeli, 1968.

Schaff, A., *Marksizm a jednostka ludzka*, Warsaw, 1965; Italian translation, *Il marxismo e la persona umana*, Milan, Feltrinelli, 1966.

Schwartz, H., *Russia's Soviet Economy*, Englewood Cliffs, Prentice-Hall, 1961.

Šik, O., *La verità sull'economia cecoslovacca*, Milan, Etas Kompass, 1968.

Spulber, N., *State and Economic Development in Eastern Europe*, New York, Random House, 1966.

U.N. Economic Commission for Europe, Sections on the State of the Economy in Eastern Europe, in *Annual Reports*.

Wellisz, S., *The Economics of the Soviet Bloc*, New York, McGraw Hill, 1964.

Wiles, P. J. D., *The Political Economy of Communism*, Cambridge, Mass., Harvard University Press, 1962.